IN THE FOOTSTEPS OF THE BAND OF BROTHERS

ALSO BY LARRY ALEXANDER

Biggest Brother:
The Life of Major Dick Winters,
the Man Who Led the Band of Brothers

Shadows in the Jungle:
The Alamo Scouts Behind Japanese Lines in World War II

IN THE FOOTSTEPS OF THE
BAND OF BROTHERS

A RETURN TO EASY COMPANY'S BATTLEFIELDS WITH SERGEANT FORREST GUTH

LARRY ALEXANDER

NAL
CALIBER

NAL Caliber
Published by New American Library, a division of
Penguin Group (USA) Inc., 375 Hudson Street,
New York, New York 10014, USA
Penguin Group (Canada), 90 Eglinton Avenue East, Suite 700, Toronto,
Ontario M4P 2Y3, Canada (a division of Pearson Penguin Canada Inc.)
Penguin Books Ltd., 80 Strand, London WC2R 0RL, England
Penguin Ireland, 25 St. Stephen's Green, Dublin 2,
Ireland (a division of Penguin Books Ltd.)
Penguin Group (Australia), 250 Camberwell Road, Camberwell, Victoria 3124,
Australia (a division of Pearson Australia Group Pty. Ltd.)
Penguin Books India Pvt. Ltd., 11 Community Centre, Panchsheel Park,
New Delhi - 110 017, India
Penguin Group (NZ), 67 Apollo Drive, Rosedale, North Shore 0632,
New Zealand (a division of Pearson New Zealand Ltd.)
Penguin Books (South Africa) (Pty.) Ltd., 24 Sturdee Avenue,
Rosebank, Johannesburg 2196, South Africa

Penguin Books Ltd., Registered Offices:
80 Strand, London WC2R 0RL, England

First published by NAL Caliber, an imprint of New American Library,
a division of Penguin Group (USA) Inc.

First Printing, May 2010
10 9 8 7 6 5 4 3 2 1

LIBRARY OF CONGRESS CATALOGING-IN-PUBLICATION DATA:

Alexander, Larry, 1951–
In the footsteps of the Band of Brothers: a return to Easy Company's battlefields with
Sergeant Forrest Guth/Larry Alexander.
p. cm.
Includes bibliographical references and index.
ISBN 978-0-451-22991-5
1. United States. Army. Parachute Infantry Regiment, 506th. Company E.   2. Guth, Forrest L.,
1921–2009. 3. World War, 1939–1945—Campaigns—Western Front.   4. World War, 1939–1945—
Regimental histories—United States.   5. United States. Army—Parachute troops—History—
20th century.   6. World War, 1939–1945—Personal narratives, American.
7. Soldiers—United States—Biography.   I. Guth, Forrest L., 1921–2009.   II. Title.
D769.348506th.A45 2010
940.54'1273—dc22   2009046990

Set in Baskerville
Designed by Patrice Sheridan

Printed in the United States of America

PUBLISHER'S NOTE
While the author has made every effort to provide accurate telephone numbers and Internet
addresses at the time of publication, neither the publisher nor the author assumes any
responsibility for errors, or for changes that occur after publication. Further, publisher does not
have any control over and does not assume any responsibility for author or third-party Web sites
or their content.

Dedicated in fond memory of
FORREST LEROY GUTH
1921–2009

CONTENTS

IN THE FOOTSTEPS OF THE BAND OF BROTHERS

In the summer of 2008, my agent, Dave Robie, and I traveled to New York City for a lunch meeting with my editors, Claire Zion and Brent Howard of New American Library (NAL). This foray to the Big Apple was a chance for me to talk to my editors face-to-face, rather than via the phone or the even more impersonal e-mail. It was, in part, a get-acquainted meeting, but it was also to provide me with an opportunity to bounce some ideas for future books off of them.

My first book, *Biggest Brother: The Life of Major Dick Winters, the Man Who Led the Band of Brothers*, had been out for about three years and my second book, a Pacific version of *Band of Brothers* entitled *Shadows in the Jungle: The Alamo Scouts Behind Japanese Lines in World War II*, was with the publisher and set for a February 2, 2009, release.

But what was next?

I presented a few suggestions, one of which drew some interest, although none was greeted with banners and ticker tape. Then I rolled out a concept I had tucked away in the corner of my brain reserved for off-the-wall, "I'd like to do this, but don't know if it's practical" ideas.

I'd fallen in love with World War II—if one can fall in love with a war—around 1959. I was eight years old and I had just gone to the old Main Theater in my hometown of Ephrata, Pennsylvania, and seen my first war movie, *The Naked and the Dead*, Hollywood's attempt to bring to the screen Norman Mailer's gritty novel. (That book introduced us to the term "fug," which Mailer created after he was banned from using the actual four-letter word in print.)

Up until then I doubt if I'd even been aware that there had been such a thing as World War II, because I recall asking my grandparents, "Was there a war in 1944?" which was only seven years before I was born.

From that time on, I became engrossed in learning all I could about this huge conflict that affected so many millions of lives, including my own, caught up as we were in the Cold War years that were a direct result of that earlier struggle.

At first what I knew of World War II came from comic books, both those based on fact and those grounded in fantasy, where heroes like Sgt. Fury and his Howling Commandos and Sgt. Rock single-handedly, it seemed, brought down the Third Reich. I watched and enjoyed every war movie Hollywood ever made, even those flag-waving wartime flicks that overflowed with propaganda and racial slurs. ("Scratch one squint-eye," a marine says when he shoots a Japanese sniper in the 1943 film *Guadalcanal Diary*.)

The comic book phase was followed by novels and historical works, especially those with lots of photos. And the more I learned, the more I wanted to actually see the war-ravaged places that appeared in those mostly black-and-white pictures, and walk those bloody grounds where so many fought and sacrificed.

Gradually, I became aware that the veterans of that war were all around me, and could tell me their stories firsthand. When I met my wife, Barbara, I discovered that her father, Israel S. Gockley, was one of these men. Issy had been in Easy Company, 334th Infantry Regiment, 84th Division, rising from a private to a sergeant and assistant squad leader during the Battle of the Bulge. Like many vets, he didn't talk much about the war and, indeed, tried to bury it deep within and forget it. At this he was successful. But one terrible engagement at Beho, Belgium, on January 23, 1945, during which his company, out in front of the regiment, held their ground and were nearly overrun by an SS Panzer unit, was one even the determined Issy could not forget.

In 1983 I had the honor of taking Issy to his first—and only—division reunion, and met some of the men he talked about. Hearing their stories planted an urge deep inside me to one day walk the ground at Beho where he and his comrades almost came to grief.

The desire to visit the battlefields of World War II was further inflamed when I became a newspaper reporter. Around Memorial Day and Veterans Day, I interviewed scores of men from World War I through Desert Storm. But it was the World War II guys who enthralled me most. It was such a terrible yet heroic struggle fought on a battlefield that stretched around the globe, and against deeply evil forces.

Then came *Band of Brothers*, both the book and the miniseries, and I met and became friends first with Dick Winters, and then with Forrest Guth. Through knowing them, and seeing the movie, their story became so tangible to me that I knew I just had to visit their fields of glory.

I had to walk in their footsteps.

That was the idea I now laid out over that luncheon meeting in Manhattan, a historical memoir and travelogue that involved me traveling to these sites accompanied by an Easy Company veteran, recording his memories and emotions, and weaving into that my own impressions of those fields today, both as a historian and a writer.

I was not at all certain how I would accomplish this task, or even if it was feasible, which is why I tucked it away in my mind's "later" file. But since my other suggestions seemed to crash and burn (publishing is a tough business), I thought, "What the hell?" and brought my idea out. As I described my project, I saw Brent's eyes light up. He especially liked the part about taking a veteran along.

At this meeting, we did not agree that this would, indeed, be my next book for NAL, mainly because I still wasn't sure I was good enough to pull off this huge plan. But the favorable impression it left on Brent encouraged me, so I began looking into the possibility.

The first thing I had to do was line up an Easy Company veteran. I knew Dick Winters, at age ninety, was out, so my first choice was Forrest Guth.

I had met Forrest in 2001 around the same time I met Dick Winters. After the war, Forrest had attended and graduated from what was then called Millersville State Teacher's College in Millersville, Pennsylvania. Forty years later, I graduated from what is now called Millersville University, and in 2001, after I had become a journalist, I was asked to write an article for Millersville's alumni magazine about the school's *Band of Brothers* alumnus.

I did, interviewing him over the phone at his home in Delaware.

After that, Forrest and I ran into each other a number of times over the next couple of years, including at a birthday party for Dick Winters, and our friendship developed.

In December 2007 Forrest's wife of almost sixty years, Harriet, a lady I had met many times and grew to enjoy, passed away. I thought about this when I called Forrest in August 2008 to propose the trip, thinking it would be a good way to get his mind off his grief. He agreed to go along without hesitation.

The trip was not a definite yet. I still had to line up guides and my itinerary, and get the whole package blessed by NAL.

For the guides, I turned to my Internet friends of the Wild Bill Guarnere and Major Dick Winters Web sites. These folks responded admirably. Both Linda Cautaert, living in Holland, and a San Francisco woman, BK Masterson, recommended Paul Woodadge of Battlebus. Paul, a Brit who lives in Normandy, specializes in *Band of Brothers* tours. I contacted Paul, and he readily agreed to guide Forrest and myself over Easy Company's French battlefields. Paul also recommended (as did Linda) Reg Jans for the Belgian part of my tour. I contacted Reg, who quickly agreed. Reg then went above and beyond. I spoke to him about Beho, asking how close it was to my tour route. Reg offered to do some research on the fight at Beho that my father-in-law was in, and possibly take me there during our visit. Not only that, but he hooked me up with a Beho veteran who had also contacted him, seeking information. That man was James Morgia, who had been the officer in command of the company during that fight. (Issy and I had met Morgia at the 1983 reunion, but I had had no contact with him since.)

For the England part of my tour, I called on Keith Sowerby, who resides in Aldbourne and whom I had met at Toccoa in 2005. In addition, Neil Stevens, who is also quite familiar with the history of Aldbourne, agreed to meet me there and share his research.

It was all coming together. Then we had a setback.

Our original departure date was set for the end of September, and the tour was to start in Aldbourne and end at Hitler's Eagle's Nest high in the Bavarian Alps. We could not leave earlier because Forrest, along with the Easy Company vets Clancy Lyall, Bill Guarnere, Babe Heffron, and Don Malarkey, were flown by the USO to visit American troops in Iraq. The trip was a success, but took a toll on the aging veterans, and Forrest ended up being hospitalized in October.

I postponed the trip a month and, with much reluctance, considered having to put it off until spring, but Forrest, ever the trooper, wanted to go. His doctors advised against it, but they did not prohibit him, and so, with their grudging agreement and the blessings of his family, we were off.

The problem was, we were now forced to leave on October 31, the same day the Eagle's Nest closes for the season. Since the Eagle's Nest was out, I scratched Germany off my itinerary entirely. I did this reluctantly, but felt I could since Forrest, who had won a furlough home at the time Easy was in Germany, had not been with them there. Plus, the company did not actually experience combat in the Fatherland.

At Forrest's suggestion, and because of time constraints, I also scratched off Haguenau and decided to focus on Easy Company's—and Forrest Guth's—primary fields of combat, Normandy, Holland, and Belgium. But even though we did not visit Haguenau, I include it in this book because it was, technically, a Band of Brothers battlefield, and also to correct a grievous error committed by the screenwriters of the miniseries, much to the detriment of Forrest Guth.

After a lot of work and phone calls and e-mail exchanges, the trip finally became reality. For convenience's sake—our flight home was to leave from Amsterdam—we made the journey out of chronological order, leaving Normandy and going to Belgium and then Holland, rather than the other way around. However, for the book, I have arranged the chapters in their proper, historic sequence to minimize confusion.

For me, the trip was the fulfillment of a lifetime dream. In Aldbourne, I strolled the same streets the paratroopers had walked. I sat on a bench in St. Michael's cemetery, exactly where Dick Winters had sat when he met his adopted British family, and I had been in the house where he and Harry Welsh had stayed. I had stood in Colonel Sink's office, where he dealt with the anti–Herbert Sobel "mutiny" committed by Easy's noncommissioned officers.

In France, I walked the field at Brecourt Manor and followed the company's path to Carentan. I also had the deeply moving opportunity to walk the sand of Omaha and Utah beaches, and visit the U.S. cemetery where nearly ten thousand Americans lie at rest.

Moving to Belgium next, I had the opportunity to stand in Easy's foxholes in the Bois Jacques and view their attack field into Foy. Here, too, I fulfilled my promise to myself to visit the Maison de Neuve, the farm outside Beho where my late father-in-law and that other Easy Company fought so desperately for their lives. (I have included a chapter covering that fight in this book, because I feel it is also a story of heroism worth telling.)

Ending our trip in Holland, I stood at Easy's Market Garden drop zone and followed the company along Hell's Highway. At the Crossroad on "the Island," I walked on the field across which Easy Company had charged and defeated a superior number of enemy troops. I later had my photograph taken by the Schoonderlogt arch, where Dick Winters had stood so young and strong and proud in an October 1944 photograph.

And all along the way, I was touched by the interest and heartfelt gratitude and admiration extended to Forrest from *Band of Brothers* fans and other grateful people, who greeted us at nearly every stop, including a young World War II reenactor from Liverpool who portrays Forrest Guth.

This book recounts that pilgrimage, which, for me, began in Toccoa and ended in Amsterdam. It records the memories of Forrest Guth as he traveled by my side across England and Europe, as well as recollections from my interviews with Dick Winters, Clancy Lyall, Herb Suerth, Brad Freeman, Ed Tipper, and James Morgia, this latter with that other Easy Company at Beho, plus the writings and remembrances of other men of Easy and, when possible, the civilians whose lives the GIs touched.

I have also replayed the historical events that took place at these sites, and added my own personal recollections to create, I hope, a unique blending of the past and present—a then-and-now book that is, for me at least, a fitting final chapter in the Easy Company saga.

So I invite you now to walk with Forrest Guth and me as we retrace this heroic legacy and walk together *In the Footsteps of the Band of Brothers*.

CHAPTER 1

THE JOURNEY BEGINS

Toccoa and Currahee

For almost as long as time itself, the mountain has kept its silent vigil over the valley that flows out at its base some nine hundred feet below. Dubbed Currahee by the Cherokee Indians who once hunted amid its thick blanket of evergreen and hardwood trees, its name means Stands Alone, which, indeed, it does. The highest point in Stephens County, Georgia, the mountain is the last, or southernmost, peak of the Blue Ridge range, a solitary edifice that is now embraced by the Chattahoochee National Forest.

Six miles east of the mountain lies Toccoa, a city of about ten thousand souls and the seat of Stephens County.

Prior to the 1700s, what is now Toccoa was inhabited by the Cherokee and Creek Indians. One of the larger Cherokee villages was called Tugaloo, located as it was on the lower Tugaloo River, near the joining of the Toccoa Creek. With a population of about six hundred people clustered in a log council house and two hundred lodges, the place became a trade center, a religious meeting ground, and a social gathering place for the Cherokee.

During the Revolutionary War, the Cherokee had the misfortune to ally themselves with the British. As a result, Tugaloo was attacked and destroyed by units of the Georgia and South Carolina militias. The only evidence of the Cherokee town that remains is a large earthen mound rising above the waters of Lake Hartwell.

Modern-day Toccoa began in the early 1870s when three land speculators, Dr. O. M. Doyle of South Carolina, and B. Y. Sage and Thomas Alexander, both of Atlanta, anticipating the coming of the railroad through post–Civil War Georgia, purchased 1,765 acres around the old village of Tugaloo. Surveyed into individual tracts, the land was sold off in 1873. Within a year, the city of Toccoa was chartered.

By the late 1930s, a small but prosperous city had emerged. The two largest industries in town were a cotton mill owned by J & P Coats Company, which would remain a manufacturing fixture for almost seventy years, and an earth-moving equipment plant owned by a flamboyant industrialist named R. G. LeTourneau.

The coming of World War II was a boon to LeTourneau, as his plant churned out construction equipment for the U.S. military that would be used in every theater of combat. Employment at the factory grew to as many as two thousand during the war years.

In addition, during those war years, LeTourneau's Lake Louise facility, which later became the Georgia Baptist Assembly, was converted to a hospital to treat wounded servicemen.

But as vibrant as Toccoa became, it was the solitary mountain that carved the city's name permanently into American history.

Motoring west from Toccoa along Old Highway 123, formerly Highway 13, it's doubtful that many people notice the mountain, or if they do, they see only its height. Perhaps they also note that its rocky peak bristles with communication towers, which it stoically wears like a man-made thorny crown.

Only those who know its history are aware of the role this mountain played in the defense of the nation during World War II. For in a sprawling army camp that once lay within Currahee's shadow trained some of America's toughest soldiers, paratroopers of the 501st, 506th, 511th, and 517th parachute infantry regiments, rugged men who would take the war to our country's enemies.

Among these men was a company of soldiers whom a bestselling book and a widely acclaimed television miniseries would convert into national heroes, the Band of Brothers of Easy Company.

On January 17, 1940, under the auspices of the federal Works Projects Administration, or WPA—one of President Franklin D. Roosevelt's alphabet soup of organizations, such as the Tennessee Valley Authority (TVA) and the National Recovery Administration (NRA), aimed at putting a Depression-mired America back to work—construction crews began clearing a wooded meadow at Currahee's northern base. The place was to become a training area for the Georgia National Guard, and was called Camp General Robert Toombs, after a Southern firebrand and Confederate Civil War leader from Washington, Georgia, about sixty airline miles south of Toccoa. Although incomplete, the camp, adjacent to Highway 13, was dedicated on December 14, 1940.

By early 1942, the nation was at war, and the United States Army took over the National Guard camp and began expanding it, converting it from an infantry-training center into a training ground for parachute infantry, a new concept among America's armed forces. The first batch of trainees to arrive at Camp Toombs during that hot, dusty Georgia summer were designated the 506th Parachute Infantry Regiment (PIR), which would become one of the three regiments that would constitute the as yet to be formed 101st Airborne Division.

These men were true citizen soldiers, drawn from cities, towns, and farms across America.

Richard Davis Winters hailed from Lancaster, Pennsylvania. The only son of a foreman for Edison Electric and a gentle woman raised in the pacifist Mennonite tradition, he had worked his way through Franklin & Marshall College, majoring in business. He had enlisted in the army shortly after graduation in the summer of 1941, opting to get his military obligation out of the way before embarking on a career. Beginning his army life as a private at Camp Croft, South Carolina, Winters found he enjoyed the rugged, athletic military life, and soon asked to be assigned to officer candidate school at Fort Benning. His request was granted.

In mid-August 1942, Winters stepped down from a Southern Railway passenger car at the small wooden terminal at Toccoa, Georgia, and was met by a jeep that carried him the six miles to the new camp. He would be the second man to join Easy Company of the 506th's 2nd Battalion after its commander, Lieutenant Herbert Sobel.

Within days, more trains carrying more men began arriving at the station. Among them were three Pennsylvania boys, friends who had enlisted together in Philadelphia.

Forrest Guth was born February 6, 1921. A direct descendant of German immigrants who came to America before the Revolutionary

War, Guth spent his youth in the little town of Ruppsville near Allentown, which he recalled consisted of "five houses, a hotel, and a railroad track right by our house."

When America was drawn into the conflagration that had been raging in Europe for two years, Guth was working for Bethlehem Steel, where he helped produce armored plating for battleships. But the war and patriotism beckoned.

"Two of my friends, Rod Strohl and Carl Fenstermacher, found an advertisement for volunteers for army paratroopers," Guth recalled. "It was during the Depression and we read where we could make fifty dollars extra a month in the paratroops. And it was something new, and those two dumb friends of mine talked me into it. Actually, we talked each other into it."

In August 1942, the three comrades joined the army.

Guth recalled the "long train ride" to Toccoa, made even longer because passenger-carrying trains, back then just like today, had to give way to the more important freight trains.

For many men like Guth, this trip was a new experience in their lives.

"A lot of us had probably never been on a train before," he said.

After arriving in Toccoa, this increasing tide of men was ferried to the camp by truck, or, as Guth recalled, they would walk the entire six miles. But in whatever fashion they arrived, day by day, the 506th Regiment was taking shape.

I first saw Toccoa on Friday, October 7, 2005. I was in town for the annual Toccoa Reunion, where veterans who trained at the former camp are invited to return for a weekend of commemorative activities hosted by the Stephens County Chamber of Commerce and the local historical society.

My book *Biggest Brother: The Life of Major Dick Winters, the Man Who Led the Band of Brothers* had come out seven months earlier, and I had been invited to participate in the event by Bucky Simmons of the historical society, the weekend's main organizer.

Always a fan of rail travel, I arrived by train in Toccoa at 6:30 a.m. Stepping off Amtrak's Crescent City—Toccoa is one of only two stops Amtrak makes in the state of Georgia, the other being Atlanta itself—

the first thing I saw in the predawn gloom was the yellow, wooden, 120-year-old train station at the corner of South Alexander and West Railroad avenues. As I walked past the streamlined aluminum Amtrak cars—a far cry from the Pullmans of the 1940s—toward the station, it occurred to me that I was debarking at precisely the same place and seeing pretty much the same sights that Dick Winters, Forrest Guth, Bill Guarnere, and the other original members of Easy had seen when they arrived and were preparing for God only knows what.

I had known Dick Winters for four years. I had visited him often and, with his help, had written a book about his life. I had also known Forrest Guth since 2001, when I wrote an article about him for the alumni review published by Millersville University, from which both he and I had graduated.

They had both spoken to me about this town and this place. Now, as I stood where they had stood, ghostly images of them as young men ran through my imagination.

As promised, Bucky Simmons was at the station to meet me, and we were off to start a busy day that included speaking about Easy Company and my book to various school groups, followed by a luncheon at the National Guard Armory and book signings at Cornerstone Antiques and, later, at the Old Stephens County Courthouse. There I joined other authors, like Mark Bando, a well-known airborne historian, and Richard Killblane and Jake McNiece, who together penned the wonderful war story *The Filthy Thirteen*, about a gritty, gutsy band of paratroopers of which McNiece was one.

Later that day I was introduced to another piece of Easy Company history. Through an agreement with the village of Aldbourne, England, where the 506th would be stationed prior to and after their D-day operations, the Stephens County Historical Society was able to obtain one of the two remaining stable barns that had once been home to Easy Company. A work crew in Aldbourne dismantled the long wooden building from where it had stood within the walled courtyard of a breeding farm called Hightown, and transported it to America courtesy of the Pentagon and the Mississippi Air National Guard, which flew the parts from England to Dobbins Air Base in Marietta, Georgia.

The stable arrived in Toccoa, along with the British work crew, who reassembled it inside a new wing built onto the train station, which is owned by the historical society and serves as its headquarters. Leading the work crew was Keith Sowerby, who gave me a good-natured ribbing for misspelling his name in early editions of my book. Keith and I became friends that weekend, and he would later play a major role in creating this book.

On Friday afternoon, a formal dedication was held and the stable was opened to the public for the first time. While five of the six stall areas of the stable held memorabilia, the sixth had been reconverted into a barracks, with bunk beds, a small stove, uniform jackets hung on nails, duffel bags, and GI footlockers carefully placed around the room, to make it seem as if its soldier inhabitants had just stepped out, perhaps for chow.

Other artifacts were also on display, including items found during the dismantling of the stable in Aldbourne. Among these was a letter from the mother of Easy Company's Denver "Bull" Randleman, which was found tucked away in a nook in the wall where Randleman had placed it fifty-seven years earlier and either forgot it or never had a chance to retreive it.

Although no veterans of Easy Company attended the Toccoa event—they had their own company reunion elsewhere at the same time—their presence was all around me. Even the motel where I was staying, the Country Hearth Inn on West Savannah Street, was, in its own way, part of the legend—it was the very same place Home Box Office had lodged Easy Company's veterans during the premiere of the miniseries in 2001.

After Bucky and I had dinner that evening, I settled into my motel. Sitting in a wicker chair on the motel's porch, I watched the sun go down. I was in Toccoa, I thought, I was at Easy Company's birthplace. Tomorrow, I would be visiting the camp, the airfield where Winters and the other officers qualified for their jump wings, and Currahee itself. It was in these places that Dick and Forrest and the other men of Easy Company trained and lived and forged the bond that would make them inseparable for the rest of their lives

Tomorrow, I would be walking in their footsteps.

The man who would forge these untrained recruits into a fighting unit was Colonel Robert Sink. A 1927 graduate of West Point, Sink was

Looking toward Toccoa, in the distance, from the top of Currahee.

thirty-seven years old when the 506th was activated on July 26, 1942, almost making him old enough to be the father of many of the young men he would be leading.

The soldiers who served under Sink liked him. Although he was a military professional, Sink did not display that air of superiority prevalent among so many West Point officers. Winters recalled that he admired Sink's earthiness, and the fact that he mingled freely with his men. And while he was a hard drinker—the men affectionately called him "Bourbon Bob," although not to his face—he did not consume alcohol while on duty, a fact that impressed the teetotaling Winters.

Bill Guarnere, a South Philadelphia boy who arrived at Toccoa about this time, called Sink "honest and fair," while Guth said he respected Sink but that he was "a tough bird."

Everyone seemed to appreciate that Sink, while he could be gruff, was not overbearing, and that he had a knack for making the officers and men under him feel they were a part of the team.

As commander at Toccoa, one of the very first things Sink did was to change the camp's name. Aware of the value of high morale, Sink understood the potential for superstitious fear when the men realized that to get to the camp from town, they had to travel on Highway 13, passing the Toccoa Casket Company and a cemetery, to get to Camp Toombs. Sink persuaded the Department of the Army to change the name to Camp Toccoa.

Entering the base from Highway 13 onto what was then called Camp Drive, one first encountered the bus stop, where eager men clutching passes that were as valuable as gold awaited transportation to Toccoa or other destinations. Provided, of course, they had the time.

"We didn't have much time to look around," Forrest Guth recalled. "They kept us busy training."

Just beyond the bus stop, two World War I tanks parked on concrete slabs flanked the entrance road. Next came the guard post, which stood at the apex of Camp Drive, which continued straight, and Third Avenue, a wide dirt street that turned off to the left. Along the northern side of Third Avenue stood the mess halls, latrines, and other service buildings. Across the road was a barracks area, with 142 wood and tarpaper structures standing in twelve rows and bisected by four streets named First through Fourth. It was here that the men who wore the circular red, white, and blue patch of FORSCOM—the U.S. Army Forces Command—were billeted. These men would eventually comprise the 506th Regiment.

More buildings, mostly used by the motor pool and headquarters personnel, stood just south of the barracks, along Utility Street. Beyond Utility Street was the spacious drill field and parade ground. Here, and on cleared ground across Camp Drive to the west, were located the jump towers and the obstacle course needed to transform these raw recruits into finely honed weapons of war.

Also across Camp Drive from the parade ground along Warehouse Drive stood regimental headquarters, as well as the quartermaster, paymaster, waterworks, a warehouse, the camp fire station, the officers' club, and the regimental bowling alley and movie theater.

Between the drill fields and the main camp, along what was called A Street, was Cow Company, where new men coming in stayed until assigned to a company. This was also the final bivouac, where soldiers who had washed out of paratrooper training waited to be reassigned. Subsequently, Cow Company became known as W Company, with the

W standing for Welcome or Washout, depending on which direction a man was heading.

Men who stayed in Cow Company long remembered the ordeal. Set in a swale, when the heavy rains swept up from the Gulf of Mexico, the place turned into a morass of mud, and men who lay down on their cots the night before often awoke to find water gurgling past their faces as their beds' legs had sunk into the muck.

Don Malarkey had a dread fear of ending up in Cow Company. He initially had problems just getting his bed inspection-ready, but even worse, he happened to run into an officer with whom he had been friends back at the University of Oregon and happily greeted him by blurting out "Eugene" rather than by saluting him.

Beyond Cow Company, flanked by Regimental Street to the east and Camp Drive to the west, were rows and rows of large, olive drab, twelve-man squad tents. This tent city, bisected by five company streets labeled A through E, expanded as the camp grew and was fully operational by the time the 511th PIR arrived. In fact, Camp Toccoa grew so overcrowded that the 507th PIR eventually completed its training elsewhere. Across Camp Drive from this sea of tents was Officers Drive.

None of the roads in Camp Toccoa were paved, so when the rains fell, the whole place was quickly converted into a quagmire of red Georgia mud. Guarnere recalled the camp as being "a sloppy mess" with "dirt and mud everywhere." When it rained, he said, "your cot floated away."

But mud aside, there were nearby diversions the men grew to enjoy. Drawn to the soldiers like moths to a candle, barrooms and eateries sprang up almost overnight around the camp, the closest being the Wagon Wheel just across Highway 13 and a little west of the gate, or the Hi-Dee-Ho, just down the road toward town. Others included the Tadpole Inn, the Pines, Nubs Place, and the All Night Lunch. These quickly became popular spots to separate the men from their pay. However, some, like Forrest Guth, "pretty much stayed on base." Unless, of course, he managed to wangle a pass that would allow him and some friends to catch a bus or train to Atlanta, where they checked into places like the Peach Tree Hotel on Peach Tree Street.

"One guy would rent a hotel room and about ten guys piled in," he recalled.

* * *

Today, Camp Toccoa is slowly being converted into an industrial park.

Turning off of Route 123 onto Camp Drive, now Ayersville Road, Bucky stopped his truck. Unlike Camp Drive, Ayersville Road is paved.

As would be expected, the guard station that once blocked the road is long gone, as are the two World War I tanks that once stood sentinel.

Pointing to his left, where Ayersville Road intersected the highway, Bucky said, "That was where the bus stop was. They'd get their weekend passes and line up and wait for the buses to Atlanta. This was a busy place."

The most obvious feature at the intersection today is the monument commemorating the four regiments that trained at the camp. The monument, located on the right as one turns onto Ayersville Road, features a black marble marker about six feet high, engraved in gold leaf with jump wings and "Camp Toccoa, 1942–1945." A smaller stone to the left of the larger, cut diagonally right to left, depicts two legs, jump boots, and the lower portion of a rifle. On the rear of the monument is engraved the number of casualties suffered by each regiment that trained at the camp.

Behind the monument is a granite base in the shape of a deployed parachute with a small stone dedicated to each of the four regiments that trained there, the 501st, 506th, 511th (11th Airborne), and 517th combat team, this latter including paratroopers, an engineer company, and a battery of artillery. On each stone is also engraved the number of combat jumps each unit made, and where those jumps took place. A flag in the center of the parachute-shaped slab is permanently at half-mast.

Beyond the monument, almost all vestiges of the former training camp have vanished beneath the bulldozer. Third Avenue, Utility Street, and First through Fourth streets, and the more than 170 barracks buildings, classroom structures, and regimental and battalion offices are all gone. In their place is the large Milliken & Company textile plant— which employed three hundred people before closing its doors in 2006—a parking lot and manicured lawns, all surrounded by security fencing. However, sitting alone between the plant and the highway, along where Third Avenue once ran, stands an oblong white concrete structure that sixty-plus years ago had served as a mess hall, but today seems to be used for storage. It is Camp Toccoa's sole surviving building.

Continuing along Camp Drive, Patterson Pump, which provides about 380 jobs, stands off to the right, replacing the army structures that once lined Warehouse Street. In the cleared land beyond Patterson Pump, any trace of the jump towers, scaling walls, and other training equipment used to get the men ready for war is long gone.

Beyond the Milliken factory, as the old camp leads toward the mountain, part of the parade ground still remains as a grassy area inside the chain-link fence. Beyond that, Camp Toccoa becomes hidden beneath a wild profusion of tangled weeds, vines, and scrub pine trees. Despite this growth, the footprint of the company streets that cut through the tent city can still be discerned, and at places, concrete curbing remains. Rusted fire hydrants stand like silent sentinels at the end of each street, A through E, as if safeguarding the past.

As for the clubs and bars that sprang up around the camp, they have all vanished, most without a trace. However, if one gets out of the car along the highway just west of the camp entrance and takes a few steps into the brush, the rotting remnants of the Wagon Wheel may still be seen.

In that summer of 1942, some 5,300 enlisted men and 400 officers descended upon Camp Toccoa, from which just 1,800 enlisted men and 148 officers would graduate and become the 506th PIR. Men arriving straight from civilian life were divided into platoons of three rifle squads and a six-man mortar team with a 60mm mortar, and one .30-caliber machine-gun team in each squad. The platoons were formed into companies, and the companies folded into battalions.

Second Battalion was assigned to Lieutenant Colonel Robert Strayer, an able administrator who set a training schedule that would get his troops fit for action. While most of the men under him seemed to like Strayer personally, some questioned his ability as a decision maker in combat and felt his true strength was in selecting competent officers to serve directly under him. Winters, for example, once told me he thought Strayer's executive officer, Major Oliver Horton, was the more capable combat leader. Guarnere later wrote that Strayer "had a knack for picking the best officers, so it made his job much easier." Men like Horton and Lieutenants Clarence Hester, Lewis Nixon, and George Lavenson contributed immeasurably to Strayer's success, and most of the men knew it.

"We admired Strayer because he got all the credit, while all the officers underneath him had all the brains," Guarnere recalled.

Comprising Strayer's 2nd Battalion would be three companies, Dog, Easy, and Fox, each led by a first lieutenant. In the case of Easy Company, that first lieutenant was the Chicago native Herbert M. Sobel, a stern martinet of a man with a great ability for training, offset by a mind that sorely lacked the nimbleness to make the quick life-or-death decisions required of a combat leader.

One thing that becomes quickly obvious to anyone who has spoken to or read the memoirs of the men of Easy Company is that reactions vary when the name Herbert Sobel is tossed out.

"He was a good man, even though they didn't depict him well in the book or the movie," Forrest Guth told me. "He's the one that trained us. We were tough, and he's the one who did it."

Forrest's observations are shared by a number of men who hated Sobel personally but felt his rigidity forged their bond. On the other hand, Winters, who, as Sobel's executive officer, drew the brunt of the man's disfavor, once remarked to me that it was the vigorous training program laid out by Sink and the men's own determination that made them tough. Sobel, Winters remarked, "just made things more difficult."

The training Winters referred to was a steady routine of calisthenics that included push-ups, pull-ups, an obstacle course that was to be run in three minutes, climbing log walls, crawling through large pipes, jumping hurdles, and log tossing. And when they finished, Guarnere recalled, they did it all "over and over until we could barely stand." The whole time, Sobel cursed and yelled at them as the men silently cursed him in return.

The training area also boasted several thirty-four-foot jump towers, where each soldier slid down a sixty-foot cable while suspended from a fifteen-foot static line. It was, one recalled, like "jumping off a three-story building." As they did their jump training, the men were taught the five points of performance: check your body position and count, check your canopy, check initial oscillation, get your back into the wind, and prepare to land.

In addition to jumping, the men learned the use of hand signals, field phones, and radios. Although they did not know it at the time, the woodland around the camp, with a number of certain species of European trees added by the army, was selected because of its resemblance to what they might encounter in Germany. In these woods, the troopers studied compass reading, map reading, and how to navigate at night. (Later, when they arrived in England and their destination was known, German army tactics and the use of enemy weapons were added to their curriculum.) Forrest recalled that the woods around the camp were home to "a lot of chiggers and ticks."

Camp Toccoa had no rifle range, so the men were marched forty miles to Clemson College, where they learned to fire every weapon in the American infantry arsenal.

"The army was training us to be killers," Guarnere remembered. "We didn't want any goldbricks or sissies next to us in combat."

One long-remembered facet of Sobel's training program was the twelve-mile night marches, which stretched into eighteen miles if Sobel so chose, which he often did. On more than one occasion, Easy Company would be on the hiking trail while the rest of 2nd Battalion was in camp or on leave.

"All the other companies would be done and we'd be out there running with gas masks on our heads," Guarnere later said.

Sobel's favorite exercise was the Friday night thirty-five-mile nonstop hike with full gear. He would order canteens to be filled with water at the start of the hike, and expected them to still be full when they got back. Harsh punishment awaited any man who sneaked a sip.

Fatigue was also not tolerated by Sobel.

"If the guy in front of you fell asleep, he would drop his rifle, so you just poked him to wake him up," Guarnere said.

"We wanted to kill him, but we also wanted our wings. So we did exactly what we were told," Forrest remembered.

During the company runs up Currahee, Don Malarkey recalled how Sobel would yell, "The men of Easy Company do not quit. Do you understand me?" and "Gear up. We're going up Currahee. Now! Heigh-ho, Silver."

Just as Sobel made training harder, he also made it more difficult to obtain relaxation time. He relentlessly inspected the men, their weapons, and their bunks, and would yank a man's pass, or even the entire company's, for the slightest infraction—real or contrived.

"It was hard enough to get a pass in the first place, and you could lose it in a hurry," Forrest told me. "Sobel was trying to make a name for himself."

Sobel would find "someone to make a fool out of and not give them a pass," Guarnere later recalled.

"Your tie wasn't tucked. It was. Your shoes weren't shined right. They were. Your sleeve wasn't buttoned. If he had it in for you, you were done," Guarnere wrote.

Sobel's inspections, Malarkey recalled in his excellent memoir, *Easy Company Soldier*, occurred at any hour, and heaven help the man who met Sobel's disfavor.

"Sobel would look you eye to eye—he was tall—and start sneering at you and raising his voice just enough so you wanted to start choking him," Malarkey recalled.

The tension was too much for some, and men began disappearing from the platoons, heading for Cow Company and reassignment.

"Guys couldn't cut it. Couldn't cut Sobel. Maybe both," Malarkey wrote.

Despite their dislike for Sobel, the men grudgingly admitted that whatever exercise he ordered, or however many runs up Currahee he demanded of them, Sobel was right there, doing it with them. Sobel "did what we did," Malarkey recalled.

The men felt they understood why Sobel was so hard on them.

"In a strange way, it kind of filled you with pride," Malarkey wrote in his book. "You got the idea he was hardening us for tougher times to come. That he truly wanted us to be the best of the bunch—and believed we could be. We wrestled, boxed, did decathlon events, and ran, ran, ran. Soon we established the finest fitness record in the 506th. . . . We were becoming exactly what Sobel wanted us to be; the best . . . not that he ever told us he was proud of us. He'd find a way to suck it right out of you."

Quite the opposite from Sobel was Dick Winters, for whom the men had nothing but respect. Guarnere called him a "good guy" who led by example, and Forrest Guth said Winters was "an excellent leader." But while he was considerate of the men in training and in camp, Winters had yet to be tested in battle. Guarnere, whose Philadelphia home was just sixty miles from Winters's home in Lancaster, was well aware of

Lancaster County's Mennonite/pacifist heritage. He often referred to Winters as a Mennonite or Quaker, thus questioning Winters's will to fight. Later, of course, he would revise this assessment, saying of Winters that the men "would follow him anywhere."

The training went on for thirteen weeks, starting with reveille at 0500 and breakfast an hour later. Then it was off to work, as men ran the hillside obstacle course, over stacked lumber, and through wooden chutes that peppered their hands with splinters. They did sit-ups, windmills, somersaults, and the unpopular forced Friday night marches through the Georgia countryside and along rural roads.

Through it all, the men formed a tight bond, prompting Guarnere to recall, "By the time we were done, we'd know each other's thoughts."

Thanksgiving 1942 found Easy out on maneuvers. It was so cold water froze in the men's canteens, and while others back in camp feasted on turkey, Forrest and his buddies dined on C rations, only because, the men believed, the army had nothing worse to give them.

"Had it been known that there was a form of concentrated ration infinitely more distasteful than C rations, there might have been serious consequences," the *Currahee Scrapbook* bemoaned.

The exercise most remembered by the men, even sixty years later, occurred in November 1942 and would be forever known as the "hog innards problem." To add a touch of grim realism to the training, Sink had hog entrails brought in from a local meatpacking company. This bloody debris was strewn over an area twenty feet wide and fifty to sixty feet long. Barbed wire was strung from stakes eighteen inches off the ground. Machine guns loaded with live ammo were mounted on two-by-four wooden supports with the tripod legs sandbagged down so the gun remained stable. The men were required to crawl through the bloody gore, heads kept low, as .30 caliber bullets whizzed by above them.

Forrest recalled that the training was intense and required "the stamina and will to be able to perform beyond the ordinary." The men worked hard not to let each other down and had the feeling "if Sobel can do it, so can I."

"We learned respect for the abilities and talents of our comrades, which has stayed with us for our lifetimes," Forrest told me. "We were a band of brothers."

Indeed they were, for despite the difficult training, hard work, running the mountain and Sobel's harshness, it was here in this camp that the men of Easy forged bonds of friendship that would last them the rest of their lives.

Besides Fenstermacher and Strohl, with whom he enlisted, Forrest drew especially close to Carwood Lipton, a West Virginian, who would become Guth's leader when Lipton took over as 3rd Platoon sergeant, and later company first sergeant. Throughout the campaigns in Europe that lay in their future, Forrest and Lipton shared a foxhole.

In his postwar writings, Wild Bill Guarnere shared Forrest Guth's liking of Lipton, whom he referred to as a "smart kid, very conscientious," and a leader who "used his brain." He "was tough as nails," Guarnere wrote, and "looked out for the other men."

Forrest also befriended Paul "Hayseed" Rogers, "a farm boy from Kansas City," and Walter "Smokey" Gordon, a Southern boy who enlisted in Philadelphia after he was rejected in Mississippi for having flat feet. Gordon was "a big guy," Forrest recalled, who seemed to enjoy griping about having to carry the heavy .30-caliber machine gun. Forrest was fond of Gordon, who was a good, intelligent soldier, although he did not take things with appropriate seriousness, a flaw that may have cost him a chance to move up in rank.

"He could have been an officer, I'm sure, except that he never got down to business," Forrest said.

There was also Floyd Talbert, who, Guth recalled, underwent intense ribbing due to being "deathly afraid of anything that crawled."

"We were always putting something in his footlocker or in his bed," Forrest remembered with a chuckle. "We even put things in his ammo belt. He'd go wild."

Jokester George Luz, a Rhode Island boy, was a company favorite. Guth recalled how, when the company was out running, Luz, who was good at disguising his voice, would call out, "Captain Sobel to the rear." Sobel, who always ran at the head of the column, would dutifully double back to see what was up. Finding no problems, and undoubtedly perturbed, he'd run back to lead. Later, the joke would be repeated. This particular prank caused Sobel to run more than the rest of the men.

"Sobel never caught on," Forrest said.

The men also assigned nicknames to each other, and Guth became "Goody" "because of my last name. Sometimes they also called me

'Chowhound' because I loved to eat." Gordon was known as "Smokey" or "Lard," Talbert was "Tab" or, oddly, "Bunny," and Francis Mellet was "Mel" or "Pope."

Wild Bill, as Guarnere would be known after Normandy, had a special affection for John Martin. Guarnere remembered the future 1st Platoon sergeant as a "loner" and "goldbrick" who would "beg, borrow or steal" what he wanted. However, Guarnere wrote, in combat, Martin proved to be an excellent leader.

The first of his fellow Easy Company paratroopers that Don Malarkey met was Rod Bain from Ilwaco, Oregon, "right across the Columbia [River]" from Malarkey's hometown of Astoria. The two became good friends.

Malarkey also recalled one of his other friends, Joe Toye, whom he called the "toughest guy in the unit, bar none." But the boy from Oregon was probably closest to Warren Harding "Skip" Muck of Tonawanda, New York. An adventurous kid who once swam the Niagara River, Muck was assigned to the mortar squad, along with Malarkey.

"I'd sight. He'd drop the rounds down the tube," Malarkey recalled.

When they ran Currahee, it was side by side.

Malarkey described himself and Muck as both being "ornery, mischievous and athletic." Many times, he recalled, they would drop by the PX, buy a Coke or a beer, sit on the floor with their backs to the wall, and play the jukebox "until I thought we were going to wear out the grooves in those 78 rpm records."

Malarkey believed the unassuming Muck was the best-liked soldier in the company, with a personality that "drew people to him like cold hands to a fire."

"Skip was the real deal; didn't have a phony bone in his body," Malarkey remembered.

After the war, the two made plans. Muck would show Malarkey where he swam the Niagara and Malarkey would take him fishing on the Nehalem River, where he had spent many happy days of his youth.

The thought that either of them would not get back home was never discussed.

Another of Malarkey's Easy Company friends, Robert "Burr" Smith, would later write that Muck was "a happy guy, and those who knew him basked in the warmth of that happiness and were happy, too."

Thinking back on the men he served with, Forrest told me, "It was a great group of guys from all over the country, and we had a lot of fun, even though the training was hard work. They're the best friends I ever had. When one dies, it's just like losing a family member."

But amid the mud and heat of the camp, the hard training, the tight friendships, and the frivolity of spending leave time in Atlanta and elsewhere, it was Currahee mountain, looming up just behind the camp, that drew everyone's attention, and almost every man who saw it knew that locating the camp at its base was no coincidence. Speaking for all of the 506th, Dick Winters told me in 2002, "The first time I saw that mountain, I knew we'd have to climb it."

He was correct, and whether it was running shirtless, wearing just blue shorts and combat boots, or in full battle gear, those "three miles up and three miles down" left a lasting impression.

"We ran Currahee every day and sometimes twice," Forrest told me. "It was hell. We ran up that son of a gun no matter what, and if you couldn't make it, you were thrown out. You did everything you could to get up there and back. It was a grueling route."

Forrest said had the trail been "nice and smooth" like the one depicted in the miniseries, the run would have been easier.

"But it wasn't," he said. "It was full of rocks."

Malarkey recalled the first time he ran Currahee. After half a mile, he was "sucking eggs," he wrote. Prior to the company running the mountain, Malarkey was encouraged to go for an evening run with his buddy Rod Bain to see what he "was up against."

"Near the top, I thought I was going to lose my dinner," Malarkey later wrote. "On the way down, I thought I was going to lose everything I'd eaten since high school. It took about two hours, but, wheezing like an aging outboard motor, I made it."

Upon completing the run, Bain congratulated him. That night, Malarkey's thoughts were not of home three thousand miles away, but of the special nature of the unit he was joining, and how "guys who didn't even know me would run up a mountain just for my benefit."

This, he said, was his initial bonding into the Band of Brothers.

The ideal time for running Currahee was fifty minutes or less. The 101st record was forty-two minutes. Winters's best time was forty-four.

A relatively calm stretch of the "three miles up and three miles down" trail winding up Currahee.

Often their regimental runs were on Saturdays. The 506th would jog past Colonel Sink and his staff perched on the reviewing stand by the drill field, then continue on Utility Street, turning left onto Fourth Street, which connected to the mountain trail, and head for the top. Army ambulances followed to the rear.

On occasion, Sobel made the difficult run even tougher. Forrest recalled the time Sobel had the mess hall serve the men a spaghetti dinner, then had them run Currahee. It left many of the men "heaving their guts" on the trail, my friend remembered.

"It was tough," he said. "When I look at that mountain now, I wonder how I ever did it. I can't even walk up there anymore."

For me, the high point of my trip was coming face-to-face with Currahee, and as I climbed into Bucky's truck for the trip to the mountain—I wasn't about to run it—my excitement grew. By standing on this ground, I would truly be walking in their footsteps.

While the camp, as described earlier, is slowly disappearing,

Currahee, rising up behind, continues to mark the passing of the years. The road so many men ran along during those wartime days is now called the Col. Robert Sink Memorial Trail, and was dedicated by veterans of the "Five-oh-Sinks" on November 4, 2000, with two of Sink's daughters in attendance.

Just as daunting now as it was in 1943, the first two miles of the dirt road are relatively smooth, but as it wends its way up the ever-increasing slope, beneath the silent canopy of trees, the final mile becomes more rutted, with numerous loose rocks on which a fatigued runner could turn an ankle. In 2001, during the miniseries premiere, the actors who portrayed the men of Easy, most of them in fine physical shape thanks to the intensive boot camp they underwent prior to filming, actually ran Currahee. The veterans, having done it in their youth, contentedly watched from the comfort of the vans in which they were riding. Only one actor, Frank John Hughes, who portrayed Wild Bill Guarnere, succeeded in running the entire distance to the top. For his achievement, Winters stooped down and picked up a rock from the mountain's summit and handed it to Hughes.

"If anyone was going to make it," Winters told the young man, "I knew it would be you."

The Currahee Challenge, where hearty souls are invited to run the Col. Sink Trail "three miles up and three miles down," is still a part of the annual Toccoa Reunion, although participation has dropped off in recent years. Still, the few who make it to the top and back down have the satisfaction of knowing they have re-created history. Not to mention that they are treated to a spectacular view. Rippling hills and fields of green roll away across the valley toward Toccoa, visible off in the distance. The only annoyance to the beauty of this setting is the squat, ugly concrete building behind a hostile-looking wire fence, and the array of steel communication towers that dwarf the surrounding trees on Currahee's summit.

Despite that, the runners who reach the peak have the satisfaction of knowing they are standing in the shadow of great warriors.

Jump training for the officers took place at LeTourneau Field. To see who would have the honor of being the first man to hit the silk, Sink organized a Junior Officers' Olympics. Competition was intense and included excelling at push-ups, chin-ups, and the fastest time on the obstacle course. The Olympics culminated in a race to see who could make the best time up and down Currahee. The athletic Dick Winters won and was awarded the first seat in the first stick for the first of the five qualifying jumps.

After a hair-raising takeoff from the undersized airfield, the C-47 circled the drop zone. Winters recalled standing by the open door, a mixture of excitement and fear coursing through his mind. He was eager, yet nervous, and he asked himself, "Am I nuts? What the hell am I doing here?" Pushing his fears aside, he jumped, coming down in a cornstalk-stubbled field just northwest of the camp.

The fifth and final qualifying jump for the 506th's officers was a morning exercise. Upon its completion, the officers were permitted to blouse their boots by sticking their pant cuffs inside—the mark of a paratrooper.

However, because of the inadequacies of the airfield—and the fact that Sink's lone C-47 later crash-landed on the runway, luckily without injuries—jump training for the enlisted men was shifted to Fort Benning. Thus, the 506th packed up in preparation for leaving Toccoa.

While looking for a way to make the trip to Benning more memorable, Sink had an inspiration. He had read an article in *Reader's Digest* about a Japanese unit in Malaya that marched 100 miles in seventy-two hours while en route to defeat the British at Singapore. Determined to prove his regiment was better than anything the emperor could field, Sink decided that his men would walk the 118 miles to Atlanta and beat the Japanese time.

Marching in column, the 506th tramped out of the main gate on the morning of December 1, and turned left onto Route 13. Almost immediately, the weather turned against them. The sky clouded over and a cold rain began to fall.

"It was rainy," Forrest remembered. "We had sleet and it was muddy as heck."

Worse, Sink often left the road to march his men cross-country.

Forrest recalled, "We were carrying full field equipment and rifle, and were taking the most beating a Georgia winter had to offer. When we arrived at bivouac at 2100 hours, we had already accomplished forty miles on windy, rainy, muddy backcountry roads. The weather was so miserable that we couldn't get the field stove started. During the night, the temperature dipped to the low twenties and everything we had when we woke up was frozen solid."

The next day they marched another forty miserable miles.

"On the ice-caked mud roads, we suffered sprained ankles, and some fellows ended up limping along with one man on each side supporting them," Forrest said. "Other soldiers would relieve those men of their rifles and they would walk along with as many as three rifles slung across their shoulders. There was many a sore and blistered foot by the time we reached our destination, two of which were my own."

Lacking a tent, Winters recalled rolling out his sleeping bag on the ground. He removed his wet boots and tried to settle in as best he could. Temperatures plunged below freezing overnight and Winters awoke to find his sleeping bag frozen to the hardened mud and his boots stiff to the point where he could barely get them on, even with the laces totally undone.

Guarnere said the men "ate slop, slept on wet ground, and we were freezing." Many wanted to "take off our boots and wiggle our toes," he said, but were unaware that their feet had swelled. As a result, some could not get their boots back on, so they slit them with a knife, put them back on, but left them unlaced.

"Everybody was in pain," Guarnere wrote. "Our backs were killing us, our feet were killing us."

Malarkey remembered that for mortarmen like himself and Muck, the hike was "like being asked to climb Mount Everest with a pack full of bricks on our backs." During one stop, Malarkey wrote, he was invited by the lady of a nearby house to get some water. Thirsty, but knowing it was forbidden, he glanced both ways to see if either Sobel or Winters was watching. Not seeing them, he ran across the road and filled two canteens. Sobel spotted Malarkey as he dashed back and yelled, "I want that man's name." However, at that precise moment, the column resumed its march, and Sobel never learned the culprit's identity.

Whatever aches and pains the men experienced on the march disappeared when the column reached Atlanta on December 3. After bivouacking in a rest area overnight, they marched down Peach Tree Street the next day amid cheers and newspaper photographer flashbulbs. At the other end of town, they boarded a train for Fort Benning. They had marched the 118 miles in seventy-five hours, fifteen minutes (actual marching time: thirty-three hours, thirty minutes) and earned a unit citation.

"It was a big to-do," Guarnere wrote. "We beat the Japanese record."

They also proved their toughness. Of the 586 men of 2nd Battalion who started the march, only 12 failed to make it, none of whom were from Guth's 3rd Platoon.

"Third Platoon made it without anyone falling out or having to be carried," he told me. "That was one of our feats."

Still, the men ached for days afterward and Malarkey, his legs swollen, spent the next three days in bed.

The second day of my trip to Toccoa, Saturday, October 8, was taken up by activities at the Toccoa–Stephens County Airport. The landing strip had been built in the late 1930s by LeTourneau so he had a place to land his private, twin-engine DC-3, the civilian equivalent of the C-47, during jaunts between his Toccoa plant and another in Illinois. (LeTourneau's use of a corporate plane put him years ahead of other industrialists, who, in those days, mostly moved about in private railcars.)

I spent much of the afternoon signing books and answering questions about Dick Winters, but during my breaks I had the opportunity to recall Dick telling me about his experiences here when he made his qualifying jumps. He recalled how the runway at what was then called LeTourneau Airfield was not long enough to handle a fully loaded C-47. Pilots taking off were forced to dive parallel to the slope of the hill to gain flying speed. When landing, pilots reaching the end of the airstrip had to cut left or right and run along the edge of the hill. It made for a hellish ride for paratroopers and flight crews alike.

"It was safer to jump out of the plane than to land in it," Winters remembered.

Today, Toccoa Airport is a modern facility that could more than handle any plane Sink cared to land there. During the Toccoa Reunion, the field was the site of artillery-firing demonstrations, and helicopter-borne U.S. Army Rangers performing modern methods of inserting and extracting men from a hot landing zone. The event was capped off by a small World War II battle reenactment between U.S. and "German" troops.

By early December, much of Easy Company's initial ground training was behind them. Now it was time to learn what they were being paid $50 a month extra to do—jump from an airplane into the enemy's midst.

To add a bit of levity to the idea of leaping from a perfectly good airplane, not to mention the overall rigorous training, in August 1942, Sink's executive officer, Colonel Charles H. Chase, issued the Paratrooper Insurance Benefits Plan as follows:

Broken back—1 case Scotch whiskey

Broken arm or leg—3 bottles Bourbon whiskey per limb so affected

Broken ankle or wrist—2 bottles Scotch whiskey per ankle or wrist

Broken finger—Family-sized beer per bone involved

Sprain, assorted types—12 ounce bottle of beer per sprain

Contusions or lacerations—12 ounce bottle of beer per five such

The Secretary Treasurer of the mess, upon receipt of certificate signed by the Reg'l Surgeon covering injuries falling within the categories listed in vertical column I will, without delay, and at the expense of the mess fund, present to the injured member the benefit listed in vertical column II.

Putting their jump training into practice at Benning, the men were taught how to land properly by jumping into piles of sawdust from dummy plane fuselages, and were dropped under a deployed parachute from a 250-foot tower. Finally, it was time for the real thing.

"We knew who had arms and legs," Don Malarkey wrote after the war. "Now, aboard C-47s heading into the skies over Georgia, we were going to find out who had balls."

In jump training, the men of Easy came to understand the rigors of their previous training. The *Currahee Scrapbook* notes, "You wondered why you learned parachute packing and all about panels, until the day you floated to terra firma with the beautiful stretch of silk, and you looked up to see (just in case). Then you were sure you had learned everything."

On his first jump, Malarkey recalled how, as he drew closer and closer to the C-47's yawning doorway, his "stomach churned harder." Everything he had worked for up to this point boiled down to this brief moment in time. He knew the others felt the same way, too—scared and nervous. Then he was in the doorway and out of the plane and the "wind rippled my face, far worse than any gale-force storm I'd experienced on Oregon's windy north coast." He drew a sigh of relief when he felt that blessed tug as the chute opened. He landed with a "quick jolt of pain" as his chute swirled around him.

Recalling his first jump, Forrest Guth told me, "I had no idea what was going to happen, so I just didn't think too much about it. I always got jarred on landing, but I never broke any bones."

Forrest equated jumping from a C-47 with riding a roller coaster.

"When you got down, you wanted to go back up," he said, a smile creasing his lips at the memory.

Guarnere recalled that he wasn't afraid until he actually jumped from the plane, after which, at fifteen hundred feet, "all my training went out the window." He tried running in midair, arms flailing to the point where "I almost broke my neck." Somehow, he managed to land safely. His second jump should have been easier, but wasn't. Panicking again, he pulled his emergency chute, yanking the ripcord down rather than out and away from him. That caused the parachute to open between his legs, with the result that he now had two open canopies pulling him in different directions. Again, in spite of himself, Guarnere landed safely on the ground, whereupon he "caught holy hell" from his commander.

For many men like Guarnere and Guth, the first jump was the toughest, yet few refused to leap from the plane, knowing that to do so meant instant washout. Some did wash out, and that meant not just a personal failure but public humiliation. Malarkey recalled the "drumming out" ceremony, where the men were lined up and forced to watch as the unlucky soldier was stripped of his patches. Next, a jeep rolled up and dumped his barracks bag on the ground at the man's feet, and he was marched off to a mournful drumbeat. Malarkey called the ceremony "sickening" and that it was "not the proudest day in American military history."

Still, most made it. Forrest Guth received his letter of qualification from Sink on December 8, 1942, and celebrated by purchasing a civilian version of the army air corps leather jacket, which he adorned with the 506th "ParaDice" patch depicting two red dice, one showing the five, the other a six. Between them was a large zero adorned with an eagle. The patch was not authorized once the 506th was formally attached to the 101st Airborne Division in June 1943, but that did not stop Forrest from wearing it on his jacket throughout the war.

Malarkey called the day he got his wings "one of the proudest days in my life." It meant not just the culmination of a lot of hard work, but also he would now be getting that extra $50 a month, which he sent, along with $15 from his regular pay, home to his mother to assist her in his absence.

After Guarnere's final jump, he celebrated by blousing his pants and pinning on his gold jump wings.

"Everyone knew you were the best of the best," Guarnere wrote. "You were different from any other soldier. Those wings made you different, and you never took them off."

The final phase of Easy Company's training began in early March at Camp Mackall, North Carolina. Here the men underwent the most extensive maneuvers they had yet experienced. Emphasis now shifted from just learning how to jump and land to quick movements and operating behind enemy lines. Within Easy Company, though, the increased field training seemed to heighten the tension, as Sobel's leadership deficiencies became more and more glaring and his treatment of the men grew correspondingly harsher.

During one night exercise, the company lay in a strong defensive position in a wooded area waiting for the "enemy" to walk into their carefully set ambush. In the silence of the woods, a breeze stirred the leaves. Springing to his feet, Sobel, his nerves taught, yelled, "Here they come! Here they come!"

"Jesus Christ," Winters heard a nearby soldier mutter. "I'm going into combat with this man? He'll get us all killed."

Nicknamed by his men "the Black Swan" or, later in England, "Herr Black Swan," Sobel seemed "awkward," Guarnere recalled, and "all he did was scream."

"He was high-strung, ranted and raved, criticized everything," Guarnere remembered. "A mean son of a bitch."

The men retaliated against Sobel's harshness with a host of pranks. His maps were sometimes "mislaid" so he would get lost on field exercises, and once medics, as part of an exercise on treating the wounded, put Sobel under anesthesia and performed a fake appendectomy, complete with an actual scar. He never discovered who was responsible.

"He was mad as hell, but nobody would confess," Guarnere remembered.

Sobel drummed into the men the importance of their rifle, telling them to eat with it, sleep with it, and "make it your wife." He had them memorize the weapon's serial number. In an attempt to catch men who failed to do this, Sobel and First Sergeant William Evans slipped around the encampment late one night, stealing all the weapons. The next day when the men fell out, Sobel's jaw dropped when he saw each and every man had his rifle. It seems that, in the dark, Easy's commander had gotten into the wrong camp and stolen the weapons of Fox Company.

In the field, Guarnere wrote that Sobel "didn't know what to do under any circumstances." He lacked common sense, the men believed, and did not have the mentality for combat, relying on Evans instead. In combat scenarios, Guarnere recalled how Sobel would "make noise and holler when we were supposed to be hiding." Worse, he was "nervous and jumpy, he would overreact."

Sobel's abilities now became more and more the focus of concern. In war games, he made crucial tactical errors that resulted in him and his men walking straight into the enemy. He lingered too long over simple map questions, got lost, or would make a decision, then suddenly reverse himself.

Guarnere was convinced that the men knew if Sobel screwed up in combat, they would die. Subsequently, drastic action was contemplated.

"There were a hundred forty-eight of us, and a hundred forty-seven talked about 'accidentally' killing Sobel as soon as we got in combat," Guarnere said.

By summer 1943, the training was over, and on August 22, the 506th arrived at Camp Shanks on the Hudson River, an embarkation center in New York. Red Cross "Donut Dollies" saw them off with pastries and coffee as the men prepared to board the ship that would carry them to war. The night before they boarded, the men had a big party, Guarnere recalled, and "everybody got drunk."

It was a memorable send-off.

Camp Toccoa continued to function after the 506th departed, graduating men of the 511th PIR, who would see action under General Douglas MacArthur in the Philippines, and the 517th PIR, which would make the war's last jump in Europe, Operation Varsity, by descending on Germany's industry-rich Ruhr Valley.

The end of the war meant the end of the camp, which later in the 1940s saw duty as a Georgia State Prison site, housing primarily youthful offenders. However, too many escapes forced prison officials to close the facility and move its population to a newer, more secure facility at Alto, Georgia.

Thus the camp that once turned out so many of America's elite fighing men was left to be reclaimed by nature.

My weekend at Toccoa concluded with a banquet held Saturday night at the Georgia Baptist Convention Center, the same place the cast and crew of the miniseries, along with the Easy Company veterans, had gathered in July 2001 to dine and view the "Day of Days" episode of the film.

As they watched the film that evening, Bucky told me, "Some of the men had tears in their eyes, the others were ducking as if the bullets were really flying past. Winters was just sitting there in deep thought."

During the Brecourt portion of the movie where Private Hall was killed, Bucky said of Winters, "you could tell he was back in Normandy." Later, Bucky said he spoke to Dick and could sense the fatigue in his voice.

"No one was paying Winters any attention," he told me. "You would never guess he was the star of the movie that had just been shown. He was like a regular grandfather. He talked about the town now and about other things."

I thought of that other banquet six years ago in this very room. Today, in 2005, they were honoring in part the dedication of the stable that had once stood in Aldbourne. In 2001, they honored the men who lived in it.

Then it was time for me to leave, and a member of the historical society drove me to the train station.

Standing alone in the darkness outside Toccoa rail station that Saturday night, awaiting the 11:30 p.m. arrival of the Crescent City that would carry me back to Pennsylvania, I had time to ponder the past two days. I remembered the descriptions of the camp and training that I had heard from Dick Winters and Forrest Guth. I thought back to their recollections of Sobel and Sink and their never-to-be-forgotten runs up Currahee.

Then my thoughts turned to where I was standing at that exact moment, alone and in the dark at the Toccoa rail station, and I pictured Winters, Guth, and the other soldiers milling around there as well.

Now I had been where they had been, seen what they had seen and walked where they had walked, and that night I made the decision that if I could walk elsewhere in their footsteps, I would do so.

The narration that follows is a fullfillment of that pledge.

Chapter 2

"A NICE, QUIET LITTLE TOWN"

Aldbourne, Wiltshire

Forrest Guth and I departed from Philadelphia International Airport on the night of Friday, October 31, 2008. As the plane climbed to its cruising altitude of thirty-seven thousand feet, I watched the lights below. Many were stationary, but countless others moved in ribbons along invisible streets and highways. Then an inky blackness began to creep into my window from the east, growing broader and broader, as the expanse of lights below grew narrower until it was completely gone. With nothing below us now except the absolute darkness of the Atlantic Ocean, I settled back in my seat.

This was my first trip across the ocean, but Forrest, seated beside me, quietly listening to music through headphones, had made this trip many times. The first, of course, was the one he had made in September 1943 with his comrades of Easy Company—all expenses paid by Uncle Sam—when they departed from New York, sailing toward an uncertain future.

That earlier journey had been aboard the SS *Samaria*, a 19,602-ton, 601-foot-long cruise ship pressed into service as a troop carrier. Launched in 1922 by Vickers Ltd. along with her sister ships, the *Scythia* and the *Laconia*, the ship could accommodate 2,165 passengers—1,500 in third class, 350 in second class, and 315 in first class—along with 434 crew members. On the day it ferried Easy Company to war, her decks were jammed with some 5,000 GIs.

While Forrest and I flew to England in relative comfort, with flight attendants serving us a hot meal and drinks, Forrest's first trip was far less pleasant. The ship was crowded, he told me, and so dirty and hot below that "most of us stayed on deck." Possibly worse, he recalled, was being served fish chowder for breakfast.

"There was a rumor that the British were getting all sorts of American rations, but that they kept those for themselves rather than serve them to us," Forrest told me.

As the ship rolled up and down the ocean swells, many men, Forrest remembered, "turned green and started puking." To pass the time, men gambled, at least when Sobel was not running them through calisthenics.

"It got our minds off the rancid boat," Guth said. "The boat stunk. We stunk. The food stunk."

In his book, *Parachute Infantry*, David Webster, then with Fox Company, wrote of the voyage, "At times our sooty, disheveled Cunard Line transport took on the air of a floating mad-house. There was simply not enough fresh water to go around. To remain even tolerably clean, we had to resort to salt-water showers. This required special salt-water soap, which was in very short supply. I rubbed ordinary soap on my hands for five minutes and produced nothing but wet slime—no lather. The salt-water soap left you very sticky. Our clothes got very dirty, very quickly from sleeping in the filthy corridors, and we had to keep our life jackets on at all times, even when sleeping. . . . We had to wash our mess kits and utensils in salt water and discovered, to our sorrow, that they were starting to corrode and rust. After three days at sea, my spoon was so rusty that I cut my lips when I ate with it. Anyone who was lucky enough to have an aluminum mess kit guarded it with their life."

Fresh drinking water was only available at fifteen-minute intervals and shaving time was limited. The coffee was horrible, and the men ate meals twice a day in a crowded, unventilated mess hall on the lower deck. Luckily the trip across the unpredictable North Atlantic was relatively calm and U-boat-free.

Ten days after the men lined the ship's rail to watch the Statue of Liberty fade into the distance, they again piled on deck for their arrival in Liverpool. Sergeant Bob Williams of 2nd Battalion, 506th headquarters, later wrote, "We crowded the rails on the starboard side and the dockhands below showed up and asked us if we had any extra cigarettes. Packet after packet rained down onto the dockside."

Before they debarked from the ship, the men, who already had been prohibited from wearing their Screaming Eagles shoulder patches during this move to Europe, grumbled after receiving orders that they were to wear infantry leggings over their much-prided jump boots to further disguise their identity.

"This did not sit well with the men, as they had worked like hell to achieve the status those boots represented and were damn proud of the fact," Williams noted.

At Liverpool, the men boarded trains that ferried them to either Hungerford or Ogbourne St. George, where they transferred to fleets of army trucks, bound for camps being established for them in the Wiltshire villages of Ramsbury, Chilton Foliat, and Aldbourne. Eventually, almost every town and village was in some way involved in what was becoming known as the "friendly invasion," which involved some 1.5 million troops between 1943 and 1945. Of those, the County of Wiltshire, to the west of London, probably accommodated the most. By April 1944, this land of small hamlets and rolling green fields was home to 136,340 American soldiers.

For the 506th, they would mainly be stationed in and around Aldbourne and Ramsbury, while Colonel Sink established his headquarters at Littlecote House, a two-thousand-acre, 193-room Elizabethan estate near Chilton Foliat. The regiment's service company was set up at Manor Farm, beside the A4 at Foxfield between Hungerford and Marlborough, which today is a housing development called Manor Park.

To transport the paratroops, the 436th Troop Carrier group built its hangars and landing strips at nearby Membury, while the 437th Troop Carrier group did the same thing at Ramsbury, about five miles southeast of Aldbourne.

The trucks loaded with paratroopers of the 506th's 2nd Battalion bound for Aldbourne rolled along the quiet roads under strict blackout conditions. About a mile outside the village, the trucks drew to a halt and the men were ordered to unload. To avoid disturbing the local villagers with this late-night move, the men would walk to their new home.

The American authorities "were pretty considerate of the residents," Forrest told me. Prior to encamping at Aldbourne, which Forrest called "a nice, quiet little town," the GIs were "lectured on what to do and what not to do while we were here. Of course, we didn't always follow the rules."

Once in the village, men were bivouacked in at least two different locations. Some moved into what was called Camp Aldbourne, a cluster of rounded Quonset huts that occupied what had been a football field—or to Americans, a soccer field—along Farm Lane on the town's western edge.

Williams of Headquarters Company recalled, "A gloomy light was shining through an open door of a Quonset hut. We entered and found wooden double-deck bunks lined down both sides. The hut was of corrugated iron construction and not insulated. We were issued a mattress cover and shown a pile of straw with which to fill them. I got into bed, dog-tired, and could not stop shivering. The cold air came up through the mattress and it was impossible to sleep. I found some old newspapers and put them under the mattress, which made things marginally better. Awake at 0600 the next morning, we headed for the mess hall. I got my first view of the camp and I was not impressed. Shaving in cold water and sitting on a stinking honey-bucket in the latrines on a cold September day was not my idea of fun. This was, however, to be our home for the next year, so we simply got on and made the best of it."

Guth and Easy Company were billeted in Camp Aldbourne. One of Guth's memories of that time revolved around the mess hall and of being in line, "waiting and waiting." Forrest told me of how his friend Darrell "Shifty" Powers, tired of the long wait, yelled to the cooks, "Feed us or fight us."

"The cook came out and punched him," Forrest recalled. "He made the choice."

I asked my friend if the food was worth the fight.

"It was good, but I keep thinking that it's a miracle we didn't get sick from the unsanitary conditions," he replied.

By that, Forrest referred to the army's practice of having the men swoosh their dirty mess gear into barrels of hot water.

"Rinse it out, and that was it," Forrest said. "Sometimes it didn't rinse too well, but I don't recall too many people getting sick. I just think we had a lot of stamina."

For David Webster, one memory was seeing the thatched-roof cottages that dot the hill known as the Butts, which overlooks the football field. Seeing them, he wrote, reminded him of being "on a Hollywood set."

Hightown in Aldbourne. Easy Company was billeted in stables beyond these walls.

Men not camped in the Quonset huts ended up in the village at Hightown, a manor house with a walled courtyard that sits on the northwestern edge of the Green. A breeding place for horses, Hightown's stables had been transformed into barracks. Don Burgett of A Company was with one group that occupied this area.

Years later Burgett recalled, "We arrived in the village by truck and a sergeant took us through an iron gate in a brick wall and told us that this used to be the stables for an English mansion. The stables, or barracks now, were built of wood and ran the full length of the courtyard with four stalls protruding out at right angles. This gave the appearance of a large multiple E laid out top to bottom. There were four men to each stable, with a Dutch type door and two small windows. The inside had a cobblestone floor, a double bunk on both sides and a small stove in the center of the back wall. They were the best barracks I had ever seen—small, neat, comfortable and large enough for four men to live in, with a certain amount of privacy—something almost unknown in the service."

On a return trip in 1991, Carwood Lipton came back to Hightown,

entered the stable he had lived in, looked around, and located the nail
he had driven into the wall on which he had once hung his field jacket.

Officers, including Easy's Lieutenant Lynn "Buck" Compton, were
billeted in the Hightown manor house itself, which also contained the
officers' mess. A few, like Dick Winters and his friend Harry Welsh,
found accommodations in the homes of the local population.

But whether sleeping in a converted stable or an uninsulated, corrugated iron hut, the men of the 506th were at the only home they
would know until they came to grips with the enemy.

Forrest Guth's entrance into England and Aldbourne in 2008 wasn't
nearly as dramatic as it had been in 1943. By dawn the lush green of
Ireland was passing beneath the wings of our plane, followed soon by
the checkerboard countryside of England itself. It was a typical dreary
English morning when the wheels of the jet touched down at Gatwick
Airport, about a dozen miles south of London. Passing through customs
and getting our passports stamped was somewhat intimidating for me,
for while mine was virginal, Forrest's, thanks to the popularity of *Band
of Brothers*, bore more stamps than I could count. But that intimidation
was nothing compared to when I picked up our rental car, a blue Vauxhall Vectra, and tried to acclimate myself to driving a vehicle that has
the steering wheel and pedals all on the wrong side. Thus, cautiously at
first, we motored out the M23 toward London, then turned west on the
M4 toward Aldbourne.

Aldbourne is a Saxon village that dates back at least to the sixth
century. Located on the south slope of the Lambourn Downs, the village's name comes from a stream that flows through southeasterly toward Ramsbury, where it joins the Kennet and Knighton rivers. Three
valleys lead out of the village. Those to the northwest and southeast
meander off to Swindon and Hungerford, respectively. In the northernmost valley, the Swindon Road carries travelers away from Aldbourne.
The nearest railway stations today are in Hungerford and Swindon.

In 1943, Aldbourne was home to around a thousand people.

I had read so much about Aldbourne and seen so many photos that
I recognized the village as soon as we entered it. In particular I spotted
the quaint village plaza where six streets come together by Dabchick

Pond. The Crown Inn, where we would be staying, is in this plaza. After parking the car by the pond and walking toward the Crown, I looked to my left and immediately recognized what had once been the store owned by the Barnes family, where Dick Winters and Harry Welsh had been billeted. Except for the layer of white paint covering the redbrick walls, and the television aerial on the roof, it remains just as it appeared sixty-five years ago.

Interestingly, Aldbourne was never actually used in the HBO *Band of Brothers* miniseries, as the producers considered the village to be too far away from the other major shooting locations. Instead, Hambledon, outside of Henley-on-Thames, was substituted as Aldbourne's movie double.

Considering that Aldbourne had been home to men of the 101st and the fame that has come down upon the village thanks to Stephen Ambrose, I was perhaps a little disappointed that no one made mention of it when Forrest and I checked in. In fact, except for my friend Keith Sowerby, whom I had met at Toccoa, and his son Stephen—both of whom soon joined us —no one from the village gave us any sort of greeting. It made me recall Bill Guarnere's words when he wrote of Aldbourne, "everything and everybody we saw during the war is all gone. Today they don't know who we are. Me and Babe went over there and they threw us out of the pub. They close it from two to four p.m. What kind of joints are these?"

Even when I spoke to Bill on the phone briefly about a month before my trip, and told him Aldbourne was on my agenda, his reply was, "Hell, no. I don't go there."

The reason Bill and Babe may have gotten a less-than-warm reception, according to Neil Stevens, a historian who, along with his brother Clive, did much research on Aldbourne in the late 1980s, is that the town has changed drastically in recent years. Today Aldbourne, Neil told me, is a bedroom community. People live there, but their jobs are in Swindon, Hungerford, Reading, and even London. Since their incomes are higher than the local standard, real estate values are up.

"If you're born and bred here, you probably can't afford to stay living here," Neil told me.

While Forrest and I were, perhaps, somewhat ignored by the villagers, we never felt unwelcome, as evidently Bill Guarnere and Babe

Heffron had. Our host at the Crown, Geoff Eccleston, and his staff were most accommodating. But no villager we met, aside from the Sowerbys, mentioned the war years or the 101st Airborne.

As for Brits living in places other than Aldbourne, it was a different matter. Forrest and I were still finishing our lunch when I spotted a World War II reenactor outside, walking toward the Crown. Dressed as he was in full uniform and bearing a 101st Airborne patch on his left shoulder, he entered the pub.

"Are you looking for us?" I asked him.

He was.

His name was Jonathan Hodson, a seventeen-year-old lad whose father, Graham, had driven him here from Liverpool specifically to meet Forrest Guth. Not only was Jonathan a member of a reenactment group that has assumed the identity of Easy Company, but he specifically portrayed Forrest Guth. His eyes lit up when he shook Forrest's hand.

This meeting was to have taken place over the summer when some Easy Company vets visited Aldbourne. Jonathan's dad drove him from Liverpool, only to find that Forrest had not been able to make the trip. The boy was devastated and nearly in tears, his father told me. But not today. Jonathan could have hit the lottery, and he would not have been happier.

What drew Jonathan to Forrest was the man's uniqueness. For one thing, Forrest had a passion for cutting pockets off of old uniforms and sewing them on the one he was wearing. Besides the usual pockets found on an army fatigue jacket, Forrest attached one to the left sleeve between the shoulder and elbow, and two on the back of his jacket, low near the hemline.

"I sewed extra pockets on my jacket while I was in the marshaling area at Upottery," Forrest recalled. "I removed the pockets from a jump jacket and sewed three of them on the suit I was going to wear in combat. I needed those pockets to carry all the stuff I wanted to take with me. On one sleeve I'd sewn half an ammo bandolier to carry cigarettes and pipe tobacco, but that didn't work too well, so I replaced it with another pocket."

Jonathan's uniform jacket sported the extra pockets and the ammo bandolier.

Forrest also wore something else unique, especially when colder weather set in—a hooded sweatshirt under his jacket. Jonathan also wore the sweatshirt, although he told me that other reenactor know-it-alls, guys who think their expertise is much greater than it truly is, give him grief, telling him that the men during World War II didn't have "hoodies." His response is to take out a wartime photo of Guth. "And there it is," he says. It never fails to quiet the critics.

There was one problem, though. The lining of Jonathan's hoodie was light blue, and when Forrest quipped that his lining had been gray, a concerned look crossed the boy's face.

I looked at his dad, Graham, who was wearing a gray sweatshirt, and told him he'd better guard it closely, or he'd wake one morning to find a huge hole in it.

One of Forrest's quirks did confound the boy. Though right-handed, Forrest fired his rifle as a lefty.

"Now I have to learn to shoot left-handed," Jonathan said.

I'm certain he was serious.

Eager to begin retracing the footsteps of the men of Easy, I decided to walk to the Barneses' store, leaving Forrest at the Crown to rest after the long journey. Jonathan accompanied me, while Keith Sowerby waited with Forrest. The building sits at the corner of Marlborough Road and Castle Street, maybe seventy-five yards from the Crown. As I approached the two-story cottage with two big store windows on street level and a round red Royal Mail box standing as if on guard to the right of the door, I was truly stepping back in time. Even the words painted on a green sign across the front of the building proclaiming "General Store," "Post Office" and "Fully Licensed" are there, as is the round red post office sign hanging above the door on a wrought-iron bracket.

Dick Winters had met Francis and Louie May Barnes, the village storekeepers, in the cemetery at St. Michael Church, where he had gone to meditate following a Sunday service. They had come there to lay flowers on their son's grave. A friendship ensued, and when a request of the villagers to take in American officers was made, the Barneses agreed to welcome two men, provided Winters was one of them. That was how Dick Winters and Harry Welsh came to live here in this corner house.

Jonathan Hodson, a young Easy Company enthusiast who portrays Forrest Guth at World War II reenactments in England, meets the real thing in Aldbourne. Note the many pockets and hooded sweatshirt—Guth trademarks.

As I approached the store, it felt surreal, just being there. I looked up at the second-floor window on my left. Beyond that glass pane was the room Winters and Welsh shared, both before D-day and after their return from France in July 1944, until they departed for Holland the following September.

Besides being the town grocer, Francis Barnes was a lay minister at the Methodist Chapel on Lottage Road. Louie May was the church organist. Another villager, Nancy Barrett, best friends with the Barneses' daughter, Stella, told Neil Stevens during an interview how she recalled Winters attending services at the church as well.

"I'm not sure if it was out of obligation to Mrs. Barnes, or whether he was a religious man," she said. "I would think possibly it was a combination of the two."

At the Barneses' home, Winters and Welsh slept on army cots, and both were happy to be away from the crowded officers' billet and in a place that afforded them a modicum of privacy combined with the pleasure of living in the heart of the village. Winters made many friends in town, especially among the kids who tagged along with him when he went for walks, giving him the thumbs-up sign or asking, "Any gum, Yank?" And every morning, he'd exit from the home's side door on Castle Street for a five-mile jog along the village roads and streets.

Besides privacy and the family-like atmosphere provided by Mr. and Mrs. Barnes and their daughter, Stella, he also now had a new "sister." At thirteen, Elaine Stevens was the same age as Ann Winters, his kid sister back in Lancaster. Blond, five feet tall, and chipper, despite being separated from her family, Elaine was one of thousands of children evacuated from bomb-battered London to the countryside, where German planes seldom roamed.

Life at the Barneses' residence was not too unlike life at home. Around nine p.m. each evening, Mrs. Barnes would climb the stairs and knock on the Americans' door and ask if they'd like to come downstairs and listen to the news on the radio. Often they joined the family around the dining room table, where Mr. Barnes would read Bible verses while Louie May cut up bread for snacks and served tea.

That done, around ten p.m., Mr. Barnes would announce authoritatively that it was time for bed.

The store owned by the Barnes family in Aldbourne. The room Dick Winters and Harry Welsh shared was beyond the second-floor window at left.

Winters told me he enjoyed the quiet moments in this cozy house, which allowed him time to study and reflect on his job and himself. Decades after the fact, he said he felt living with the Barnes family was one of the luckiest breaks of his life, allowing him the needed time to mature as a man and build the strong sense of character that he would carry with him for the remainder of his life.

In 1991, Dick Winters, on a tour with other Easy Company vets and the author Stephen Ambrose, walked to the store, just as I was now doing. He hoped to see his old room, but the store was closed. He never got back.

As I entered the Barneses' store sixty-four years after Winters last did, all of those moments came back to me and I felt as if I had witnessed those experiences firsthand, they were that familiar. Of course, the Barneses are both gone, as are Stella and Elaine Stevens. The three Barneses are buried at St. Michael's graveyard, while Elaine died in Australia many years after the war.

For the past six months, the store has been owned and operated by Mark and Sue Rendell, who were "somewhat aware" of its past in regards to the *Band of Brothers*, Mark told me. The room on the second floor that Winters and Welsh called home is now the Rendells' sitting room. I did not get the opportunity to visit the room, but just being under the same roof and in the store, which probably still looks very much as it did then, minus the modern freezers and refrigerators, was most satisfying for me.

After leaving the Crown, we piled into two cars and drove to Farm Lane. Stopping by the town soccer field, it was almost impossible to envision this lush green expanse, surrounded by a low white single-rail fence, as ever having been a busy army camp. But it had been. Nancy Barrett, whose home was one of several laundry places used by the GIs, years later recalled the sight as she looked out of her windows at the Quonset hut camp.

"I can see it in my mind as plain as day. I can see the huts, the jeeps, the uniforms, the soldiers eating lardy cakes. I can see Dick Winters walking down the Butts toward the field in his dress uniform, brasses shining and the face of the young GIs knocking on my door and asking if I could wash their pants. The men that left Aldbourne . . . to lay down their lives were my neighbors. . . . I can't imagine how any of those men ever came back alive. Just what they went through and how they survived is quite unbelievable and it explains why they were like they were when they lived in Aldbourne. And to think I was living opposite the camp where all this history was taking place on a day-to-day basis."

Don Malarkey lived here at Camp Aldbourne, recalling the potbelly stove in each hut and, with less delight, the outside toilet facilities, or "honey pots," which, Malarkey recalled, "stunk to high heaven."

Today, only two remnants of the old camp remain. One is a cream-colored concrete structure, once a mess hall, tucked among modern houses just a few dozen yards from the field. The other is at Keith Sowerby's home, which overlooks the soccer field on Farm Lane. That remnant is nothing less than the sole surviving Quonset hut, moved from the soccer field to this site before Sowerby bought his house. Furnished with power saws and lathes, the corrugated iron hut, with heat and insulation now added, serves as home base for Sowerby's woodworking business. Walking around inside the Quonset hut, Forrest wondered if this had

The last remaining Quonset hut at Aldbourne, now Keith Sowerby's woodworking shop.

been the one he had lived in prior to D-day. Considering the odds, probably not. But one never knew.

We left Sowerby's and drove the four miles to Ramsbury, our goal being to locate the airfield used by the 506th for jump training. Surprisingly, or perhaps not, a few of the old airplane hangars still stand, mostly empty and in a state of deterioration. Locating a gravel lane that led to the airfield, we found the concrete hardstand still there, despite weeds and grass pushing up between the cement slabs. The runways have largely returned to meadowland, but their imprint can still be seen. Again, as I so often found myself doing, I tried to envision the peacefulness of this rural hilltop suddenly inundated by the incessant drone of C-47 engines and officers shouting orders to men laden with jump gear, climbing aboard the planes or loading into parked gliders attached to the rear of the Skytrains, all heading off to war. My effort was futile. Only the men who were there could picture it accurately. And even then I'm not so sure, for Forrest himself had trouble describing it sixty-four years later.

* * *

The next day, Sunday, Forrest and I were joined by four more Easy Company reenactors. Keith Sowerby soon arrived at the Crown, and we prepared for a brief tour about the center of the village. We left the inn and turned left, slowly walking along the Green, a street that leads past the village Green and straight to St. Michael Church, which loomed on the high ground directly ahead of us. The first house on the Green, directly behind the Crown, had once been home to a woman who took in laundry for the soldiers, Keith told us, one of several local women so employed.

In fact, almost the whole of village life, economic and social, revolved around the American troops, who outnumbered the residents. For one thing, the soldiers were shocked by the wartime shortages being experienced by the civilians and the realization that, in some ways, they had more luxuries than the villagers. The GIs grew to respect the town's inhabitants and were very generous. They especially took to the kids and old people. The children, in turn, were fascinated by the soldiers and could often be found clustered around outside the cookhouse at Hightown or by the Quonset huts, especially when donuts were being made.

One big social event was the Saturday night dances at the Memorial Hall. Audrey Barnett later recalled, "There was no shortage of partners at the dances in the village. . . . For the paratroopers, it was a welcome relief from the rigorous training and practice jumps. Most of the men had never left home before enlisting and were naturally homesick. They would readily talk about their homes, parents, siblings, and quite often about their girlfriends or young wives whom they had married before embarking overseas. I found them to be extremely well behaved, very friendly, generous and outgoing, and full of life and good fun."

Of course, there were also some problems between villagers and GIs. Nancy Barrett, a young mother whose husband was stationed at Gibraltar, told Neil Stevens, "The trouble with the Americans was that they were just so forward. I recall one spring morning opening the front door to shake the hearthrug out, and being almost bowled over by the number of young soldiers wanting to chat. The problem was, of course, that deep down they were very lonely, very far from home, and just weren't familiar with the English ways of reserve. On another morning, there was a knock at the door and when I opened it, the first words this GI spoke were, 'Can you wash my pants, please, ma'am?' . . . I agreed to take this man's trousers and wash them for him, but made it clear that this wasn't to be his regular laundry house. It wasn't a case of being rude, but you had to be firm from the outset, otherwise things would easily spiral out of control." Still, she noted, "The Americans stationed in Aldbourne were far from all bad, and when they left the village, it seemed like a huge void then appeared."

The soldiers tried not to stir up trouble.

"We were told to behave and I think we did pretty well," Forrest told me.

But soldiers are soldiers, and nighttime found them crowding into the Crown and, even more so, the Blue Boar, which sits on the eastern fringe of the village Green.

Malarkey said the men were "first-class hell-raisers."

"We were all in our early twenties and had never had such freedom, such opportunities," he later wrote.

Malarkey relates how, during one night of rowdiness, he stood atop the pub bar and loudly recited every line of Kipling's "Gunga Din."

"No wonder my jump boots smelled like stale beer," he wrote.

When we reached the village Green, Keith pointed out Hightown, still standing serenely behind its stone wall and iron gate. The house and grounds today are the home of the same Geoff Eccleston who owns the Crown. The thirty-six stables Easy Company and other troopers once slept in are all gone, of course. As mentioned previously, six of them now reside in Toccoa, Georgia, where I had attended their dedication three years earlier. The last was dismantled and shipped down the road a few miles to Littlecote House, Colonel Sink's headquarters.

At the Green, Keith told us the history of the Blue Boar, which sat across from where we were standing. The immaculate-looking fourteenth-century pub with its white walls, he said, was reportedly built to house workmen sent to the village to rebuild the St. Michael Church tower, which had collapsed. Legend says the Blue Boar is built of rubble from that original tower.

"How much truth there is to that, I don't know," Keith Sowerby said.

Ahead of us stood St. Michael, where Winters met the Barneses and where, after the war, Easy Company's last commander, Captain Ronald Spiers, was married.

"There's been a church on that site since Saxon times. That's a thousand years," Keith said.

I looked around the center of Aldbourne, trying to visualize what this quiet village had been like in 1943–44. To my delight, the town, at least the older part of it, had not changed much, an observation reinforced by Forrest Guth.

"The houses are kept up better now," he told me when asked about the village. "But it still looks the same."

Aldbourne must have been a bustling, hectic place during the war years. Homes, people, even the land itself, all had a share in the war effort. That included the village Green, which now lay spread out before us on this dreary November morning.

Tom Barnes, then fourteen, told Neil Stevens how "the village Green was being used to park large British army tank transports. They were lined up in rows, sometimes with Churchill tanks on board and other times empty. The combination of the soft ground and the enormous weight of these vehicles really used to tear up the village Green and leave muddy ruts almost a foot deep."

Aldbourne had become home for the men of Easy. Carwood Lipton told of returning from five days of maneuvers out on Salisbury Plain. Marching back, the column topped Ewin's Hill and was glad to see Aldbourne laid out in the valley below. Visions of hot food and their own bunks filled them with joy. In 1991, Lipton, thinking back on that event, recalled, "Having been on exercise for a week, living in a wet foxhole— seeing the church tower and the village in the valley was the prettiest sight imaginable, and we knew we were nearly home."

Forrest told me the residents were very easygoing and accepting of the Americans' presence.

"It must've been tough for the people to change their way of living to put up with us," he told me.

And the men never forgot what the civilians did for them. In the 1960s Nancy Barrett heard a knock on her door. Upon opening it, she found a former GI who asked her if this was the mayor's home. He said he had walked from Ogbourne St. George, a distance of about three miles, to hand-deliver a letter thanking the villagers for their treatment of the soldiers of the 101st. Aldbourne has no mayor, but Nancy's father was chairman of the parish council, so evidently when the man asked at the Crown for the mayor, he was directed to her home.

"To think that this chap had walked all the way from Ogbourne," Nancy recalled, "up that very steep hill, to hand-deliver this letter and make quite sure that it got to the right person, really touches me. It surely shows that they must have felt that their stay in the village was one of their happier times."

In 1994 Les Hashey, an Easy Company replacement after D-day, made a pilgrimage back to Aldbourne. He visited the stables at Hightown and found his old billet. Likewise, Ed Shames, then a sergeant with I Company and stationed at Ramsbury, revisited that village in 1999. He found the house on High Street where he had stayed during the war, and he knocked on the door. The owner greeted Shames and showed his guest the very room where he had lived.

Following our walk to the village Green, we returned to the Crown. I wanted to walk up the hill to St. Michael Church, but did not want to fatigue Forrest. So I left him seated on the brown leather couch in front of the Crown's blazing fireplace, surrounded by reenactors. Knowing he was in the best of care, I left the Crown and hiked toward the church.

Dick Winters and I had talked long about this place, and as I reached the steps leading to the imposing medieval stone edifice, I recalled Dick's story about another Sunday in 1943. Dick told me how he had left the church service and strolled along the cobblestone walkway that I now stood upon. Then he stopped, turned right, and walked through the grass, around the side of the church, and entered the silent graveyard. Retracing his steps, I did exactly the same thing.

The sky was gray and a slight breeze rippled the St. George's flag atop the bell tower, its red cross on a snow-white field flapping against the steely heavens. No rain was falling, but the grass was still wet as I entered the cemetery. Dick told me about the two benches that sat atop the sloping graveyard and how, seeking solitude, he had walked up the hill to them and sat on one. So imagine my delight when I rounded the church to find almost the same scene Winters had described. Other than the fact that the two benches had been replaced by a single bench built

Dick Winters's view of St. Michael's cemetery, Aldbourne, from the bench atop the hill. It was here he met Mr. and Mrs. Barnes.

into a brick memorial that was dedicated in 1963, it was probably just as Winters had found it.

Though the wetness of the grass began soaking my feet through my shoes, I was drawn up the hill toward that bench by the spirits of the past. I sat down, damp wood be damned, and contemplated the cemetery, much as Winters must have done from this same spot. I remembered Dick telling me about the older couple who came into the cemetery, walked to a grave about halfway up the hill, and stopped to place flowers. As related earlier in this chapter, this was Mr. and Mrs. Barnes, placing flowers on the grave of their twenty-six-year-old son, Leonard.

That thought led me on a second search, and I walked down the center lane of the cemetery, checking names on headstones. Then, on a creamy white marker, I found the quiet grave of Royal Air Force Corporal L. J. Barnes, who died June 12, 1942. Now, placing myself in the shoes of Mr. Barnes, I mentally reenacted the events of that day as I looked up the hill at the bench where a young blond-haired American officer sat watching. It would be the start of a friendship that would last a lifetime.

I stood there for I don't know how long, haunted by my mind's vision of that meeting in this churchyard six decades ago. Dick had spoken of it in a voice choked with emotion, and I had written about it in my book, and related the story in countless book talks I had given since then. But, as I would discover so many times over the next two weeks, none of that compared to actually standing on the same ground.

Mr. Barnes, in declining health, died sometime after Dick left for Holland in September 1944. Dick returned to see Mother Barnes shortly after the war's end and before he shipped home, and they would continue to correspond until her letters suddenly stopped in the 1970s. Both were buried in this churchyard somewhere, so I went in search again, but failed to find them. Now, with my feet thoroughly soaked and the chill of the late autumn afternoon penetrating my coat, I returned to the Crown, where Forrest still kept the reenactors hanging on his every word.

I doubt they missed me.

CHAPTER 3

LITTLECOTE AND LARDY CAKES

FINAL PREPARATIONS

Upon my return to the Crown from St. Michael, it wasn't just the reenactors who were waiting for me. Sitting with Forrest was Bruce Steggles, who oversees the airborne museum at the luxury hotel that is now Littlecote House. Steggles was going to take us to visit Sink's headquarters, so Forrest, myself, and Jonathan and Graham Hodson, along with two other reenactors, loaded into two cars and were soon off.

With parts of it dating back as far as 1275, Littlecote House, about four miles east of Aldbourne near Chilton Foliat, encompassed some two thousand acres of fields and woods. In 1943 the estate was owned by Sir Ernest Wills, a tobacco magnate who had made his fortune manufacturing Woodbine cigarettes.

"This was their country home, basically," Steggles told us as we drove along the lengthy tree-lined entrance road, through a pair of iron gates, and parked on the circular drive in front of the main doors. During the war, Steggles said, Wills spread the story that he had "loaned" the house to the Americans "for a year and two days." In fact, Wills, despite his wealth and power, didn't have much choice in the matter, although the family continued living in the part of the estate not commandeered by Sink and his staff.

Inevitably, there were problems between the upper-crust English baronet and his citizen-soldier American guests. Wills was constantly complaining, often angrily, to American authorities about GIs shooting deer on his land and catching "his" fish in the nearby Kennet River, generally by tossing hand grenades into the water.

"If you got caught killing the wildlife on the property, you were fined twenty dollars," Steggles told us. "If you didn't own up to it and got away with it, then it went to your platoon or company commander, and he ended up paying fifty dollars. That was about a third of his monthly wages."

That's what happened to Jake McNiece of the 101st Airborne's famed Filthy 13. McNiece and a comrade shot a deer and hung the carcass in a tree to bleed it. MPs were summoned to the scene, Steggles said, and actually stood under the very tree, looking for suspects or evidence. The MPs, evidently not hunters, failed to glance upward. Subsequently, McNiece's CO was slapped with a $50 fine.

The poaching continued, unabated.

Only officers stayed within the walls of Littlecote House. Noncoms and others were billeted in Quonset huts along the entrance driveway.

Entering Littlecote House through the main double doors, we found ourselves in a huge foyer. Steggles ushered us to the left into the high-ceilinged Great Hall. Built in the fifteenth century, the walls are paneled in dark oak wood and adorned by antlers, swords, banners, and Elizabethan period portraits of lords and ladies. In Wills's day, these walls also held an array of matchlock and flintlock rifles used during the English Civil War. The weapons have since been sent to the Royal Armory in Leeds.

The Great Hall's most prominent feature is the five-hundred-year-old solid oak table and benches that run the length of the room. Sitting upon the flagstone floor, the 3-foot-wide, 29.8-foot-long table is so heavy that the artisans of the day had to build it in place inside the hall. It can seat forty people.

In 1943–44, this room served as Colonel Sink's mess hall. Sink sat at the far end, nearest the door leading to his office. Sometimes Lady Wills was invited to join them, and she would be seated next to the colonel. On the wall behind Sink would have hung the crossed flags of the United States and the 506th Regiment. Today, a suit of armor stands watch behind where the colonel sat, as if guarding the door to his private lair.

We walked the length of the room to the library, entering through the tall double doors. Elegantly furnished, with built-in ceiling-to-floor bookcases, polished hardwood floors, Persian rugs, and a fireplace, this had been Sink's office. The room is also called the Round Library because the wall opposite the double doors is concave. With his desk placed

Colonel Sink's office at Littlecote House.

by the long bank of arched windows so he could turn and watch his troops train on the fields outside, it was in this room that Sink made the decisions that affected the lives of his men. Ed Shames, for example, received his commission as a second lieutenant here after transferring into Easy Company.

But perhaps most important, from Easy's perspective, it was in this room that Sink dealt with a problem that threatened the very core of the company.

As combat drew nearer and training switched more and more from the classroom to tactical field problems, the friction between Sobel and Winters increased as the former's deficiencies as a combat leader became ever more apparent. Don Malarkey recalled how Sobel was bearing down relentlessly on the men. Malarkey thinks Sobel was "scared stiff," knowing he was in over his head and believing, rightfully, that the men did not respect him.

"And worse," Malarkey said, "he knew he wasn't Dick Winters. . . . Winters was that rare leader who could be tough as nails but who respected us deeply." As a result, Malarkey said, "We respected him."

Winters, Malarkey believes, was "everything that Sobel wanted to be but couldn't." The man's pride, he said, "got in the way." So Sobel's only recourse, in his mind at least, was to beat respect into the men.

The tensions bubbled over in October 1943, when Sobel ordered Winters to inspect the latrines at the Quonset hut camp at 10:00 a.m. But when Winters arrived at the appointed time, he found Sobel already inspecting them, with latrine orderly Private Joachim Melo trailing along behind, mop in hand.

After completing his inspection, Sobel made some notations then left without a word. Winters proceeded to conduct his own inspection, finding that Melo had done an excellent job.

A short time later, First Sergeant William Evans found Winters and handed him a paper that read:

Subject: Punishment Under 104th AW

To: 1st Lt. R.D. Winters

1. You will indicate by indorsement *[Author's note: The misspelling was Evans's]* below whether you desire punishment under 104th AW or trial by Courts Martial for failure to inspect the latrine at 0945 this date as instructed by me.

HERBERT M. SOBEL, CAPT. COMMANDING

Winters hurried to Sobel's office to confront his commander, who told him he had changed the time to 9:45. He said he had tried to phone Winters about the change, and had also sent a runner with the new time. Winters, who up until the inspection time had been censoring the men's mail by order of Colonel Strayer, knew Sobel was trying to "gig" him, that no runner had been dispatched and that Sobel knew there was no phone in the orderly room. "Bullshit!" Winters told himself, anger welling up. "This is it." He returned to the orderly room and wrote, "I request trial by Courts Martial for failure to inspect the latrines at 0945 this date" on the bottom of Sobel's memo, signed and returned it. Winters was soon transferred to the kitchen until the issue could be settled.

Angered by Sobel's blatant attack on Winters, Sergeants Terrence

"Salty" Harris and Mike Ranney convinced all of the company's sergeants to turn in their stripes in protest. When word of this "mutiny" reached Sink, he called the rebellious NCOs into his office. He busted Harris to private and transferred him from the regiment. He also busted Ranney to private, and severely reprimanded the rest. Not long after that, Sink, realizing the problem lay in Sobel, transferred Easy's commander, placing him in charge of the jump school at nearby Chilton Foliat. He replaced Sobel with Lieutenant Thomas Meehan of A Company, and brought Winters back to Easy. Throughout E Company, tensions eased remarkably when word came down that "Sobel is gone."

"Sobel was a gambler who thought he had a hot hand and could trump Winters easily," Malarkey said. "Sobel was wrong. He'd underestimated the man's integrity."

Malarkey, in his book, wrote that he is convinced Winters orchestrated the event in order to force Sobel out, "not for his selfish gain, mind you; that wasn't Winters's style." Winters himself has always denied the claim, and having myself spoken to him at length on the topic, I agree. But Malarkey wrote, "I will go to my grave believing that out of compassion for his men, he believed he had no other choice."

Either way it happened, it was for the best insofar as Easy Company's future was concerned. And now I was standing in the room where this important event had taken place.

I asked Forrest if he had ever been in this room. He said he had, and although he could not recall the exact reason, he quickly added, "It wasn't because I was in any trouble."

To commemorate the history of this room, two bronze plaques hang on one wall. The first, recognizing Colonel Sink, was dedicated on September 17, 2004, the sixtieth anniversary of Operation Market Garden, and unveiled by Sink's daughter, Margarette Swenson. The second plaque honors the 101st Airborne and 506th PIR.

Besides his office, Sink's bedroom was somewhere on this floor, but Steggles said no one is sure precisely which room.

The ground-floor level also boasts an indoor pool in the conservatory, Steggles told us, and when Colonel Sink had a party, the water was heated.

"They'd go upstairs, have the party in the Long Gallery, and by midnight they'd be drunk as skunks, and have a lady on one arm, a bottle of champagne in the other hand, and end up in the swimming pool," Steggles said.

The Long Gallery Steggles referred to is on the second floor. At 110 feet in length and 18 feet wide, this room served Sink as a ballroom and a place for musical concerts. Opposite the entrance is a door leading to the Jerusalem Staircase, a heavy oak stairway between five hundred and a thousand years old, that leads to the upper-floor rooms. During Sink's stay, there was but one bathroom in this part of the house and officers queued up to wait their turn. Steggles told us of one man who would consistently take his time and lounge in the bath, backing up the line. The other officers cursed and grumbled, but two of them, Lieutenant Colonel Harold W. Hannah and a Major King, got thoroughly fed up. Waiting until the offender was settled in the tub, the officers lobbed a smoke grenade into the bathroom and shut the door. The man was never a problem after that.

The Haunted Bedroom also occupies the second floor. According to legend, in 1575 Wild William Darrell, who owned Littlecote at the time, brought a midwife into the room and directed her to deliver the child of a pregnant woman and make sure the mother's life be saved. She obeyed, after which Darrell took the newborn baby, who, the story goes, was illegitimate, from the midwife, threw it in the fire, and held it down with his foot until it died. Later, to satisfy debts, Wild William mortgaged the house. During a visit in 1589, William fell from his horse and was killed. Legend has it that he was startled by the appearance of the infant's ghost. Since then, it is said, Wild William haunts the infamous bedroom. Hannah and King were billeted in this room, but neither ever reported encountering the spirit.

Near the Haunted Bedroom is a Cromwellian chapel, one of two still existing in their original states anywhere in England. The chapel has a pulpit, but no altar, and worshippers during bygone years sat for four hours, listening to the preacher. Anyone who failed to show up for church was fined. While Sink was at Littlecote, Sunday services were held in the chapel, both Catholic, led by Father Jack Maloney, and Protestant, under Reverend Tilden McGee.

A trip down the nearby staircase leads to the Oak Room, which the Americans, always in search of entertainment, stocked with billiard tables. As D-day and, later, Market Garden approached, these tables would be covered with maps as Sink and his staff refined their plans. It is believed, but not known for certain, that General Dwight D. Eisenhower visited here just prior to D-day, possibly in the company of Winston Churchill.

Back on the ground floor, tucked away in a small room, is a museum run by the Kennet Valley at War Trust and dedicated to the 101st Airborne, displaying weapons, photographs, and artifacts. Steggles said more items have been acquired and the room was earmarked for expansion. We toured the small museum and Steggles asked Forrest to sign the guest book reserved for distinguished visitors.

Our last stop was the Aldbourne stable that sits in a small grove of trees to the east of the main house.

Today, Littlecote House retains only a remnant of its past grandeur. Trimmed down from two thousand acres to about a hundred, it is a luxury hotel complete with tennis courts and a soccer or cricket field. It is no longer owned by the Wills family, although they still hold much of the surrounding land.

By the time we arrived back at the Crown, all of the other reenactors had headed for their homes and their real lives, happy with the experience of sharing time with Forrest Guth. Only Jonathan and his dad remained, but they too had to make that long trek to Liverpool. Following a few farewell photos with his idol, Jonathan left a very happy boy, and Forrest and I spent some quiet time by the Crown's friendly fireplace.

On Monday I left Forrest at the Crown and drove to Hungerford train station to pick up historian Neil Stevens, who was arriving from London. Neil and his brother Clive began their research into Aldbourne's wartime history in 1988, well before the publication of *Band of Brothers*. Their interest had been piqued after learning that a sister of their grandmother was a war bride, having married a GI. After the war, she had gone to live with him in Portland, Oregon. Neil was interested in what her soldier-husband did during the war, and where he had been stationed. While the man was not a member of Easy Company, he had been a paratrooper in Aldbourne, spurring the Stevens brothers' interest in the village.

In 1989 the brothers were joined by another local historian, Colin Spencer, who owned a World War II–vintage Willys jeep. Together, they explored the area in depth, which sometimes got them into trouble. Once, while lingering by the old hangars at Ramsbury, they were approached by the local gamekeeper, who suspected these strangers might be poaching pheasants. They explained their mission to the man's satisfaction, although he still told them to get off the land.

During their search for local history, Neil said they had discovered a tree with the word "Eagles" and a Nazi swastika carved into it by some eager paratrooper. Unfortunately, in 2001, the tree was felled during woodland management work.

As we arrived back in Aldbourne from Hungerford, the sun peeked out from behind the clouds for the first time since Forrest and I arrived in the UK. Neil and I walked back to St. Michael in yet another attempt to locate the Barneses' graves. Sadly, we again failed, but in that, we were not alone.

In June 1991, Ambrose, researching his *Band of Brothers* book, led three Easy Company vets, Dick Winters, Carwood Lipton, and Don Malarkey, back to England and Europe. Ambrose intended to visit the Airborne Museum in Aldershot, but surprisingly, Aldbourne was not on the itinerary due to time constraints. This oversight prompted Neil to travel to London, where he arranged to meet with the group in hopes of enticing them to come to Aldbourne since their travel route would take them through Hungerford, just six miles away.

"For goodness' sake, you're going to be in Aldershot. Aldbourne is just up the road," he told them.

Neil said Winters was "an easy sell" because he had a yearning to visit the Barneses' graves and home. Ambrose was persuaded, and their bus arrived in the square by Dabchick Pond. There they were greeted by Spencer in his jeep and Neil, driving a World War II–era Dodge weapons carrier. Neil guided them on a tour. Winters expressed a desire to visit the Barneses' house, but as related earlier, the store was closed and he could not get in. Later, accompanied by Neil, Winters walked to St. Michael. They went into the cemetery, where Winters asked Neil, "Could you give me fifteen minutes on my own?"

"I like to think he sat on the bench here and contemplated on the intervening years," Neil told me as we stood in the cemetery. When Winters returned, Neil said, "He was at peace with himself."

Afterward, the two searched for the Barneses' graves. Like Neil and myself seventeen years later, they failed to find them.

Nancy Barrett, the best friend of Stella Barnes, in a 1988 interview with Neil recalled Winters's relationship with the Barnes family. She said, "I can recall seeing Lieutenant Winters walking around the village on numerous occasions and as I was best friends with Stella, she very often used to talk about him and held him in very high regard."

She told Neil that Stella died young, at about age fifty, and is also buried at St. Michael.

"I wonder whether, when he returned to the village in 1991 looking for Mr. and Mrs. Barnes' graves, he had any idea that Stella had passed away so young and was also buried in the same churchyard?" she said.

After our futile visit to the cemetery, Neil, Forrest, and I loaded into my Vauxhall and headed for Ramsbury, where Neil said we could taste some authentic lardy cakes.

The lardy cake, also known as Lardy Johns or Fourses Cakes, originated in Wiltshire, an area long noted for pig farming. A heavy, doughy pastry made from rendered lard, flour, sugar, spices, and currants, and topped with raisins and toffee, lardy cakes were a sweet treat the GIs grew to savor.

"I ate them all the time," Forrest recalled. "I loved them."

Forrest had not tasted a lardy cake since he left England that last time in September 1944, and Neil promised him a taste of the old days. Our stop was the Midway Store on High Street, where Neil purchased the cakes. Then we stopped on the sidewalk outside, unwrapped them and dug in.

"Delicious." Forrest smiled, crumbs falling from his chin. "It's just like I remember it."

After wolfing down the lardy cakes, we drove back toward Aldbourne, heading for the Membury airfield. Located, Neil said, two to three miles from Aldbourne "as the bird flies," it is the airstrip from which Easy Company departed for their Operation Market Garden jump.

In 1944, as the troopers prepared for their combat jumps, this whole area between Aldbourne and Ramsbury was quite a different sight from the serene, undulating hills and fields that greeted Forrest and me in 2008. Trucks and jeeps rolled along the roads, carrying supplies, equipment, and paratroopers to the airfields. There, the men loaded onto planes for practice jumps in preparation for their next action.

Tom Barnes recalled the "endless stream of C-47s flying" overhead and how they "would be dropping paratroopers in their hundreds throughout the entire area."

Mary Devlin of Hungerford recalled, "I can remember walking up the garden at home and turning to look across the valley toward Chilton Foliat. As far as the eye could see the sky was almost black with aircraft dropping paratroopers and landing in the distance."

In May the division made over three dozen practice jumps. During one, Malarkey recalled being ordered to jump with his mortar intact and ready for immediate action. That meant the tube, base plate, and bipod—a total weight of sixty-five pounds—was stuffed into a canvas bag. Adding to the discomfort, Winters told him, "If you're not killed, that's how we'll do it over Normandy."

On occasion, the training was marred by tragedy. Sergeant Bob Williams of 2nd Battalion headquarters recalled seeing two C-47s collide.

"Our squad was making its way down a rough trail on a stony hill when over the hillside came a tight V of three C-47s," he remembered. "They were obviously on a practice mission, flying a tight formation pattern."

As he watched, two of the planes touched wings.

"One aircraft started to bobble around momentarily, violently turned through 180 degrees, and then plunged directly into the ground. The other two aircraft continued on for a few moments when the second aircraft involved in the collision did exactly the same thing. . . . Both aircraft exploded on impact in a ball of fire."

The squad hurried to the crash site, and Williams said, "The burnt remains of the flight crew, still at the controls of the aircraft, will live in my memory forever."

Neil Stevens said the crash took place near Whittonditch, between Aldbourne and Chilton Foliat. The planes fell on either side of a small road leading from the crossroad, up to Membury, adjacent to Whittondale Farm.

Today, many of Membury's hangars still stand, more even than remain at Ramsbury. Several of them have been refurbished and are used by local industry. Traces of the concrete hardstands and roadways can also be seen. However, the incessant drone of airplane engines is gone, and the only sound that interrupts this pastoral English country scene is the distant hum of traffic along the M4 connecting London to Bristol, which passes by out of sight, but not out of hearing.

*   *   *

By late May 1944 the 101st was making preparations for its part in the invasion of Europe. Duffel bags were packed and sent ahead and personal items stored. The men knew the time for action was drawing near, but were yet to be told when and where. Some met combat veterans from North Africa or the Italian front who related stories of grim reality, "crystal-clear stories," Malarkey wrote, "of American soldiers fighting, dying, being wounded, and being taken prisoner," and suddenly, he recalled, "the war started having context."

Before leaving for France, Winters asked Malarkey to take on the job of squad leader. Malarkey agreed, not because he wanted to climb the command ladder, but simply because he was getting tired of "being jerked around by nitwits" like First Sergeant Evans, ex–company commander Sobel's toady, whom Malarkey did not respect in any way.

Orders were finally cut, and the paratroopers loaded onto trucks for airfields to the west in Essex County. How the villagers viewed this is uncertain. Neil said, and Forrest agreed, that their departure did not stir up a lot of fanfare in Aldbourne. Since Operation Overlord was cloaked in secrecy, there was no reason to assume that this move was not just another training maneuver. On the other hand, Bill Guarnere remembers people flocking around to say good-bye.

"There were tears in their eyes; they were sad to see us go," Guarnere said. "They got close to us. Nice people."

Either way, they were off.

After our trip to Membury, I drove Neil Stevens back to the rail station at Hungerford, and Forrest and I headed for the Channel port city of Poole, leaving Aldbourne and Wiltshire County behind us.

As for Aldbourne, it remains forever locked in history, side by side with the 101st Airborne in general and Easy Company in particular, even though others came after them.

"It's not just the 101st," Neil Stevens told me. "The 17th Airborne came here after the 506th left. But try to find something about the 17th Airborne being here. It's very, very difficult."

No formal historical records exist, he said. One must rely "on meeting somebody" who was there during the time.

"Even ascertaining the units who had been here was not easy," Neil said. "They were paratroopers. Yeah, but which ones?"

That night found Forrest and myself aboard the Brittany ferry *Barfleur*, bound for Normandy. Around midnight the ferry glided from its berth and headed across the dark English Channel. I walked out on deck to the rail, braving the cold November wind that whipped along the ship, and watched the lights of England recede. I thought of the men heading for France on the night of June 5–6. I reflected on the spectacle of some five thousand ships of all sizes dotting the Channel and the hundreds of troop-laden planes droning overhead, many with silent gliders in tow, all heading for France, just as I was now doing. Granted, when I arrived in Normandy, pissed-off Germans with machine guns and shore batteries would not be waiting for me, at least I hoped not, but I was still aware of the sense of history.

Like those thousands of men sixty-four years earlier, my next stop was Normandy.

Chapter 4

"WE WERE ALL
SCARED TO DEATH"

D-day

The convoy of trucks ferrying the 506th Regiment from Aldbourne deposited them some 110 miles away in Upottery, 20 miles west of Southampton. Here the men learned for the first time that they—along with the 82nd Airborne—were bound for Normandy, to be dropped 5 miles behind the infantry landing beach code-named Utah, where they were to seize and hold the causeways leading inland from the beach. Forrest told me they were further ordered "to kill any Germans we encountered and take no prisoners."

For the next several days they studied the enemy's defenses, along with the towns and landmarks, with such intensity that by the time they took off they could sketch the road networks around their drop zones from memory. The men pored over sand tables that featured every detail laid out in miniature—beaches, villages, artillery positions, trees and hedgerows—all gleaned from aerial reconnaissance and thousands of vacation postcards sent to military authorities by Englanders who had toured northern France in prewar days.

On June 3, Lieutenant Thomas Meehan led Easy Company to the supply dump to draw ammo and grenades. The paratroopers took hot showers that, unbeknownst to them, would be the last they would enjoy for weeks, and they stockpiled candy and cigarettes.

At the marshaling area, the troops were sealed away from the outside world. No letters were sent or received, and they lived in tents by the airfield, the entire area patrolled by armed guards. Forrest Guth and Joe Liebgott made some extra money giving haircuts.

"The guys who went to Joe got a better deal," Forrest recalled. "He was a real barber. I just gave the guys the best haircut I could."

While awaiting the word, the men reviewed tactics on how to take machine-gun positions, bridges, and causeways, how to dig foxholes and knock out enemy artillery. They checked their equipment, and then checked it again. They sharpened bayonets and had the "flash/thunder" password and countersign hammered into their memory.

The paratroopers were also handed a small British-made brass toy called a cricket, stamped "The Acme, made in England," to facilitate them in identifying friend from foe. When a soldier probing through the darkness heard a rustle in the bushes, he was to click the cricket once. If the other man was a GI, he would respond either with two clicks of the cricket or with the countersign, "Thunder."

The cricket, according to the historian and author Michel De Trez, a friend of Forrest Guth's and owner of the Dead Man's Corner Museum at Carentan, was the brainchild of Maxwell Taylor, who had combat jump experience in Sicily and knew the confusion that could result from a night jump.

Crickets were carried in a variety of places by the men. Many punched small holes in the toy and wore them on strings around their necks or on their dog-tag chain, while others taped them to the stocks of their weapons or attached them to their helmets, either via the chin strap or bound to the helmet by tape.

Forrest carried his in one of his many pockets.

As the date of the invasion drew nearer, activity increased, both on the ground and in the air. Buck Compton recalled, "Great formations of bombers flew overhead, as high as you could see in the sky. . . . They came back at night, some limping with one motor out, straggling through the air."

With the invasion originally scheduled for Monday, June 5, on June 4 each trooper was issued $10 in French francs, newly minted in Washington, D.C., and a map of the Normandy area, printed on silk. That evening the cooks served up a feast of steak, mashed potatoes, white bread, peas, ice cream, and coffee. The meal was accompanied by the usual cracks about "fattening us up for the kill."

General Taylor took the opportunity to give the men a pep talk that would later be recalled with wry humor. "Give me three days of hard fighting," he said. "And then you'll be withdrawn."

Forrest recalled, "When we were in England, ready to go to Normandy, my mother sent me a package of cookies, cakes and stuff, a sweatshirt and a wristwatch with my serial number on it."

The watch was later stolen, but he took the aforementioned hooded sweatshirt into combat. He also secured a .45-caliber automatic.

"We stole these pistols from the air corps, we ordered them from home, we traded for them, we got them any way we could," he said. "Every man carried one into action."

Forrest's friend Walter Gordon recalled that Guth's .45 automatic, carried as it was in a shoulder holster under his left arm, "made him look like a mean Chicago gangster."

Inclement weather forced postponement of the invasion to Tuesday, June 6, which was a mixed blessing to the men gearing up to go. On the one hand, the adrenaline was pumping and they wanted to get started, to put all of their training into action. So the delay was a bitter disappointment. However, Don Malarkey recalled a more positive side of the postponement.

"Even if we'd been anxious to go, somehow the thought of a nice hot meal and a movie instead of jumping into the unknown had a certain appeal," he wrote.

On the afternoon of June 5, final preparations began, and by eight thirty p.m., the 506th were once more headed for the airfield. After stopping at a hangar to pick up prepacked chutes, the columns of men proceeded to the hardstands, where eighty-one C-47s, many with bundles of ammunition strapped to their underbellies, awaited them.

"We were told it was on for tonight," Forrest recalled. "Only a few showed emotion. After all that hard training, it was a relief. We were finally going to do something. We would finally go into action."

Forrest tried not to think too much about what lay ahead. He knew when he volunteered for the paratroopers, he'd soon "be in the thick of the fighting."

"Once we got to France," he said, "I didn't think I'd live to be too old."

As they prepared to climb into the plane, Forrest said he and the others "donned our equipment, blackened our faces, and were given copies of letters from Ike and Sink. I folded my copies and put them between my liner and steel helmet."

The letter from Eisenhower, headed "Supreme Headquarters Allied

Expeditionary Force," or SHAEF, told the men they were "about to embark on a great crusade, toward which we have striven these many months." It continued, "The eyes of the world are upon you. The hopes and prayers of liberty-loving people everywhere march with you." At the end it wished them "Good luck! And let us all beseech the blessing of Almighty God upon this great and noble undertaking."

Sink's letter said they were heading for the "great adventure for which you have trained for over two years."

"Tonight is the night of nights," the memo read. "Tomorrow throughout the whole of our homeland and the Allied world, the bells will ring out the tidings that you have arrived and the invasion for liberation has begun."

As ten o'clock approached, the soldiers, loaded down with gear, began the arduous task of climbing into the aircraft. Guarnere recalled, "It took three men to pick you up and put you on the damn plane."

Don Malarkey, straining under about two hundred pounds of ammo and equipment, wrote, "It took four guys—two pushing and two pulling—just to get me into the plane."

Malarkey and Guarnere were members of Stick 70, along with Joe Toye and Buck Compton, who as jumpmaster had the task of handing out airsickness pills, which someone higher up in the command chain decided the men needed, but which had the unfortunate effect of making the men drowsy.

"I threw mine the hell away," Compton later wrote.

At 11:13 p.m. the lead Skytrain, engines at full throttle, roared down the runway and lifted off the ground, its propellers biting into the night air. The invasion of Europe was under way.

The flight across the English Channel and into Normandy took two and a half hours, and the men spent the time in different ways. Winters, about to lead men into battle for the first time, asked himself, "Can I handle it? Will I make the right decisions? Or will I end up getting myself and my men killed?"

Forrest Guth told me, "I guess we should have looked scared but we didn't. Guys were still horsing around, smoking like mad."

Forrest was seated near the rear of the plane, and the motion sickness pills distributed to the men prior to takeoff had made him drowsy, although he did not fall asleep. He recalled the view of the dark English Channel below him.

"The plane's doors were off and I looked down below and there were thousands of ships, big ones, little ones," Forrest said.

His stick included his friends Walter Gordon, Floyd Talbert, Francis Mellet, Wayne Sisk, Ed Tipper, Campbell Smith, and John Eubanks, who were all engaged in a soldier's favorite pastime.

"There was the usual bitching about equipment, and a lot of smoking and joking took place," Forrest told me. "It seemed like just another jump. Of course, we were scared to death but we didn't dare let it show to anybody."

Buck Compton wrote that the men quietly sat on the row of hard metal bucket seats, and that no one sang or gave patriotic speeches.

"Adrenaline surged, but I did not feel nervous," he recalled.

In the plane carrying Compton and his stick, a C-47 crewman removed the aircraft's door. Compton stood, took off the leg bag with his extra gear, and shuffled to the doorway. Looking out, he noticed the peaceful coastline of France approaching.

Compton was always close to his men, a fact that sometimes got him into trouble with Winters, who felt some distance must be maintained in order for an officer to effectively do his job. But to Compton, all that separated him from the men were the gold bars on his shoulders, and he was just "a go-between for the company commander and my noncommissioned officers who interpreted the commands and got the job done." He said he felt "blessed" with NCOs like Guarnere, Toye, Malarkey, Ken Mercier, Charles Grant, and James Diel under his command.

Guarnere recalled that, during the trip across the Channel, "our stomachs and bladders were working overtime." He was wide-awake, he said, and his thoughts were on his brother Henry. Just prior to loading for the flight, Guarnere had learned that Henry had been killed in Italy during the fighting around Monte Cassino.

"I was a madman," he said. "You never want to feel that kind of rage."

Guarnere's "burning" desire to lay into the Germans would earn him the nickname Wild Bill. Still, he also understood that his first duty was to the men under him.

"I didn't want to get anyone else killed, so I prayed to the man up-stairs," he wrote. "Everyone knew what I was thinking."

The vast armada of planes took a smattering of antiaircraft fire over the British-owned islands of Jersey and Guernsey, which the Germans had seized in 1940. But other than that ineffective resistance, the quiet flight was punctuated only by the engine drone of the planes until the C-47s crossed over the coastline and entered France. There the Nazi defenders, caught unaware at first, responded with vigor, and streamers of colored tracer rounds arced across the black sky, straight at the para-troopers. They were "spectacular and deadly against the night sky," Buck Compton recalled.

Guarnere thought the flak "looked like ten thousand Fourth of Julys," and the men in the plane just wanted to get out, even though they were not yet over their drop zones.

"Making it through the jump alive was a feat," Guarnere said.

Malarkey, who was the fourth man from the doorway, recalled stand-ing up and hooking his static line from the ripcord of his parachute to the overhead cable. His "guts tightened," he recalled, and he just wanted to "get the hell out of this plane." Not out of fear, he was quick to add; there was far too much going on around him, so there was no time for fear. He just knew, he said, that "the ground was our friend" and the sooner he was on it, the better off he'd be.

Forrest told me, "I didn't think about the jump much until the anti-aircraft fire started coming at us. Then we just wanted to get out."

He recalled how shrapnel passing through the plane's fuselage "sounded like shooting into a tin can.

"Luckily they didn't hit the right spot and we kept on flying, but the pilot sure did some evasive action," he said. "We were bounced all around in the plane. We were very vulnerable in the sky."

Near to Forrest was Smokey Gordon, who, because he was the tall-est man in the platoon, was the machine gunner. He carried the weapon in a canvas Griswold Bag, having first dismantled it and packed it so neatly, he told the historian Michel De Trez, that "it looked like a tube." He had wrapped an ammo belt around himself and loaded a short belt of ammo into the gun so it was ready for action upon landing. His as-sistant, Mellet, lugged more rounds and the bipod.

Gordon told De Trez, "I remember standing in the aircraft and thinking, 'What in God's name am I doing up here? I really don't belong here. I shouldn't be here,' and about that time, I was out."

Forrest recalled the violent bobbing and weaving of the C-47. The pilots were eager to get out of there, he said, "just like we were."

After what seemed like forever, the green "go" lights flashed on and the paratroopers leaped from the planes and into the maelstrom of battle that had become the sky over Normandy.

"It was sure a relief when the green light switched on," Forrest told me.

Forrest told me that as he looked out the doorway, "I could see the German tracers coming up at us."

Because of the flak, the C-47 pilots, many under fire for the first time, did not slow down their aircraft as instructed, but rather flipped on the green light while they were doing speeds of over a hundred miles per hour. The wash from the plane's propellers was tremendous.

"We jumped out right behind the left engine and it gave you a good blast," Forrest said. "It was bad enough when they went slow, but fast like that. That's why a lot of guys lost those leg bags and their equipment. They were just ripped right off."

Forrest Guth and thousands of his comrades had arrived. It was 1:10 a.m.

The *Barfleur* docked in Cherbourg at 6:30 a.m. Forrest and I debarked at the Quai de Normandie and were transported to the terminal on a small bus the ferry company had provided specifically for us. The harbor has seen its share of history. It was here in 1864 that the Confederate raider CSS *Alabama* sailed out to do battle with the USS *Kearsarge*, within sight of the city's population. The *Alabama* lost, and her remains lie out beyond the breakwater. Cherbourg was also the *Titanic's* first port of call on her first—and last—voyage in 1912. During World War II, Cherbourg was a major German naval base for surface ships and submarines prowling the North Atlantic. As such, the harbor suffered extensive damage from Allied bombers. Following the June 6, 1944, invasion of Normandy, and as the American forces drew ever closer, the place was rigged for demolition. When it became evident the city would fall, the Nazis blew up dockside facilities and sank ships in the channels. The

Americans seized Cherbourg on June 27, 1944, but it would be months before it became fully serviceable. The Cherbourg we saw on November 4, 2008, was a vibrant and modern port that shows no sign of the wartime destruction it had suffered.

Forrest Guth and Easy Company had first come to this historic city in July 1944, after the fighting around Carentan, and prior to their return to Aldbourne for rest and replacements. Following their hard-fought battles in Normandy, Winters treated his men by springing for the cost to have their uniforms spruced up at one of the local dry-cleaning shops.

A cab waiting for us at the terminal whisked Forrest and me away from the port and into the city to the car rental agency on the rue du Val de Saire. As I slid behind the steering wheel of our shiny black Opal, I expressed to Forrest my relief at once again being able to drive on the "correct" side of the road.

Leaving Cherbourg, I could see in the distance Fort du Roule, the nineteenth-century bastion perched on a hilltop overlooking the city, which the Germans had converted into a formidable strongpoint. Continuing east out of the city, we turned onto the E46/N13 and headed toward Carentan.

The trip was pleasant and uneventful thanks to the invaluable Global Positioning System unit I had with me. (GPS! Don't leave home without it.) During the trip I asked Forrest how he felt about coming back to these fields. My friend, who has returned to this part of Europe maybe a dozen times, said each trip is a little easier.

"Time eases a lot of things," he said, thoughtfully.

Exiting off the N13 at the Saint-Come-du-Mont-Carentan exit, I quickly spotted our guide, Paul Woodadge, parked on a gravel pull-off. Paul, who had met Forrest before, has escorted veterans, including Easy Company's Buck Compton, Bill Guarnere, Babe Heffron, Ed Tipper, Don Malarkey, Earl McLung, Ed Shames, and Paul Rogers, as well as other travelers across the battlefields of Normandy for the past twenty years. A Brit who lives in Normandy with his French wife, Myriam, Paul founded Battlebus in 2002, and since the *Band of Brothers* miniseries, he, along with his staff of knowledgeable guides, has become a specialist on the subject of Easy Company.

We pulled up behind Paul's big red Battlebus van, shook hands, then followed him a brief mile to our accommodations. We would be staying at the Blazing Sky bed-and-breakfast at Haute Addeville, a handful of homes along a narrow country lane just three miles north of Carentan. Upon our arrival, we drove through an iron gate and into a courtyard totally surrounded by walls and buildings. During the war, Blazing Sky was a farm located in an area known as Les Drouries. Most of this farm dates back to the 1600s; however, one entire section was rebuilt following the war after being destroyed by fire as a result of naval gunfire from the cruiser USS *Quincy*, firing inland from Utah Beach less than four miles to the north.

Language was no problem at Blazing Sky. Its owner, Dick Cooper, is British, as is the inn's manager, Spencer Henry, an ex–British army officer.

After we checked into our rooms, Spencer showed me around the farm. On D-day, all of the land around here had been the designated assembly area for E and F companies of the 501st Airborne, under the command of Lieutenant Colonel Robert A. Ballard.

Fighting roared around the farm where Forrest and I were now staying, and its ancient buildings still bear the scars. In the loft of the building where Forrest was staying, a German sniper had hacked a hole, through which he shot at oncoming paratroopers. One of his rounds mortally wounded Lieutenant George Schmidt, who, even as he fell dying, raised his weapon and peppered the sniper's position. His comrades joined in as well, and whether it was Schmidt or one of his men who killed the German, the pockmarked wall around the sniper's firing hole, which is preserved with a Plexiglas covering, bears mute testimony to this deadly exchange.

And it wasn't just small-arms fire that left its mark on the farm. Spencer pointed out holes in one building made as shells from the *Quincy* passed through without exploding.

After our mini-tour, Forrest and I climbed aboard the Battlebus with Paul and we were off. Our first stop in Normandy would be the same as Forrest's in 1944: Marmion Farm.

Like most of the paratroopers that night sixty-four years ago, Forrest Guth did not hit his drop zone, which was Drop Zone C, just west of

Sainte-Marie-du-Mont. In fact, he and his stick were three miles off target, most likely somewhere between the villages of Ravenoville and Foucarville.

As we drove, Paul said, "People argue about where Forrest landed. But one of my guides, Allan Bryson, interviewed Forrest by telephone a few years ago and they marked on a map where they think Forrest came down."

All Forrest could recall about that night of confusion was landing in a cow pasture by a hedgerow, and that the first sound he heard was Germans "chattering" in the darkness.

"Obviously I wasn't where I was supposed to be," he told me.

He waited quietly until the voices faded, then began looking for his comrades. The first one he met was Smokey Gordon.

"I was by myself for five, six or eight minutes before I found the first guy, Walter Gordon," Forrest said.

Gordon had also landed by a hedgerow, possibly the same one as Guth, and quickly assembled his machine gun. At first he thought he was "the only SOB in the ETO," until he saw a figure approach. He recognized the shadow as Forrest Guth.

"We were so familiar with each other we were able to recognize our men almost from their shadow," Gordon later recalled. "We could distinguish a silhouette at night or watch a man walk and tell who he was. We knew by the way he was standing or by the way his helmet sat on his head or how he slung his rifle."

Moving on, they next picked up John "Georgia Jap" Eubanks, who had not only lost his cricket but had forgotten the flash/thunder sign and countersign. Surprised by his sudden appearance, his comrades almost cut Eubanks down in the dark.

"He almost got shot before he could see France," Forrest said. "We almost killed him. Luckily we recognized him."

Continuing their journey through the predawn darkness, the group saw another man approaching in a crouching run. Gordon told Guth and Eubanks to hold while he crept along a ditch.

"I suddenly encountered these two eyeballs looking up at me and the muzzle of a pistol pointing right at my face," he later wrote. "I heard, 'Smokey. Is that you?' and replied, 'Yeah, Tab. It's me.'"

Floyd Talbert was overjoyed to find his friends. He had made it

Forrest Guth and Paul Woodadge at Marmion Farm in 2008. Forrest saw combat for the first time here on D-day.

safely to the ground, got out of his harness, and crawled into a ditch because he heard German voices on the other side of the hedge.

"I was scared to death," he wrote after the war. "I remained quiet while they passed and decided I should get to another location."

Moving quietly to another hedgerow, he heard a noise and pulled out a .45-caliber revolver his father had sent him, a gift from his hometown police department. That was when he recognized Gordon, Guth, and Eubanks.

"The four of us began making our way along a narrow road and we finally met with some other troopers who were from other outfits," Talbert recalled.

Marmion Farm sits at a T intersection where the D15, approaching from the west, connects to the D14 at the southern edge of Ravenoville. It consists of a large stone manor house and three stone outbuildings, including a barn, set in a quadrangle, surrounding a grassy courtyard.

The Germans, realizing that Allied aircraft would photograph their mainline beach defenses, needed to establish a second line of resistance should the invasion come ashore from the coast about a mile to the northeast. Marmion Farm was perfect, not just because of its thick stone walls, but also for its placement overlooking a crossroads connecting Sainte-Mère-Église to Cherbourg.

The area was occupied by about two hundred Germans, most of whom were billeted at Ravenoville, and not at the farm itself. This divided their command with the result that, when paratroopers began descending on them from the sky, the Germans were confused and disorganized.

One group of paratroopers now heading for the farm was led by Major John P. Stopka, executive officer of 3rd Battalion, 502nd Airborne. Stopka had assembled a mixed bag of men from various regiments, including at least one man from the 377th Parachute Field Artillery. It was this group with whom Guth, Gordon, Talbert, and Eubanks fell in.

"Our group was led by a very colorful major," Walter Gordon later told the 101st Airborne historian George Koskimaki. "About dawn of D-day, we joined twenty-five to thirty other paratroopers from various regiments and wrested a large quadrangle farmhouse from the Germans."

While the group of GIs Forrest and the others had fallen in with attacked the farm from one side, Tipper told me in 2009, he, Smith, and the rest of their "pick-up group" struck the Germans from another angle. They were attacking, he said, what they initially thought was a communication center with "a couple of German vehicles parked outside," and not an enemy strongpoint.

The initial fight, Tipper recalled, was "very, very quick" with no casualties. The Americans had killed some Germans and took twenty German prisoners.

"We took that place, but I thought the chances were pretty good that I would die there," Tipper told me. "We were running out of ammunition and they counterattacked every hour or so for a day and a half."

He said the ragtag bunch of paratroopers, who were "a pretty good bunch of men," had no automatic weapons, but that luckily, the Germans did not know.

Stopka was "a wild man," Tipper said, but he "did a very good job" in holding the farm from repeated counterattacks. Then, just as their ammo was giving out, Tipper said, infantry coming in from Utah arrived.

"They came over the horizon and the Germans took off," Tipper said.

The fight at Marmion was brisk, but brief.

"They were the first Germans I shot at," Forrest said. "It's funny. You never know if you really killed them."

Casualty numbers are unknown, although Forrest said, "we killed a few." Luckily for the Germans, none had been captured, since the paratroopers had been ordered to take no prisoners.

"Number one, you didn't have a place to put them," Forrest recalled. "Number two, you get pretty mad at those fellas shooting at you and angry because of some of the things you see in combat. There was a war to be fought and you don't do wars without killing anyone. After all, that's what we were trained for."

Stopka organized a defense of the farm, including setting up a machine gun manned by men of A Company, 506th, under Lieutenant Bill Muir, to guard the road intersection. This gun crew included Don Burgett. With this collection of waifs and strays, Stopka held the farm for the remainder of D-day. Of course, after the farm's capture, the men took time to clown around. A German helmet had been found and Forrest placed it on his head and smiled into the camera. Several men also posed holding a Nazi flag Forrest had taken down from a wall inside the farmhouse. Forrest snapped such a photo of Gordon and Eubanks. Then he folded the flag and brought it home as a souvenir.

It's uncertain how long the Easy Company men remained with Stopka. Gordon told Koskimaki in 1969, "We defended the billet all of D-day." Forrest, however, in 2008, recalled staying there only a few hours, before pushing on in the direction of Sainte-Marie-du-Mont. Gordon was most likely correct, given the length of time they were separated from the rest of Easy, and the tricks the passage of the years play on memory.

Tipper's comments to me also support Gordon's time frame, saying the Easy Company men left on June 7. Initially, they all moved together, Tipper recalled, but during the course of "a few brief skirmishes," he

Forrest at Marmion Farm, June 6, 1944. Note the captured German helmet on his head. *Forrest Guth*

and Smith became separated from the others, and continued on alone, linking up with them again later at Sainte-Marie-du-Mont.

One thing that did happen at Marmion Farm is that the Easy Company men picked up another of their comrades, Francis Mellet, Gordon's assistant gunner. Unfortunately, Mellet had thrown away the machine gun's bipod, which meant when Gordon fired the weapon, his only methods of aiming would be to use the weapon's sights or watch the path of the tracer rounds and adjust accordingly. He preferred the latter, so the loss of the bipod, he said, "didn't really bother me too much."

Standing in the grassy center of the quadrangle at Marmion Farm in 2008, Paul Woodadge told Forrest and me that, had the farm been properly defended by the Germans, it would have been a much tougher nut to crack. Researching the defense of the farm, he and his guide staff have discovered over half a dozen German bunkers, three of which he showed us, one by the main house and two more by outbuildings.

"Everywhere there is an uneven patch of ground, you'll find a bunker," Paul said.

Stopka and his men benefited not just from the Germans' disorganization, but also because of good timing.

"The ironic thing is, had the Germans been here in force with maybe a hundred and fifty guys in these bunkers, and had the attack come ten hours later, the paratroopers might all have been killed," Paul told us.

The American success, he said, symbolizes the difference between them and the Germans. While the latter were reluctant to break routine, and operated under a stringent guideline of training and tactics, the paratroopers proved more resilient, telling themselves, "I don't know where we are. I don't know how many men the enemy has, but let's just move in and do it, and do it quickly."

Marmion Farm still stands today, its appearance little changed from June 6, 1944. The land is owned and worked by the same family who owned it then, but the large house stands empty. Paul tells the story of how, during the war, a German officer, for whatever reason, hanged himself from a rafter in the house. After the war, the family, aware of the suicide, moved back in. According to local legend, they lived there for the next fifteen years, until the mother, driven by that suicide a decade

Forrest revisiting Marmion Farm in November 2008.

and a half earlier, hanged herself from exactly the same rafter. Her surviving family now believes the home to be haunted, and moved out. It has been vacant ever since.

Looking through the ground-floor windows at the austere, eighteenth-century interior with its wooden beams and empty, wide plank floor, I felt a pang of pity for this grand house. The scene of one of the many struggles during the liberation of France, it is now abandoned and left to its memories.

On June 7, Forrest, Smokey Gordon, and the rest struck out toward the east "in the vague direction" of Sainte-Marie-du-Mont, where Easy Company was to congregate.

In a field south of Marmion Farm, the Easy Company men encountered four or five civilians, probably displaced persons who had fled the bombing at Cherbourg. They were "very happy to see us," Forrest said, and offered them wine. Forrest was carrying Rod Strohl's camera, which he and Gordon shared, and they posed for photos with the French farmers. Forrest and Talbert appear in one picture, while Gordon and Talbert are in another.

"When I'm in the picture, Gordon was working the camera," Forrest told me. "And when he was in it, I had the camera."

Paul told us he had researched the photo many times, and narrowed it down to one of three fields near Marmion Farm. Which one it was exactly, however, may never be known.

Continuing their trek, Forrest recalled, the men came across scenes of previous fighting. In some spots, Forrest remembered, the ground was "strewn with bodies, American and German. Many of the bodies had been looted for handguns and possessions. Some had fingers cut off so their rings could be removed."

The booming of the naval bombardment at Utah Beach just a mile or so away, supporting the troops moving inland, was clearly audible. At first, Forrest and the others trekked along the D14, but then shifted course and cut across country, possibly encouraged by the U.S. Navy, which was shelling inland targets. Quite likely it was these American shells dropping on the road ahead that led the tiny group to swerve off onto a lane that ran between hedgerows separating farm fields. This path would lead them to a gruesome discovery.

Around dawn they neared the small crossroad village of Beuzeville-au-Plain, about two miles northeast of Sainte-Mère-Église. There, in a field beside the lane, lay the mangled, smoldering remains of an American C-47. The Skytrain, obviously shot down in the early hours of

D-day, had smashed into this field and exploded in a ball of fire. It burned for hours. Getting as close as they could, Forrest and the others found grim evidence that the plane had borne fellow paratroopers.

"It was still very hot," Forrest told me. "We looked around. We saw bodies scattered about, but we couldn't get too close because of the heat."

Forrest took out his camera and snapped some shots. Then they turned their backs on the scene of carnage and moved on. At the time, none of the men had any way of knowing that the plane they discovered had been carrying their commanding officer, Lieutenant Thomas Meehan, First Sergeant William Evans, and all of Easy Company headquarters.

"We didn't spend much time here," Forrest told me. "We had a job to do."

Grim reminders of that crash were recovered forty-five years later when the scene was excavated. Although the twenty-two bodies, paratroopers and crewmen, had been buried, first at Sainte-Mère-Église in 1946, then removed and reinterred in a mass grave at the Jefferson Barracks National Cemetery near St. Louis in 1952, many personal items were found. Among these were parachute clasps still locked, dog tags, a wristwatch with the hands stopped at 01:12, a flattened helmet, and, saddest of all, a ring engraved "T.M.," which could only have belonged to Thomas Meehan.

Although the exact route Guth and the others took after leaving Marmion Farm will never be known—it was dark and even they couldn't recall—Woodadge took us along what he believes was their route, based on his years of studying events of that day and the terrain itself. Logic based on facts discovered during that research, he said, plays a large part in conducting his tours and trying to reconstruct the events from the confusion that is inherent during combat.

"The [Meehan] crash site is not on a straight line from Marmion to Sainte-Marie-du-Mont, so something had to have turned them off the road," Paul said, answering the question of why the men deviated from their set course. "So if it's a given fact that we know there was naval bombardment here, and it's a given fact that Forrest Guth ended up taking a photo of the Meehan aircraft, to me it makes sense he turned off here to avoid the shelling."

Paul believes Lieutenant Harry Welsh of Easy Company landed

near the Meehan crash site as well. Welsh recalled drifting over a burning plane, whose intense flames nearly sucked him into the inferno. Welsh had to cut his risers with a switchblade knife he carried in order to better maneuver himself away from the flaming wreck.

The day we stopped at the crash site was one of the few sunny days Forrest and I were blessed with on our trip. The lane leading back from the road to the site was still soggy from the previous day's rain, so Paul drove as far as he dared, then we walked the rest of the way. We stood in the farm lane Forrest, Gordon, Talbert, Mellet, and Eubanks had walked along, and looked upon the muddy, vacant field. Here, in this otherwise uninteresting plot of barren farmland, an entire stick of highly trained paratroopers had died without ever seeing the enemy or firing a shot. It is impossible to imagine the violence visited upon this serene stretch of ground that night.

Today a monument stands along the roadway at Beuzeville-au-Plain honoring the dead and listing the names of the seventeen paratroopers and five crewmen who died at 1:12 a.m. on June 6, 1944, in that forlorn field about 150 yards away. We parked our car by the monument and got out. Although Forrest had been here on previous visits, he gazed intently at the monument, contemplating the names cast in bronze. He returned to the car without saying a word.

While Forrest and his friends were trying to link up with Easy, the rest of the company had been assembling in dribs and drabs since landing.

Brad Freeman of 2nd Platoon landed "not too far from Sainte-Mère-Église." Not a Toccoa man, Freeman had joined Easy Company in Aldbourne in February 1944. Unlike later new men coming into the company, he was readily accepted. This was probably because the Mississippian was not replacing any man who had been killed or wounded in combat, since Easy had yet to face the enemy. Freeman, however, told me—tongue firmly planted in cheek—that he thinks his acceptance was because "they liked my Southern drawl."

On the night of June 5–6, Freeman—a member of the same stick that included Don Malarkey—was unsure where he was. The only Easy man he found was Sergeant Chuck Grant of 1st Squad, and they struck out together to find the company.

Buck Compton recalled leaving the C-47 and being hit by the

The C-47 carrying Easy Company commander Lt. Thomas Meehan crashed in this field on D-day.

Forrest poses next to the monument that now honors Lieutenant Meehan and the men of Easy Company who died in the crash outside of Beuzeville-au-Plain.

propeller blast "with hurricane force," breaking the chin strap on his helmet as well as the straps holding on his leg bag. He tried to stop the bag from falling away by grabbing the attached rope, but it played out so rapidly it burned his hands. The bag with his gear fell away into the night, taking with it his ammo, grenades, personal supplies, mortar rounds, medical kit, rations, and his M1 carbine, one of the special weapons Forrest had converted to full automatic. All he had left was his trench knife and canteen, but he still had reason to give thanks.

"I'm just glad the force of the blast didn't blow panels out of my chute," he later wrote.

Compton landed in an orchard enclosed by hedges. Everything was deathly quiet, and aside from some cows, he was totally alone. He cut himself free of his harness after the clasp jammed, and went in search of his men.

One of the first Compton located was Guarnere. Wild Bill, the second man in his plane to jump, "landed quick and goddamned hard." He had also lost his leg bag and weapon, but soon picked up a German Schmeisser. However, Guarnere threw the weapon away when he realized that the machine pistol's distinctive sound would draw American fire. He later located an M1 Garand.

Popeye Wynn, Joe Toye, Don Malarkey, who, to lighten his load, had discarded his mortar's base plate and bipod, and Mike Ranney also linked up with Compton, and they all headed in the direction of Causeway 2.

Paul believes Winters came down in a field on the edge of Sainte-Mère-Église, about 1,500 feet due west of the church, right beside where the present-day N13 skirts around the town. Moviegoers who saw the film *The Longest Day* will recall the burning building near the town church, set alight, probably by an unexploded German antiaircraft round that had fallen back to earth. That, and the landing on the church tower of John Steele of the 82nd Airborne and the slaughter of a number of paratroopers in the town square, would not occur for another forty minutes after Winters's landing. Winters said he saw the burning building, but Paul Woodadge believes Dick made an understandable error because the time frame doesn't match the known facts.

"When Dick said he saw the burning building, I think he is mistaken," Paul told us. "I think he saw a crashed aircraft."

Our guide, Paul Woodadge, believes Dick Winters dropped into this field at Sainte-Mère-Église on D-day.

In the distance off to the north, Winters spotted the silhouette of a long row of buildings, broken by a lone alleyway, the Impasse de la Charronnerie. He headed in that direction.

Lipton, Paul told us, came down about 1,200 feet northeast of Winters and about 600 feet north of the church in what today is the parking lot of City Hall along the rue du Cap de Laine in Sainte-Mère-Église. He climbed over a wall that stood where the driveway now is, and began walking. Then, sensing he was heading the wrong way, he reversed course and found an old stone marker bearing the town's name, which he deciphered in the dark by feeling the letters with his fingers. Coming to rue du Cap de Laine, Lipton noted the same long line of buildings just across the street, and the alleyway Winters had spotted, and hurried to it. Somewhere behind those buildings, the two men joined up. Paul's statement on where the two men found each other is based on "common sense" and knowing where each man came down.

"This alley is the only gap in an otherwise unbroken row of houses," Paul said. "Whether it's one hundred percent true or not, I can't possibly say. But it works."

Earl McLung landed near a community laundry area, a spring-fed pool under a square, peaked roof set atop four stone pillars, about 550 feet northeast of the church. McLung's parachute draped over the point of the roof, while he rolled down the slanted roof and dropped to the ground five or six feet below. The chute's harness tightened around him and he struggled to get free. Two German soldiers had seen him land and walked cautiously along a trail leading from the town to the laundry area. Spotting the white parachute on the roof, they both opened fire at it, unaware that the man who wore the chute was lying on the ground. McLung managed to free his Garand, aim, and cut down both Germans. He'd been on the ground about thirty seconds. Probably the first man in Easy Company to engage the enemy, McLung cut himself free and went in search of his buddies.

We arrived in Sainte-Mère-Église around lunchtime, parking in a lot by what is probably the world's most recognizable church for World War II buffs, the Church de Sainte-Mère-Église. It was here that Private John Steele arrived in France, his parachute snagging on one of the church's four pointed finials, while inside the tower, bells clanged until his hearing was temporarily gone. Below in the plaza, Steele watched his comrades descend under German fire to certain death. Diagonally across the square, where the town museum is now located, was a burning barn whose hungry flames sucked in at least one paratrooper that night.

Standing on the broad plaza between rue de Verdun and rue Eisenhower, the church remains relatively unchanged from that night when it found itself in the center of a battlefield. To commemorate the event, one church window is dedicated to the paratroopers, and a dummy in an army uniform, representing Steele, hangs from a parachute strung over a finial, although Paul does not believe it is the correct finial. He said Steele landed on the one diagonal from where the dummy now dangles and out of sight of the parking lot.

"They hung the dummy there for the tourists," he said.

We left our car and decided to walk to a nearby café for lunch. But first we were met by a British filmmaker named Richard Lanni. He and a local man, Ellwood von Siebold, were collaborating on a documentary called *The Americans on D-Day*, and they wanted a brief interview with Forrest. The on-camera interview was done in Siebold's home, which sits by the church plaza on the corner of the rue Eisenhower and rue du General de Gaulle.

During the war, Siebold's house was owned by Dr. Monnier, a local veterinarian. On the night of June 5–6, he and his family heard the drone of planes overhead and watched paratroopers, men of the 82nd Airborne, drop from the sky. One man landed in Monnier's courtyard, almost right on top of the doctor. A German officer named Werner, who was billeted in the house and was hiding behind one of the eight live palm trees Monnier had growing in his courtyard (they are there still), stepped out and aimed a pistol at the American. Monnier placed himself in front of the GI and told the German he wanted no trouble. Werner took the American prisoner, and they all went into the family's bomb shelter. There the American opened his jacket and handed out chewing gum, then he unfolded a small map and asked where he was. When told he was in Sainte-Mère-Église, he was relieved. He was on target, and he talked freely about his unit being assigned to take the town as part of the invasion plan.

The German officer listened intently, and after a couple of hours, with the sound of fighting and the number of planes roaring overhead heralding the arrival of more Americans, Werner handed the American his pistol and surrendered, asking the paratrooper to treat him as kindly as he had been treated.

Forrest's impromptu invitation to interview with Lanni in von Siebold's home is just one of many indications of how popular World War II veterans, especially members of Easy Company, are in Europe. Everywhere we went on our journey, word of our coming moved ahead of us. It started with the reenactors in Aldbourne and continued in France. When we stopped at the Meehan Memorial earlier that day, we were joined by one of Paul's guides leading a tour group, all Americans, who were thrilled to meet Forrest, a genuine member of the Band of Brothers. This would continue throughout our trek across Europe.

I felt like I was touring with one of the Beatles, I told Forrest.

I believe Forrest felt some discomfort at all the attention. Like Winters and all of the other Easy Company men I have spoken to, he knows they did nothing different than any other group of soldiers during the war, and that it was only through Ambrose's book and the miniseries that they have risen to celebrity status.

After lunch at a little place called La Liberation, we moved on, following the route of Winters and his men as they moved toward Brecourt Manor.

About three a.m. Winters and his group, which now numbered about fifteen men, came across Lieutenant Colonel Robert Cole, commander of the 3rd Battalion of the 502nd PIR, who had with him more than a hundred men. Cole was leading his column toward his objective, Causeway 3, and the coastal batteries at Saint-Martin-de-Varreville. Since that was in roughly the same direction Winters was going, they fell in line.

Around four a.m., the approaching sound of clopping horses' hooves and the creak of wooden wheels and leather harness was heard moving toward them along the dark Norman road. Cole dispersed his men around a T intersection and they hunched down in the cover of a hedgerow. The men who had lost their weapons in the jump, Winters, Guarnere, Compton, and Lipton, stayed back. Four horse-drawn German supply wagons manned by members of an *Ost* regiment, men recruited or drafted from eastern Europe, now appeared on the road. As they drew near, Cole's trap was prematurely sprung when his men opened fire too soon. In the brief but violent blaze of gunfire that erupted, men yelled, cursed, and screamed, horses whinnied and bullets whistled through the air and thudded into flesh. Two of the wagons managed to get turned around and tore away, but the drivers of the other two, plus several of the infantrymen, were cut down. When the shooting stopped, an unspecified number of Germans lay dead and ten had surrendered. One American officer was killed.

Accounts among the men concerning this fight differ, and the miniseries, which shows the fight occurring between the Germans and Winters's little band of men, muddies the water even further. The miniseries supports Guarnere's claim that he "let loose" after the train passed, and "annihilated every last one" of the Germans. Afterward, Winters reprimands him for firing without orders. Guarnere does not remember any reprimand, but wrote, "I had so much anger I might have turned around and shot him if he tried to stop me." He "respected Winters as an officer," he said, even though he was as yet unproven in combat.

Winters, on the other hand, told me the story of how Cole had set up the ambush. He added that, like himself, Guarnere had no weapon, and therefore could not have opened fire first.

"Bill's told that story so many times, even he believes it," Winters said to me.

Much of what happens in combat is based on an individual's perspective, so what really happened in this minor skirmish is of no consequence. The reader can make his or her own determination. This narration makes no judgment.

Sixty-four years and five months after that early-morning ambush, we arrived at the site. Unlike in the miniseries, there is no railroad overpass or lined culvert. It is just a simple T junction of two roads, the D423 and D115, surrounded by fields and hedgerows and situated a mile or so northeast of Sainte-Mère-Église.

Paul believes the brief fight here is further proof of why the Allies were so successful on D-day. For while the Americans could adapt and improvise, the Germans were rigid and stuck to routine. These *Ost* men, for example, stationed at a farm named Artilly, just south of Beuzeville-au-Plain, were bringing eggs and milk to the men manning the defenses, regardless of the fact that Allied planes were flying overhead and paratroopers were dropping on their heads.

Not long after the ambush, Winters and his little band split off from Cole and moved in the direction of a rendezvous point at the small farming village of Le Grand Chemin. There, although he did not yet know it, Lieutenant Winters had an appointment with fame at a place called Brecourt Manor.

Dutifully, Paul, Forrest, and I followed in his footsteps.

CHAPTER 5

"... AN ABSOLUTE MINEFIELD OF VARYING ACCOUNTS"

THE ASSAULT AT BRECOURT MANOR

As Winters and his men continued toward their rendezvous point at Sainte-Marie-du-Mont, two and a half miles away, at the beach designated Utah, the ground portion of the invasion was getting under way. Starting at two a.m., the 865 ships of the Utah force took up station some ten miles off the coast. With dawn breaking over the eastern horizon, they began closing on the coastline, and by four a.m., men of the 4th Division landing parties were clambering down cargo nets into Higgins boats. An hour and a half later, 276 B-26 Marauder twin-engine bombers of the 9th Air Force arrived overhead and dropped their payloads on the beach defenses, filling the air with smoke and debris and shattering the morning quiet with their explosions. At six a.m., the warships pointed their guns landward and opened fire as the Higgins boats carrying the first wave of men churned their way toward the beach.

The men of Easy didn't know this, of course, but they could certainly hear it. The *ka-rump* of bursting naval shells rumbled from the direction of Utah and some larger-caliber rounds were even streaking overhead, seeking predetermined targets farther inland.

After leaving Cole and his group, Winters's band of men moved along the D14, paralleling the coast. They came across a German supply wagon that had been shot up by Allied fighters and Winters finally was able to replace his lost M1 Garand. Evidently the dead German on the wagon had picked up the weapon a short time earlier.

Buck Compton now linked up with Winters. Like many, Compton had lost his weapon in the jump, but had been given a Thompson submachine gun by Lieutenant McMillan of Dog Company, who had broken his leg on landing. During his trek, Compton, who had collected a couple of 82nd Airborne men along the way, recalled a brush with death when a naval shell "flew in like a freight train and landed about fifty feet away from us. It thudded, shaking the ground, and stuck fast—a dud. If it had exploded, it would have killed us for sure."

Easy Company was slowly coming together. Lipton later recalled, "By about eight a.m. on the morning of D-day, June 6, 1944, there were thirteen of us together from E Company of the 506th Parachute Infantry Regiment. We had joined together by twos and threes following our jump into Normandy shortly after one thirty that morning. The rest of our company was scattered over the Normandy peninsula, and it would take several days for those who had survived the jump and the combat following it to join us.

"We had two officers, Lieutenant Winters in command and Lieutenant Compton; two platoon sergeants, Guarnere and I, and nine men, and we had two machine guns, a 60-millimeter mortar, and our individual weapons. We had moved along the road network, led by Lieutenant Winters, from the vicinity of Sainte-Mère-Église, where many of us had landed, to a small village named Le Grand Chemin, near Sainte-Marie-du-Mont, joining up along the way with men from other companies in our battalion and with some of our battalion headquarters."

As the group approached the small farm village of Le Grand Chemin, about a mile and a half north of Sainte-Marie-du-Mont, Don Malarkey recalled what must be one of the war's strangest coincidences. Coming across a group of German POWs huddled along the road under the watchful eye of some GIs, Malarkey wisecracked, "Where the hell are you guys from? Brooklyn?"

One man replied, "No. Portland, Oregon."

As fate would have it, the man dressed in German field gray had lived in Portland and had worked there for the Schmitz Steel Company. When the war broke out, his immigrant family had heeded Adolf Hitler's call for all good Aryans to return to Germany to defend the Fatherland.

Malarkey, it turned out, knew the Schmitz family and had worked at Monarch Forge and Machine Works just across the street.

"Well, now, what do you think of that decision to return to your homeland?" Malarkey asked.

"I think I made a big mistake," the man replied, downcast.

"You take care," Malarkey said and moved on, thinking how odd war is.

This incident is featured in the *Band of Brothers* miniseries, although the screenwriter took the liberty of making this man one of the POWs gunned down by Lieutenant Ronald Spiers. The American-born enemy soldier was not among that group.

After arriving in Le Grand Chemin, Winters and his column finally linked up with the rest of 2nd Battalion, which now consisted of about eighty men.

Most of the inhabitants of this hamlet were farmworkers at a large estate called Brecourt Manor, whose buildings could be seen a short distance to the south. The estate was owned by a retired French army colonel named de Vallavieille, a veteran of the Marne and Verdun thirty years earlier. This latest war had cost him two sons, a captain and a sergeant, both lost during the Battle of France in 1940. Now sixty-nine, the aging army officer hid with the rest of his family, including his two surviving sons, Louis, nineteen, and Michel, twenty-four, inside their large home along with two of his farmworkers, their wives and a baby.

Just outside the village near where the D14 meets the D913, or Sonnier Road, leading toward the coast, the Americans came under German machine-gun fire from a tree line about 350 yards on the battalion's right. The dirt road was somewhat sunken here, and Winters told me how he used this opportunity to sit against the road embankment, protected from the enemy bullets, to take a welcome break. Colonel Strayer ordered D Company to do a reconnaissance of the field, a job carried out by Lieutenant John Kelly, who, Malarkey recalled, looked like "a boxer whose face was all beat up," who possibly had "taken one too many blows, not the kind of guy you want telling you to go on a do-or-die mission to capture guns that were sure to be well protected by soldiers who'd been preparing for months."

Winters said Kelly inexpertly deployed his men and tried a frontal probe without prior reconnaissance to assess the situation. Pinned down, he and his men finally worked their way back to the battalion. That was when Strayer called on Winters. Lieutenant George Lavenson, Strayer's aide, found Winters where he had been relaxing and told him, "Strayer wants you up front." Winters found Strayer and Clarence Hester talking with a harried Lieutenant Kelly. Winters stood silently near the small group. Hester soon turned to him.

"There's fire along that hedgerow there," Hester said without preamble. "Take care of it."

Hester then turned and walked away without any further instructions.

Paul Woodadge led Forrest and me into Le Grand Chemin on the afternoon of our second day in Normandy. The village is much as it was in 1944, a cluster of buildings bisected by the D14 roadway, now paved. We didn't stop at Le Grand Chemin, but rather pulled off onto a small siding just south of the village. There on June 14, 2008, a group of Easy Company veterans and friends, led by Frank Slegers and Marco Kilian— who would be our contacts in Belgium later in our trip—had erected one of four E Company monuments that mark the Band of Brothers' European battlefields. These monuments, in most cases made of brick and concrete, tell the story of what the company did and list the names of the men killed in the fighting, etched into highly polished black granite slabs.

We stopped at the Brecourt Manor memorial and got out of the van. The marker relates how Winters and his dozen men attacked and destroyed a German artillery position, just as recounted in Ambrose's book and in the miniseries. But while it recounts the story of the Brecourt Manor fight, it also muddies the water. For on a separate pedestal next to the monument is etched a map drawn by Michel de Vallavieille sometime after the war, and endorsed by Winters, that features a major discrepancy from the accepted story of the fight. I will delve into this deviation later in this chapter.

Like the Meehan marker, this one does not sit by the actual site. The field Winters and his men crossed and the line where the German guns stood is about three hundred yards and one tree line away, on private property still owned by Charles de Vallavieille, Michel's son. It is extremely difficult to see the actual field from the marker, but Paul told

Part of the German gun line, now overgrown, at Brecourt Manor. Winters and his men approached behind the hedgerow in the distance.

me we had an appointment with Monsieur de Vallavieille the next day, and would walk the field then.

Winters did not have to wait for an appointment from the de Vallavieille family to see Brecourt Manor. His appointment came directly from Colonel Strayer: Take out those guns.

Winters told me a number of times how he hated to charge into a situation without having the opportunity to assess the risk to himself and his men. To that end, on a number of occasions he undertook dangerous but, he deemed, necessary one-man reconnaissance missions. And so he did here, cautiously moving along a hedgerow to within sight of the German position. The enemy was located not in a trench as depicted in the miniseries, but in a tree-lined ditch about four hundred yards long, separating two fields. The trench in the film, with its walls of woven vines, is, as Winters told me, "what happens when you let an Englishman design the set. It looks like something out of World War One." Unlike the somewhat exposed position depicted in the miniseries, here in this heavy growth of trees and brush along the ditch, the guns were perfectly camouflaged, which is why aerial photos never revealed them.

At Brecourt, the Germans had placed four 105mm guns, which the Americans at first mistook for 88s. (The excellent German 88mm gun was so feared and respected by the GIs that throughout the war, almost every enemy gun they came up against was called "an 88," regardless of its actual caliber.) The position was manned by about fifty Germans of the 6th Battery, 90th Regiment, and protected by several machine guns. The enemy guns had been rolled into the ditch until their wheels rested against the earthen wall, with three of the guns facing Utah Beach three miles away, while the fourth faced left, toward the causeway a few hundred yards off.

But is that the way they really were? Or were all four guns on line to defend the beach? The accepted history of the fight tells us one gun was turned, but there is one convincing piece of evidence that suggests otherwise.

So which is correct? Possibly both.

Until I visited Brecourt with Paul Woodadge, I was blissfully unaware of any discrepancies in the story of the fight on this field. Our appointment with Charles de Vallavieille was on November 6, our last full day in Normandy. As was so often the case on this journey, the day was overcast with a slight off-and-on drizzle. At the Brecourt monument we had visited earlier, we turned right from the roadway onto the long lane that leads to the manor house. Charles de Vallavieille greeted us and led us into the quadrangle courtyard and then the kitchen of the big stone house. We sat around the large table where, in years past, Dick Winters, Walter Gordon, Don Malarkey, and, yes, Forrest Guth had sat before with Charles's uncle, Louis. Monsieur de Vallavieille greeted Forrest like an old friend of the family, which, indeed, he was. The de Vallavieille family has always had the utmost respect for the men of Easy Company, despite the fact that it was a paratrooper who—the man's identity is not known—shot and wounded Charles's father, Michel, who was then twenty-one. It is believed the soldier assumed the family to be collaborators since the German guns were on their land.

Monsieur de Vallavieille presented Forrest with a gold medal on a red, white, and blue ribbon, which he hung around my friend's neck, over his bright yellow *Band of Brothers* jacket, a gift in 2001 to all of the Easy Company veterans from HBO. The medal proclaimed Forrest to be a "citizen of honor" in Sainte-Marie-du-Mont. This shows how the family feels about these men, for on the day Winters attacked the Germans here on this ground, Forrest, Gordon, and the others were still at Marmion Farm.

As Forrest and Monsieur de Vallavieille chatted, Paul and I left for the battlefield. Entering through an iron gate, we walked the soggy field by the tree line that had once concealed the quartet of 105s. It is a tangle of trees, brambles, and other vegetation, running for more than 500 feet before it intersects another hedgerow coming in perpendicular from the left. This marks the famous "L" in the German "trench." Out in front and slightly to the right of the German position, barely visible through the trees, lies Le Grand Chemin and the roadway leading to the beach. To the left, and running across the fields toward the village, are two hedgerows, one of which was used by Winters and half of the men in their approach to the guns, and the other used by Compton and the rest of the patrol. Some 350 feet behind where we stood, across the broad field, is another tree line where enemy machine guns were positioned.

After picking our way across the muddy field, Paul and I stopped at the L in the German line, and he began explaining some of the variations in the Brecourt story.

The known facts are that, after his one-man reconnaissance, Winters returned to the village and briefed his men, Sergeants Lipton, Toye, and Guarnere, Corporals Malarkey and Robert "Popeye" Wynn, and Privates Mike Ranney, Cleveland O. Petty, Joseph D. Liebgott, Walter Hendrix, and John Plesha Jr. Guarnere asked Winters how many Germans they were up against. Winters had no idea.

Private Gerald Lorraine of Service Company, one of Colonel Sink's drivers, was standing nearby and asked to accompany the lieutenant and his men. Winters, knowing he needed additional firepower, agreed.

Winters had explained to me that his plan called for "a double envelopment," with Compton, Lipton, Toye, Lorraine, Popeye, and Ranney moving along one of two thick hedgerows that led toward the German line, while he led the rest of the men along the second. This would prevent both groups from being pinned down and rendered immobile. Once there, Winters told his two machine-gun crews, Petty and Liebgott on one, and Hendrix and Plesha on the second, to position themselves to lay down an effective base of fire to cover the rest when they attacked. Compton was to get his men in close and lob grenades on one of the German machine-gun emplacements guarding the artillery, and Lipton was to make sure he had the TNT he was carrying in a musette bag, to be able to blow up the guns once they were captured. He then sent Lipton and Ranney out to watch the German left flank.

"Speed is everything," Winters told his men. "We've got to hit them hard and fast, and get into that trench before they can react. Then we'll concentrate on the first gun, take it, then attack the rest one by one."

He ordered the men to drop everything except their ammo and follow him.

Malarkey liked the plan and later called Winters "a thinker."

"He'd been given a situation and he could, in about the time it took the rest of us to do an equipment check, figure out a plan of attack," he wrote.

He said Winters later told him that he had put Compton, Guarnere, and him in the same group because they "instinctively understood the intricacies of battle."

"That meant a lot to me," he said.

The attack unfolded pretty much the way Ambrose outlined it in his book, and as I did in *Biggest Brother*, with my account coming directly from Winters. At his signal, Liebgott opened fire with his machine gun, its .30-caliber slugs raking the German position. The rest of the men joined in, providing cover fire for Compton and his group.

The enemy machine guns responded, and Germans in the trench opened up with their Mauser rifles. A German helmet poked up above the trench. Winters aimed his M1 and squeezed off a round. The helmet dropped out of sight. He later found a pool of blood at the spot but no sign of the German.

Compton, Guarnere, and Malarkey slipped grenades from their web gear, yanked out the pins, and hurled the "pineapples" at the machine gun. Seeing that, Winters yelled, "Come on! Follow me!" He leaped to his feet and ran forward, the others close behind. The exploding grenades knocked out the MG 42 and its crew, but bullets from Germans in the trench and machine guns in the distant tree line buzzed around the Americans like hornets, kicking up dirt devils at their feet as they charged.

Compton and his men ran forward, getting into the German earthworks. Compton saw two Germans in the end of the so-called trench running perpendicular to the hedgerow.

"I figured I could take out the two Germans easily enough first," he said and ran toward them along the ditch. Closing the distance, he stopped and raised his tommy gun, the one he had been given earlier in the day by the injured McMillan, and squeezed the trigger. Nothing happened. Frantically he yanked the cocking lever and tried again. Nothing. The weapon's firing pin had been broken in McMillan's landing. The Germans heard Compton and wheeled in his direction, looks of surprise and horror on their faces. Then suddenly Guarnere, who was behind Compton, brushed by him and opened fire. One German went down right away; the other turned and ran. Compton tossed a grenade that burst over the fleeing man's head, killing him. Compton later said throwing the grenade was not something he had thought about, but rather was an automatic reaction.

"That was my first kill," he wrote. "I have no idea who he was, what he did outside the war, or if he had a wife or family. You just don't think. A man is trying to kill you, and you either kill him first or be killed waiting to assess the situation."

By now Winters and the others had also reached the trench. Diving behind the earthen wall for cover, Wynn yelped as a bullet struck him in the buttocks. Writhing on the bottom of the ditch and bleeding into his ripped trousers, he kept apologizing to Winters.

"I'm sorry, sir. I goofed," he cried. "I messed up. I'm sorry, Lieutenant."

A German potato masher grenade thrown from the nearby artillery position landed almost at Toye's feet.

"Grenade!" Winters yelled.

Men dove in all directions. Toye flopped over backward as the grenade went off, shattering the stock of his M1. Recalling that moment,

Guarnere later said Toye's rifle took the brunt of the blast, "otherwise he'd be singing soprano." The Americans tossed grenades back. As they exploded, Lorraine, Guarnere, and Winters stormed the gun position, weapons blazing. Three Germans leaped from the trench and ran across the open field toward their comrades in the opposite tree line.

With a quick attack, Winters and his men took the first German gun. But where was that gun? Was it at a forty-five-degree angle to the other three, firing at the causeway, as is the accepted version of the fight? Or was it on line with the others, aimed at Utah Beach? Arguments can be made for both cases.

Brecourt, Paul Woodadge told me, is the part of the tour he dreads most because of the conflicting accounts surrounding it, especially in recent years as more veterans tell their stories.

"It was so easy a few years ago when you had just one version, the one in Ambrose's book," he said. "But now you've got Dick's version, and Guarnere's version and Jumbo DiMarzio's version and Malarkey's version and Compton's version. This is an absolute minefield of varying accounts."

Some of those differences involve the route of the attack and who came in from where. There is also some question as to the location of what is called Lipton's tree. As the attack began, Lipton climbed a young tree to get a better vantage point, foolishly exposing himself to enemy fire. It was the kind of error a rookie makes his first time in combat. Luckily, Lipton survived to learn from his mistake.

Paul pointed to a tree he assumes to be the one. It is about the right size for a tree that has stood for more than sixty years, and is about thirty yards west of the L in the German line. Pointing to the trunk of a felled tree, Paul said some students of the battle think that was Lipton's perch, but Paul feels that, since we know Lipton climbed a young tree, the diameter of this trunk makes the tree too old. Plus, in my own assessment, it is right by the L in the German line, making its position too close to the enemy line. From that distance, it is unlikely Lipton could have climbed it unseen. And once the Germans knew he was there, no trained soldier could have missed hitting him.

But the biggest question mark is the exact location of the first gun on the German left. As mentioned earlier in this chapter, the Brecourt monument commemorating the fight includes a pedestal, on which is etched a map detailing the battle that occurred here. That map, as previously mentioned, was drawn by Michel de Vallavieille, who lived on the land, and was endorsed by Winters as being accurate, and shows all four guns pointing at the beach.

However, a sketch drawn by Winters for me in 2001 supports the first gun being pointed away from the beach, toward the causeway, and there are aerial photos that seem to support that claim, showing not the guns but disturbed areas where the guns might have been placed.

Still, Woodadge leans very heavily toward the first map showing all four guns on line. He bases his judgment on time—the first map was drawn shortly after the actual fight—and military logic.

"Personally, I think all four guns were on a straight line," Paul said. "Dick says there was one on the corner here, in an L shape. I don't go along with that. These guns were placed here before the invasion to defend the beach. So it makes no sense to have one gun pointing toward the road. There was nothing there to shoot at."

Another who wrote about the fight, Carwood Lipton, is also not clear on the position of the first gun. Lipton wrote, "A frontal attack against those positions by thirteen men could not succeed, but Lieutenant Winters confidently outlined to us his plan to deceive and defeat the German forces and to destroy the guns. His plan was to concentrate a double envelopment attack on one gun, the one on the German left flank, and after capturing it to hit the other guns, one by one, on their open left flanks."

By "the one on the German left flank," did he mean one was turned to protect the left flank of the position? Or was he simply referring to the gun on the extreme left of the German line, since he goes on to say they would "hit the other guns, one by one, on their open left flanks?"

It could be interpreted either way.

Lipton went on to say, "These guns were sited to put artillery fire on the full expanse of Utah Beach, where the U.S. 4th Division was coming ashore from landing craft. They had forward observers along the beach to direct the fire. The capture and destruction of the guns was a major factor in the success of the Utah landings and in the almost complete lack of casualties in that division during its landing."

Again, by that, did he mean all four guns were on line since they "were sited to put artillery fire on the full expanse of Utah Beach"?

Woodadge places great weight on the earlier map because its authors lived just a few hundred yards away.

"They drew the map that shows the guns on a line here, and my logic is they were the ones who were sitting here for years after the war," Paul said. "They would have known where the guns were. Dick, Don, Bill . . . they were only here for a few hours, then moved off."

Woodadge also feels time and publicity have clouded the facts.

"The TV version has supplanted the real memories. It's fresher and more vivid," he told me. "If I saw a documentary about my old school, that would be fresher in my brain than my own memories would be."

Having now spoken to Paul, with his assumptions based on logic and that map, and Winters, who endorsed the original map, but who now says one gun was turned and who was an actual participant in the fight, I would dare muddy the water here with my own conjecture. A compromise, if you will.

Both might be correct.

Before June 6, this gun position was likely set up with all four guns on a row. That makes sense and is simple military logic, to put maximum firepower on the beach, since the goal of Field Marshal Erwin Rommel, who oversaw the defenses, was to stop the invasion at the water's edge.

Up until June 6, the position was guarded by a number of machine guns, protecting both the front and flanks of the battery. The airdrop in the early hours of D-day changed that. One of the airborne drop zones was just inland of the battery's position.

"There's twelve hundred men landing on that drop zone," Paul said, pointing inland, away from Brecourt. "The Germans would have heard the noise. There would have been patrols and gunfire."

At that time, Paul told us, the German commander of the battery shifted some of his machine guns from the battery's front to the tree line across the field to his rear. After dawn, with the sound of battle behind him intensifying and with American infantry now storming ashore on Utah Beach out in front of him, the battery commander quite likely realized that the paratroopers were attempting to seize the causeway and hold it open for the ground forces. Thus, he turned his left flank gun in that direction as a preventive measure. Later, when Michel de Vallavieille drew his map, he based it on the guns' original positions, not taking into account the change, and Winters did not correct him.

Again, that is my own conjecture. As Paul Woodadge told me, "You tell it the best you can with the information you have, throw in all the variables and let the reader draw his own conclusions.

"Anyone who wants to write the definitive history of Brecourt, they get my absolute good luck and well done," he said.

Woodadge admits that, despite his research, he has more questions than answers.

"I wasn't here," he told me. "The only thing I can use is logic. I cannot come up with a reason why they'd have a gun pointing up there. But everybody says it. Dick says it. Buck stood here and swore blind there was a gun there, so I don't know. What do you do?"

What you do is what Paul plans to do—more research. With the blessing of the de Vallavieille family, he and his staff intend to conduct an examination of the ground with metal detectors that will penetrate three meters into the earth in order to make a thorough examination of the site.

"We're going to use a huge scale map and put this into three-meter grids or something, and we're going to systematically survey each square to see what remnants of metal and shrapnel there is in the ground," Paul said, his voice sounding excited at the prospect. "We'll do the whole gun line and we're hoping that it will pick up four obvious disturbed areas where we can then put a probe in and see if we can find where the guns were because right now, it's all based on opinion."

The key to the site is the exact location of that first gun, whether on the flank or on line. After that, he said, the exact positions of the other three should be simple. While Bill Guarnere said the guns were a hundred yards apart, Paul said German artillery pieces were generally sixty to ninety yards apart and Guarnere's statement was an approximation.

"That's someone saying, 'Bill, how far apart do you reckon the guns were?' and him saying, 'About a hundred yards,'" Paul said.

Paul understands the frustration in the minds of visitors he brings here hoping to learn about the fight, only to be confronted with more questions.

"I've brought many groups here and I can sense their disappointment because it's one of the few places where I can't just say, 'Yeah, it happened here,'" he said.

That will, hopefully, soon end.

*   *   *

But regardless of the position of gun number one, there is little question about the fight that followed.

"It doesn't matter where the first gun was, on line or on the flank, they hit it from the side and enveloped it with grenades and machine-gun fire. Once the attack gets going, it becomes more factual because wherever the first gun is, two, three, and four are down there," Paul said, pointing along the tree line toward the manor house.

Lipton remembered, "[Winters] sent Lieutenant Compton and Guarnere around to our left to hit the Germans on the first gun from their right front. He sent Sergeant Ranney and me around to our right to put fire into the German positions from their left flank. He set up the two machine guns in position to put heavy continuous fire into the German positions from their front. He then organized and led the rest of our men in a direct assault along the hedgerow right into the German positions.

"With fire into their positions from both flanks, heavy machine-gun fire into their front, and Lieutenant Winters leading an assault right into their defenses, the Germans apparently felt that they were being hit by a large force. Those defending the first gun broke and withdrew in disorganization to a far tree line, and that gun was in our hands."

Guarnere confirmed the ferocity of this attack by a small group of men against a larger force.

"My heart was pounding. It was scary," he recalled.

Attacking along the trench and tossing grenades as they did with fire coming from all directions, he said, was "stupid," but "we did it so quick, so fast, they thought an entire company was attacking."

As Lipton mentioned, three Germans tried to flee the gun position. Winters yelled, "Nail 'em," and opened fire. One man fell. A burst from the tommy gun brandished by Lorraine killed a second German, but Guarnere missed his man.

"I missed my target," he later recalled. "I never miss."

Malarkey finished the man off.

A fourth German leaped from the trench and ran for the distant hedgerow. Winters took careful aim and fired. The fleeing man spun to the ground and lay still. Only about twenty seconds had elapsed since Easy Company had gained the trench, and they had already silenced one gun. Winters also shot and wounded two more Germans setting up a machine gun farther along the gulley.

About this time, Malarkey leaped from the trench and, as Winters watched, horror-stricken, raced toward the bodies sprawled in the field. Malarkey had spoken about picking up a Luger as a souvenir, and he thought he'd seen one on one of the dead men.

"Get back here, you idiot," Winters yelled. "This area is lousy with Krauts!"

Luck was with Malarkey. The Germans let up their fire, possibly thinking only a medic would dare expose himself like that. Malarkey reached the dead man only to find the "Luger" was in fact a gun sight for one of the 105s. Aware of his vulnerable predicament, Malarkey jumped up and raced madly back to the trench as bullets chewed angrily at the ground near his feet.

"Those guns opened fire like a late-spring hailstorm back in Oregon," he wrote.

In his memoirs, Malarkey recalled how the German machine gun "sounds terrifying," making a "riiiipppp" sound, compared to American machine guns and their "putt-putt-putt."

Malarkey reached the trench and dove under a captured gun. His helmet had fallen off and he lay on his back, catching his breath, until his face began getting peppered by bullet fragments from rounds striking the artillery piece, and flecks of earth from dirt being kicked up by near misses made him roll over. His return was greeted by Guarnere, who said, "Way to go, ya stupid mick."

"It was a stupid move that could have, should have, gotten me killed," Malarkey recalled in his book.

"It wasn't a Luger either, the dummy," Guarnere quipped, looking back on the incident years later.

Winters returned to the injured Wynn, who was apologizing for being hit.

"My God, it's beautiful when you think of a guy who was so dedicated to his company that he apologizes for being hit," Winters later wrote. "Now here was a soldier—hit by enemy fire in Normandy on D-day, behind the German lines, and he is more upset that he had let his buddies down than he was concerned for his own injury. Popeye's actions spoke for all of us."

Winters told his injured friend, "I can't spare anyone to help you

back, Popeye. Can you make it on your own?" Wynn said he could, so
Winters and Compton hoisted him out of the trench, warned him to
keep low, and sent him on his way. He was no sooner gone than Compton yelled, "Look out! Grenade!" He'd yanked a pin from a grenade and
was about to toss it when it slipped from his hand. In the narrow con-
fines of the ditch, there was nowhere to go but down, so the men hit the
dirt as the grenade went off, again near Toye.

"Jesus Christ," he muttered, shaken but unhurt by this second brush
with death.

Toye wasn't the only one rattled by the explosion. A German hiding
nearby came running forward, his hands in the air. He was the Americans' first prisoner. Winters tried to point the man to the rear but they
could not communicate since no one in the group spoke German.
Lorraine slipped on a set of brass knuckles and belted the man. Winters
detested such treatment of prisoners.

Winters called Lorraine off. The Nazi soldier lay moaning, and
Winters kicked him in the behind. He rose to his feet and again Winters
indicated he was to go to the rear. Winters did not approve of Lorraine's
action, but the sock to the jaw evidently broke down the language bar-
rier, and the prisoner headed rearward.

As Paul and I stood by the trench that day, right where the incident
occurred, he questioned Winters's recollection that the man who did the
slugging was Lorraine, saying he felt it was out of character.

"A guide from the D-Day Museum at Utah Beach brought Lorraine's family here a few years ago and they said he was a very quiet,
unassuming man," Paul told me.

Paul thinks the punch to the jaw was more in tune with the nature
of Joe Toye—who was depicted in the movie as the owner of the brass
knuckles. Because Winters was so opposed to such a vicious act, Paul
suspects he did not want to lay the blame on one of his own men.

Winters now needed some way to disable the captured gun. Lipton
had the TNT blocks in his musette bag, but he had yet to rejoin the
group from his position on the right. So Winters prepared to attack
the second gun. After first making prisoners of the two German machine gunners he'd wounded earlier, he left three men to hold the first
105 and moved the rest closer to the second, keeping low to avoid the
enemy fire still coming from the opposing hedgerow and from another
machine gun near the manor house that had just joined the fray. On

Winters's signal, the Americans attacked quickly, firing their weapons and tossing grenades as they charged. The enemy fled except for six men who walked forward, hands over their heads, and saying in stilted English, "No make me dead."

This gun position was also the battery's command post, and Winters discovered several maps denoting defensive positions for the entire area. About this time two other men arrived, an officer Winters did not know and Private John D. Halls, an 81mm mortarman with Headquarters Company, 2nd Battalion. (Interestingly, there was a John D. Hall and a John D. Halls in the 506th, one from Manhattan and one from Texas. The Hall from Texas died when the plane carrying him and Stick 32 crashed on D-day. Woodadge said the screenwriters of the miniseries must have been aware of the two men, hence the character in the film hails from Manhattan while Guarnere, for unexplained reasons, refers to him as "Cowboy.")

Winters was glad for the help. Keeping Halls with him, he handed the captured maps to the officer and told him to take them to the rear, and to request more ammo be sent up.

Lipton arrived about now. He had been delayed in joining Winters because he had met Wynn crawling back to the aid station and applied sulfa powder to his friend's wound. He also encountered Warrant Officer Andrew Hill. Hill had been working his way around behind the trench to join Easy Company when he met Lipton, Ranney, and an unidentified officer. (Possibly they had come across the officer Winters sent back with the maps.)

"There was German fire right over us," Lipton recalled. "Hill asked where battalion headquarters was. The officer in front of me yelled that it was back on the road. Hill raised his head—just eight or ten inches—and a bullet hit him right in the forehead. I was looking straight at him. The bullet entered his forehead and came out the back of his head, killing him instantly.

"Except that the body doesn't die instantly. The body jerks and snorts and twists, and that shook me up. The machine-gun fire was cracking right over us, and I was sure they were going to get me too. Hill was the first American I saw hit. I'd seen dead American bodies, but I knew Warrant Officer Hill very well. I managed to get out, but that was the time I was probably most afraid."

Unfortunately, when Lipton finally arrived, Winters recalled, he had forgotten to bring along the TNT. The explosives, along with the fuses and percussion caps needed to set them off, were still back in Le Grand Chemin in his musette bag, which he dropped with the rest of his gear prior to the attack. He headed back to retrieve the bag.

Lipton makes no mention of forgetting the TNT, just saying, "Our attack then continued to each gun in turn from its exposed left flank. Lieutenant Winters blew out the breeches of each gun as soon as we had blocks of TNT."

In taking the first two guns, Winters and his men had made one concerted push each time, moving rapidly along the ditch with Guarnere, still burning from news of his brother's death, leading the way. This time, Winters opted for a quick, three-prong attack. Sending Halls up the trench, while he, Compton, and Guarnere would attack on the outside, with Winters on the left, and Compton and Guarnere on the right, even though this would briefly expose all to fire from across the field. At Winters's signal, the four men charged, firing as they ran. Guarnere sprayed the emplacement with his tommy gun, killing several of the crew.

Guarnere said during the entire assault he was "hyper-alert."

"You see, hear, and smell everything," he recalled. "Your movements are quick, your body is in survival mode. You don't think, you react."

Six more Germans surrendered. Halls, however, had been killed, although the circumstances of his death are not certain. One account has him being killed by the explosion of his own grenade, or that he had been killed by a German grenade. Guarnere said Halls was shot in the head by a sniper. Compton said Halls ran by him.

"From the trench I saw him spin around and sprint back toward me," Buck wrote. "He took a bullet in the back and collapsed in front of me, dead."

But there was no time to mourn, Wild Bill said, "you just watched men fall but kept going, if you let it get to you, you're dead. You thank God it's not you, and you wonder if you're next."

Winters did stop to mourn, at least briefly. When he found Halls, he knelt over the body, getting blood on his uniform sleeve.

"He was a damned good man," Winters recalled to me.

Then he moved on.

With three of the four guns now in his hands, Winters thought about his next move. His ammo was low—so far there had been no response to his request for more sent back with the officer—and the risk of German reinforcements moving in on him was very real. So Winters told Compton to hold the position and went back to Le Grand Chemin himself. As he crawled rearward through the grass, keeping as flat as possible to avoid the machine-gun bullets flying just overhead, Winters came across the body of Warrant Officer Hill. The young man lay on his back, his right arm extended upward. Crawling past the body, Winters noticed a watch on his right arm. For some reason the watch played on Winters's mind, and after he was several yards beyond the body, Winters thought, "Hell, I could use that watch," and turned around. As he was heading back, another thought struck him. "You're nuts!" he chided himself. "This watch isn't worth it." Reaching Hill, Winters unstrapped the watch, pocketed it, and again crawled toward battalion.

At the village, Winters found Strayer and his staff sitting unconcernedly, studying the captured maps. Tired, sweaty, and with the adrenaline of battle pumping through his blood, the sight of this seeming indifference by his superior officer while he and his men were hanging on to the trench by their fingernails caused the usually soft-spoken Winters to erupt.

Winters told me he yelled, "Goddammnit. When I send for ammunition and help, I mean now! Not when you get around to it!"

None of them had ever seen Winters that angry. Standing there in the road, hand tightly clutching his Garand, his sweaty uniform streaked with dirt and grass stains, a smear of Halls's blood on his sleeve, Winters was a ferocious figure. The image had the desired effect. Bandoliers of ammo were suddenly being heaped on him. Hester said he'd send up Lieutenant Ronald Spiers of D Company with some reinforcements, and that he himself would bring more explosives.

Private Len Hicks of F Company overheard the exchange and asked Winters if he could help. Grateful, Winters told Hicks to see if any others in Fox Company wanted to assist and to bring them along.

It may have been during Winters's absence and the brief lull in the fighting that Guarnere, his adrenaline level possibly diminishing, dozed off. Toye smacked him behind the head to wake him up.

"He thought I was dead," Guarnere wrote.

The two friends "scared the hell" out of each other, he recalled.

Hester was as good as his word. He brought the TNT charges plus new instructions from Strayer.

"The battalion is moving on to Sainte-Marie-du-Mont," he said. "Strayer sent Nixon to the beach with those maps you found. The colonel wants you to mop up here then catch up."

Winters and Hester slipped the TNT charges down the barrels of the three 105s and set them off with incendiary grenades (not a German potato masher, as shown in the movie. "Hollywood thought that was more dramatic," Winters told me). The blast split the barrels like banana peels. By now a dismayed Lipton had returned with his TNT satchel, only to find the guns had already been disabled.

Spiers arrived, bringing along Hicks, Sergeant Julian "Rusty" Houch, the F Company clerk, and Privates Jumbo DiMarzio, Ray Taylor, and another man. They immediately set about knocking out the fourth gun. Houch and Hicks crawled through the grass toward the Germans. Hicks nodded and Houch rose to throw a grenade. From somewhere, a Schmeisser machine pistol opened up, its slugs tearing into Houch, who fell dead. Spiers, an aggressive leader, jumped up and led his men forward. Hicks fell, struck in the leg, and a second man was severely wounded. Spiers leaped into the gun pit alone, causing the startled Germans to flee. Spiers cut them down with fire from his tommy gun.

Recalling the assault, Guarnere later quipped, "Spiers was as nutty as I was."

After dispatching this gun as they had the other three with TNT and a grenade, Winters decided it was time to leave, even though men like Guarnere, their bloodlust up, wanted to push on the manor house, which was visible at the far end of the field. Paul Woodadge said Winters made a wise decision that quite likely prevented Easy Company's stunning victory from turning into a bloody repulse.

"Once they knocked out the four guns, they wanted to continue on to the manor house because the Germans were retreating," Woodadge told me. "But one of Dick Winters's strongest leadership qualities was the ability to assess the importance of a situation in the heat of the battle, with the smoke and the bullets flying, and say, 'The job's done now, guys. We knocked out the four guns.'"

Had Winters allowed his men to push forward, waiting for them up ahead was a well-placed and well-concealed German machine-gun emplacement.

"Bill told me Dick had to pull him back because he wanted to carry on down the road and kill more Germans," Paul told me as we stood by the now famous trench line.

But Winters might have sensed the danger, Paul continued, which is why he had Malarkey fire the 60mm mortar at the farm. Malarkey, who had neither the weapon's base plate nor bipod, was still deadly accurate, thanks to what Winters called his "God-given touch." The stone buildings of the manor still bear the scars of Malarkey's marksmanship.

"It's a true sign of Winters's leadership," Paul said. "Not only has he led his men here from Sainte-Mère-Église, five miles away, keeping the force intact through German lines. He then leads the attack in, does the job, and then doesn't lose any men unnecessarily by making a silly, uncalled-for attack."

His men seem to have agreed with Paul's assessment of Winters's skill. Years later, Lipton said, "I was in many combat operations throughout the war in Europe, but this was the most outstanding example of a combat leader reading a situation, forming a plan to overcome almost impossible odds, organizing and inspiring his men so that each one would confidently handle his part of the plan, and leading his men in the most dangerous parts of the operation."

Guarnere wrote, "Winters turned out to be a great leader in combat. He called all the shots, and we followed his orders. He was smart, quick, efficient, resourceful, intuitive, fearless. . . . He wasn't a Quaker in battle."

Winters also had a bit of luck, Paul said. On May 18, just weeks before the invasion, German command around the farm had changed. Colonel de Vallavieille had noted that the previous garrison had "been all spit and polish," while the unit that replaced them was less disciplined, and "spent more time drinking and carousing."

"It suggests that Winters and his men were fortunate when he attacked that the Germans weren't frontline quality," Paul said.

But regardless of the caliber of troops the men of Easy Company faced, and no matter if the first gun was on line or turned toward the road, Brecourt was an act of courage and daring and a huge success.

"Bottom line is, does it really matter who did what at what time?" Paul asked. "The point is an incredibly small unit attacked and knocked out a larger, dug-in German position that was firing on Utah Beach. That's it, isn't it? That's the achievement here."

Reflecting on what they did here, the men who took part had their own remembrances.

Guarnere observed, "You do stupid things, you're so full of vim and vigor, you don't care. Afterward you say, 'Holy Christ.'"

Buck thought the whole assault was "ad-lib fighting," that the men were "developing strategy as we went along."

"It was all seat-of-the-pants to me," he wrote.

"I saw a lot of combat during the war," Lipton remembered. "I lost a lot of friends. The fighting around Bastogne was bad because it went on for so long, but I think I was most frightened in Normandy on D-day when we were attacking the 105s that were shelling Utah Beach."

Guarnere said, "For what we accomplished, we were lucky and they had to be stupid."

After the fight was over, he "got the shakes pretty bad" as he reflected over the action and thought, "What the hell did I just do?" He said the men sat around thinking about who got hurt or killed, and felt it a miracle they made it out alive.

Malarkey noted, "War, I began to realize, was like a deadly athletic contest whose score you seldom knew even while you were playing the game. War was fought without context; you seldom realize how your piece fits into the larger puzzle."

Years later Malarkey recalled that he told Winters they were "luckier'n hell at Brecourt." Winters replied, "What do you mean lucky, Malark? We were effective."

For their action at Brecourt on June 6, 1944, Winters nominated Guarnere for a Distinguished Service Cross, which Strayer downgraded to the Silver Star. Compton, Lorraine, and Toye also received the Silver Star; Lipton, Malarkey, Ranney, Liebgott, Hendrix, Plesha, Petty, and Wynn each received the Bronze Star. Winters received the Distinguished Service Cross.

(Interestingly, in his book, *Call of Duty*, Buck Compton places his friend Lieutenant Robert Brewer at Brecourt as well, but his is the only eyewitness account that does so. Neither Don Malarkey nor Bill Guarnere, in their books, mention Brewer. During our interviews for *Biggest Brother* in 2003, Winters also brought Brewer's name up. "You'll hear Compton insist that Brewer was there as well," Winters told me. "But he wasn't. Buck is wrong.")

While at Brecourt I remembered the story Winters had told about how, after the 506th was pulled off the line and sent to Cherbourg, he and some other company officers were called into regimental headquarters, where, along with Colonel Sink, sat the noted historian and author S. L. A. Marshall. After introductions, Winters was asked to take a seat. Sink began to question him while Marshall took notes.

"Okay, Lieutenant, tell us about the action at Brecourt," Sink said. "You took that battery of 88s."

"Yes, sir, that's right," Winters replied.

"Tell me how you did it."

"Well, sir, I put down a base of fire, we moved in under the fire and took the first gun. Then we put down another base of fire and we moved to the second gun and the third and the fourth."

"Okay," Sink said. "Anything else?"

"No, sir, that's basically it."

"Okay, thank you very much."

Winters was dismissed. Some time later he read Marshall's account of the action, in which the author reported that Winters had led about two hundred men. I can still hear Dick Winters chuckle when he told me, "Jesus Christ. If I had had that many men, I could have taken Berlin."

As Paul and I stood in that muddy field in a misty drizzle on that dreary November day, it was so difficult for me to comprehend that I was standing on the same field where Dick and the others had made that heroic fight, which Winters had described to me so vividly. Fifteen Germans died here that day, as did Halls, Hill, and Houch. I thought about how it must have looked to them, with armed men and four artillery pieces blazing away, as they attacked amid a hail of machine-gun and rifle bullets, tossing grenades and watching men be shot down.

"Nothing looks the same to me," Guarnere wrote in his book. "Everything's changed. . . . They tried to keep it the same, the trees are there, but they're a lot bigger."

I'm sure that's true. I know Winters told me the same thing.

We turned and walked back to the manor, where Paul pointed out a pair of gun trails from one of the German artillery pieces, lying near the

Gun trails from one of the German 105mm artillery pieces knocked out by Easy Company at Brecourt Manor can still be found today.

barn after they had been salvaged from the field. Then, before we went into the house, where Monsieur de Vallavieille had hot coffee and a plate of cookies waiting, Paul mentioned that I am probably disappointed that he could not be more precise with facts concerning the fight.

"I'm standing here on the actual field of Brecourt Manor," I told him. "How could I possibly be disappointed?"

CHAPTER 6

"THE AMERICANS HAVE DONE EVERYTHING FOR US HERE"

Utah Beach to Carentan

After we departed from Brecourt Manor, Paul guided us to the D-Day Museum at Utah Beach. Created in 1962 by Michel de Vallavieille, who was mayor of Sainte-Marie-du-Mont from 1949 to 1991, the museum sits inside what was once known as Widerstandnest 5 (WN5), a German bunker that was part of a network of twenty bunkers connected by a Z-shaped trench system. One of Utah's strongest positions, WN5, under the command of Lieutenant Jahnke and manned by seventy-five soldiers, was eight hundred meters long and three hundred wide. The position was protected by minefields and barbed wire, and the low land behind it had been intentionally flooded. In addition, larger elements of the 91st Infantry and 6th Fallschirmjager were posted nearby.

Today, what was WN5 has been enlarged and modernized, and contains over thirteen hundred artifacts of the battle, including an intricate diorama of the landings and a Goliath, the small radio-controlled explosive-filled tank the Germans employed against the Americans on this adjacent stretch of beach.

Outside, a gray Higgins boat, an American antiaircraft gun, and a Sherman tank stand a silent vigil to the historic events that occurred here. Monuments include ones to the U.S. 4th Division, the 1st Engineer Special Brigade, and the U.S. 90th Division, plus the first Road to Liberty mile marker, labeled 00. The last stands in Bastogne, Belgium, but more on that later.

While we were at the museum, which in the past has been visited by many Easy Company vets, including Dick Winters, Walter Gordon, and

Forrest Guth, I took the liberty of walking to the beach. Strolling past the Sherman tank and through a gap in the dunes, I found myself there—Utah Beach. Walking across the sand to near the water's edge, I was struck by how peaceful it all was. Except for two people on sulkies, guiding trotter horses along where the water meets the sand, I was totally alone with my thoughts.

The American landing force here had been very fortunate. Either because of tides or clouded vision due to smoke screens, they had landed a mile to the south of their intended beaches, and as fate would have it, struck a much more lightly defended position at the extreme range of the German batteries at Azeville and Crisbecq. The first twenty American Higgins boats landed to either side of WN5. Twenty-eight Shermans similar to the one behind me rolled onto the beach right where I was standing, and Lieutenant Jahnke dispatched a Goliath packed with 180 pounds of explosives. However, its radio-control unit failed, although one launched a bit later in the fight did explode, killing twelve GIs.

About 23,000 men with 1,720 vehicles waded ashore here, and only 197 would die on this beach. As the fight moved inland, the Allies would sink nine old ships in a semicircle to create Gooseberry, an artificial harbor, located just offshore. Between June 6 and November 1, 1944, 836,000 men, 220,000 vehicles, and 725,000 tons of equipment would be off-loaded on this stretch of sand.

As I had at Brecourt, and would do at every stop on this trip except, for some reason, Aldbourne, I took a small jar from my pocket, stooped, and filled it with sand, an inexpensive yet priceless souvenir of my journey.

Easy Company spent its first night in France by a hedgerow in a field near Sainte-Marie-du-Mont. They settled down and tried to sleep, exhausted, both physically and mentally, by the day's exertions. But German infantry in another hedgerow across an open field kept firing their weapons into the dark and shouting. Unable to sleep, Winters decided to get up and make a personal reconnaissance. As he was walking quietly along a footpath in the dark, he heard the approaching clatter of hobnailed boots and froze.

"Krauts," he thought. He dropped into a ditch and lay silent as a German patrol walked by, passing so close Winters caught the strong

whiff of German tobacco. As the enemy moved away, he blessed the
U.S. Army for using rubber-soled boots.

Back safely with the company, Winters stretched out on the ground
by Welsh. Having no blanket to cover himself—his was still in some
farmer's field inside his lost leg bag—Winters took some newspaper he'd
liberated earlier in the day and formed a small tent over his face and
upper body. This was less for warmth than it was to keep away the mosquitoes he could hear bouncing off the newspaper.

Before closing his eyes that night, Winters realized he hadn't said
his prayers, so he rolled over and got to his knees. Welsh watched
somberly.

"He told me, 'I'm Catholic, and when I get back home, I'll go to
church every Sunday and pray. But I won't pray here,'" Dick Winters
said to me.

Welsh would keep his word. But Winters prayed, and that night he
thanked God for surviving this first, terrible day and asked Him to watch
over him the next day. That was also the moment Winters made his
personal vow that after the war he would settle down in some quiet place
and live the remainder of his life in peace.

The next morning Easy Company and 2nd Battalion were on their
way toward Carentan, fighting their way through Vierville and into the
tiny hamlet of Angoville-au-Plain, where Sink established his headquarters on June 8.

Forrest Guth, Walter Gordon, Floyd Talbert, John Eubanks, Francis Mellet, David Morris, and the recently rejoined Campbell T. Smith were still
trying to catch up to Easy Company, and on June 7, as their comrades
were attacking Vierville, this small band reached Sainte-Marie-du-Mont.

A statue of a French soldier, commemorating the men from the village who, from 1914 to 1918, fought what was then believed to be the
war to end all wars, stands in the small town plaza. As the paratroopers
trekked by the statue, the men saw a photo opportunity.

"We were just coming through and a bunch of guys wanted their
picture taken," Forrest recalled. "It suited me."

They lined up in front of the statue, Forrest on the left, then Mellet,
Morris, Talbert, and Smith. Gordon took the camera, but before he

could press the shutter, several infantrymen from the 4th Division evidently decided this was a good chance for an "I was there" picture and lined up behind the paratroopers. Gordon took the shot.

In many ways, life in the area of Sainte-Marie-du-Mont is unchanged from what it was in 1944. It is still located in the heart of farm country, and much of the food on people's tables is grown in the surrounding fields, as each week during the growing season large farm wagons laden with meat and produce gather in the town square. Their sides are dropped down, and out come tables and barrels of goods. The milk is fresh and butter is ladled directly from the churns. This farm market is a weekly event in Sainte-Marie-du-Mont, and happens twice weekly in Carentan.

We grabbed a bite to eat at a small café called L'Estamint at the edge of the town square. As we ate, Paul pointed out the large church across the street; French towns, regardless of how small they might be, all seem to have huge houses of worship. Paul told us the story of Sergeant David Rogers of 506th Headquarters Company, 1st Battalion, who climbed up into the church's tall steeple around two a.m. on the morning of D-day. He stayed up there several hours, and at daylight watched the landings at Utah Beach three and a half miles away through binoculars.

To Rogers's dismay, a naval observer noticed light glinting off his binoculars and, assuming the steeple to be a German observation post, directed naval gunfire at the church.

Meanwhile, a four-gun German battery at Holdy, near Brecourt Manor, had been seized by men under Captain Lloyd Patch. Shells from a U.S. destroyer, unaware the guns had been taken, began dropping rounds near Patch. Patch, in turn, noticed the tall steeple of the church at Sainte-Marie-du-Mont, and, like the naval observer, assumed it to be a German OP. He turned the captured 105s around and began lobbing shells at the steeple.

"So suddenly David Rogers is up in the church tower being hit from opposite sides, and in both cases, it's by Americans. He comes down very quickly," Paul said.

By one p.m., tanks from Utah Beach were rumbling into town and Sainte-Marie-du-Mont was in American hands.

Rogers survived and, now in his nineties, regretted not having carved his name in the wooden beams in the church tower. He thought about

(Front row, left to right) Forrest Guth, Francis Mellet, David Morris, Daniel West, Floyd Talbert and Campbell T. Smith in Sainte-Marie-du-Mont, June 7, 1944. *Courtesy of Forrest Guth*

Forrest in the same spot, November, 2008.

it, Paul said, but "never had the chance." In 2004, Rogers's son, on tour with Monsieur de Vallavieille, did what his father could not.

"Charles de Vallavieille took him up the tower and he carved his dad's name," Paul said. "If you go up there now, you'll see it says 'David Rogers, June 6, 1944.'"

After lunch, Paul, Forrest, and I walked the short distance from the café to the World War I monument, where Forrest talked about the photo taken there sixty-four years earlier. I placed Forrest in front of the monument where he had stood that day, and took some "now" shots. As we were reliving that moment, another of Paul's guides arrived with a three-member tour group, an American man and a female journalist from Oslo, Norway, Nina Bergerson, and her son, Felix. The reporter and her young son, holding a copy of the original photo shown to them by Paul, asked to pose with Forrest in front of the monument. Forrest was more than happy to comply, and the Norwegian pair left with a most memorable reminder of their trip, but not before Nina handed Forrest a large bar of Norwegian chocolate, which we both savored over the next few days.

A car pulled up as we were doing this photo shoot. Out of the vehicle came Henri Milet, the mayor of Sainte-Marie-du-Mont. He greeted Forrest and me, and escorted us to the nearby town hall, where, through Paul, he told Forrest how glad he was to entertain one of the town's liberators, and gave my friend a commemorative medallion.

By now, I was becoming used to this celebrity-style welcome being bestowed upon my friend.

Our next stop was Angoville-au-Plain, a scant mile from our bed-and-breakfast. Angoville-au-Plain is a tiny hamlet of forty-two inhabitants. The village's main feature is a large Norman church that has sat at the intersection of rue de l'Eglise and rue de Canteraine for over nine hundred years. But small as it is, Angoville-au-Plain has an immensely bloody and heroic history as the scene of bitter fighting on June 6–7, changing hands three times in just a few terrible hours.

The initial fighting in and around this town was done by men of the 2nd Battalion, 501st PIR, under Lieutenant Colonel Robert Ballard, the same officer whose men fought around the bed-and-breakfast where Forrest and I were now staying.

When the fighting began around Angoville-au-Plain, Ballard ordered his adjutant, Lieutenant Edward Allworth, to go into the village and set up an aid station. With him went medic Robert Wright and Private Kenneth Moore, a stretcher bearer. They established the aid station in the village church and began gathering in casualties on a farm cart.

Outside, the fighting raged as fifty-two men of C Company and the 326th Airborne Engineers under Lieutenant Harold E. Young tried to hold the village. One resident, Mrs. Levigoiroux, writing after the war, recalled paratroopers dropping all around and the road "teeming with soldiers."

"At daybreak the bullets were whizzing," she wrote. "I was so scared that I could not open the door. Mrs. Sorel came and shouted from outside, 'Do open the door, the Americans are here.' They searched the farm buildings and gave Lucienne Lecuyer some chocolate. As they regrouped in the square they managed to capture five German soldiers in the tower. Fierce fighting took place. Many Germans were killed. In the yard of a farm a dead soldier was buried on the spot. As the village changed hands several times, old Leonard turned up to tell us to go to Mrs. Lebel's cowshed. Fifty refugees were already there. A paratrooper was hidden near the door of the cowshed; another one had pushed a chest of drawers near the window of a room to rest his rifle on it."

The Germans counterattacked and the Americans had to fall back, abandoning Moore and Wright and the aid station. Years later Moore recalled, "Our own folks had come to tell us that they could not stay any longer. So we were left alone with the wounded soldiers. A German officer soon arrived. He asked me if I could tend the Germans as well. We accepted. During the night the churchyard was the scene of a battle. Two of our casualties died. But among those I could tend, none lost their lives. I tended all sorts of wounds, some were skin-deep but others were more serious abdominal cases."

Before long Wright, twenty, and Moore, nineteen, were attending seventy-five men of both armies. Bleeding Americans and Germans lay on the floor, on the rough wooden pews and even on the stone altar. As the fight raged around them, the red cross on the door, and perhaps the grace of God, spared them. Once, a German soldier holding a Schmeisser machine pistol at the ready burst in. Noticing wounded Germans among the Americans, he looked to the altar, crossed himself, and left. A German officer came in and asked Wright if he could get him anything to help with the work of tending the injured. Perhaps most miraculous of all, a mortar round—American or German, it didn't really matter at that point—crashed through the roof and landed on the stone floor in the middle of the church. It was a dud. Had it not been, most of those in the church, including by this time an injured child, would have died.

Wright, in charge of the aid station, soon demanded that any man, regardless of army, who entered the church had to leave his weapon outside.

"He believed that inside the church, the only concern was for the wounded and the dying, not the winning and the losing," Paul told us.

The battle in and around Angoville-au-Plain, which included not just men of the 501st PIR, but troopers from the 3rd Battalion of Sink's 506th, lasted until the early hours of June 8. By this time, dead men and farm animals lay everywhere. In the church, every window had been blown out, and during the second day, June 7, two Germans hiding in the thirteenth-century bell tower came down to surrender.

Sink arrived on June 7 and established his HQ in a farmhouse surrounded by a high stone wall, located just across the intersection from the church. Easy Company arrived soon after and spent the next three days at Angoville-au-Plain, listening to the distant roll of the guns, watching the billowing smoke, and scrambling for cover when the occasional German plane, risking Allied air superiority, made a token strafing run. During this time, Winters's biggest problem occurred when some of his men discovered a hidden cache of wine and freely imbibed. Winters had the alcohol seized and sternly reprimanded the offenders for their lapse of discipline.

Today Angoville-au-Plain has not forgotten the American soldiers who fought and died to free the village. A well-kept granite marker stands before the wall near Sink's former HQ, commemorating Wright and Moore, who were each awarded a Silver Star, and paperwork is in place to make both men—who are still alive as of this writing—saints upon their deaths. The two men, who arrived by parachute, are equated by the villagers with Saints Come and Damien, two angels sent from heaven by God to become doctors to the townspeople during a time of illness.

"This church is all about remembering these two medics particularly," Paul told us.

Another marker proclaiming "Place Toccoa," standing in front of the church, links the village to the Georgia camp where Sink trained his 506th PIR.

Inside the church, a round wooden plug seals the gap in the roof where the mortar round entered, and the stone floor where the dud shell hit still bears the cracks from the impact. All of the windows have been replaced, and more than half of them are gifts from private donors honoring the paratroopers. One window is dedicated specifically to the 506th PIR and another to the 101st in general.

But the most emotional, and somewhat gruesome, reminders of the horror visited upon that house of God during those two days of hell are the pews, many bearing dark stains where blood once pooled. The congregation, which still holds services in this church, wants these stains to remain as a symbol of the sacrifice of the American paratroopers.

While we stood in the church listening to Paul tell the story of what happened here, Daniel Hamchin, the mayor of Angoville-au-Plain, entered. He greeted Forrest and myself as Paul explained who we were. Hamchin, a big grin creasing his round, jovial face, overflowed with graciousness. With Paul interpreting, the sixty-four-year-old Hamchin told us how his family had been living in the village during the battle. He also began to tell how, since he had become mayor in 2000, the little village's goal has been to repair the battle-scarred church, a huge task for the tiny hamlet.

"For fifty-five years no one seemed to care about the story of the church," Hamchin told us. "The damage wasn't repaired."

When he became mayor, he and the village decided "not only should they repair the church, but they should do so in a way that pays tribute to the Americans who did the fighting," Paul translated. Damage to the thirteenth-century bell tower alone will cost thousands of Euros.

"People see the work being done to the windows and think the church is finished, but it's a thousand years old, and there are only forty-two people in the village and there are no government grants," Hamchin said.

The money raised has come through donations placed in a box in the church by tourists coming through, led by guides like Paul Woodadge, and through other American benefactors.

"The Americans have done everything for us here," Hamchin said most earnestly.

That gratitude for what the American paratroopers did for Angoville-au-Plain is felt throughout the town, even by people like Paul Langeard, who lost his entire family in the fighting here in the village. Langeard was just thirteen at the time of the battle; his parents were killed by naval shell fire from the USS *Quincy* and his sister was inadver-

Guide Paul Woodadge *(left)* translates for Forrest Guth during our meeting with Daniel Hamchin, the mayor of Angoville-au-Plain, inside the twelfth-century church.

A bloodstained pew in the church at Angoville-au-Plain.

tently cut down by an American machine gun. Yet to this day, Langeard thanks Americans for coming and setting him and his village free.

Paul said he and others like him "see the life coming back" into the old church.

"They truly love the Americans in this village," Paul said.

We got back in our car and left for Carentan.

Angoville-au-Plain is less than a mile from Haute Addeville, where Forrest and I were staying, and only about four miles from Carentan. Slightly less than halfway in between, where the D913 meets the road to Saint-Come-du-Mont, sits an intersection that, sixty-four years earlier, earned the name Dead Man's Corner. Today the fully restored house sitting by the road junction is the home of the Dead Man's Corner Museum, owned by the historian and author Michel De Trez. In 1944 this was a deadly strongpoint manned by the tough German paratroopers of the 6th Fallschirmjager, who had established a defensive position, a radio communications center, and an aid station within its walls. Its grim name came after an American M5 Stuart light tank was knocked out on the road in front of the house.

"As the crew climbed out of the tank, the Germans killed them," Forrest recalled as we parked the car by the house. "Their bodies hung there a couple of days. We couldn't retrieve them."

The tank commander's body, in fact, lay draped half in and half out of the turret, a grisly moment of war that is commemorated inside the museum.

Also, somewhere in the fields around this house, 2nd Battalion of the 506th lost D Company commander Captain Jerre S. Gross, whom Winters respected as an able and talented officer. He had been killed by an exploding artillery round.

De Trez was in Bastogne the day we dropped by the museum, but he did phone the museum and spoke with Forrest. In 2002 De Trez had written and published a seventy-two-page hardcover book about Forrest, part of his Paratroopers Portrait Series, and much of Guth's military memorabilia, uniform parts, and web gear, bearing his name, along with some of Forrest's wartime souvenirs are on display here. The display cases also hold mementos of other Band of Brothers members, including

Dick Winters. In addition to the book, De Trez created a twelve-inch-tall Forrest Guth action figure—one of four Americans he so honored, including Colonel Benjamin Vandervoort and Major Daniel "Doc" McIlvoy, both of the 505th PIR of the 82nd Division—which he sells in his store, along with World War II uniforms and equipment, authentic and reproductions, Allied and Axis. The museum store is pure heaven for World War II buffs.

The museum is just as impressive, and in two rooms De Trez has accurately re-created the Nazi strongpoint, with soldiers manning a radio and an MG 42 machine gun in a front room with a commanding view of the road junction, while medics work on injured men in an adjoining room.

At De Trez's direction, the museum staff presented Forrest with a commemorative 101st Airborne watch. The limited-edition timepiece, bearing the Screaming Eagle emblem, was numbered, naturally, 101.

We drove on down the road toward Carentan.

By the time Easy Company moved along this road and passed Dead Man's Corner, Forrest, Smokey Gordon, Talbert, Smith, Tipper, and the rest had caught up. They had rejoined Easy on June 9 at Angoville-au-Plain.

With a peacetime population of about four thousand, Carentan is the largest French town in the Utah Beach sector of the Cotentin Peninsula. Nestled astride the Cherbourg–Caen–St.-Lô highway, the town is bisected by the Cherbourg-Paris railroad. Its distinction as a transportation hub made Carentan the main objective for the 101st Airborne now that the causeways from the beaches were open and secure. The town's fall would clear the way for a linkup between U.S. troops now pouring ashore at Utah and Omaha beaches.

Initial attacks on Carentan by the 101st began on June 8, while Easy was still at Angoville-au-Plain. Four bridges stand between Dead Man's Corner and Carentan, and on June 7, the Germans blew the widest one spanning the Douve River.

In Carentan, Colonel Frederick von der Heydte's situation was precarious at best. His 6th Fallschirmjager was outnumbered and out of communication with his headquarters and seriously low on supplies and ammunition, thanks to Allied fighters that made German airdrops almost suicidal.

On June 10, General Taylor sent von der Heydte a surrender message, which the German rejected, and the fighting continued.

On June 11, Easy Company rejoined 2nd Battalion, which was headed south along Nationale 13 toward Carentan. Outside the town, the battalion swung right, across swampy fields, heading toward Nationale 803, which entered Carentan to the west. It was one of the Germans' escape routes if they had to pull back. The 506th prepared to attack their town, with Easy and Fox companies leading the assault, and Dog Company in reserve.

The plan called for being in position by 0530 with jump-off thirty minutes later, but by 0530 the men were far from prepared. The march had been long and hard and the troops were exhausted. Worse, from Winters's point of view, there was no time for reconnaissance, and despite Allied air strength, there would be no air cover, nor was any artillery made available. Winters told me he felt the entire assault was "hastily thrown together," a state of affairs that thoroughly pissed him off.

Paul, Forrest, and I drove along Easy Company's advance route. We stopped by the Douve River, parked our car on a pull-off just by the bridge, and walked down to the river's edge. The highway bridge has, of course, been replaced since the Germans sent it crashing into the brown water. But in 1944 the span was a pile of rubble, and as the Americans stood here on this bank, just to the right of the bridge, another way across was needed.

"The Douve is not the Rhine or anything, but it is a considerable hurdle," Paul said.

Forrest recalled that troops advancing earlier had "found some planking to use" and constructed a single walkway over the river and the low land beyond, which the Germans had flooded. Forrest remembered crossing the swirling water over this makeshift span.

"It was slow going," he recalled. "It was at night and we went single file."

As the attack time drew near, Winters and his men were just outside the town on the current rue d'Auvers. Winters ordered Harry Welsh and 1st Platoon to lead the assault, with 2nd Platoon next, followed by 3rd

Platoon. Mortars and machine guns were to provide covering fire. Advancing into the town, they were to turn left where the road intersected the rue Holgate and follow that street toward the heart of Carentan.

The attack began badly. At the signal, Welsh led his men forward and Winters ordered Compton to get 2nd Platoon ready. No sooner had Welsh jumped off than a German machine gun at the intersection ahead came to life. In perfect position to dominate the road, the MG 42 spat flame and death at the charging GIs. Welsh and his first six men braved the hail of lead and made it into the town, taking cover behind the nearest buildings. However, the next man in line, Sergeant Robert J. Rader, "simply put his head down and froze," as Winters recalled. Like cars in traffic, the rest of the platoon backed up behind him and, suddenly, on both sides of the road, men hunkered down in the ditches, heads low, immobile. Winters was horrified. Not only did he now have seven men alone and on their own in the enemy-held town, but the rest were in danger as well. Stopping under fire was the worst thing they could do; it converted them into targets.

"Move!" Winters yelled above the racket. "Move. Don't stop."

Heads stayed low as his words went unheeded. From behind, he could hear Strayer shouting, "Move out, Winters. Get those men moving."

Winters blew his cork. Oblivious to his own safety, he leaped to his feet and ran into the middle of the road.

"Go forward," he yelled. "You can't stay here. Move! Move!"

Guarnere, recalling the attack, said the universal thought among the men was, "Is he friggin' nuts? He thinks we're gonna get up?"

But Winters kept yelling and gesturing. He was a sitting duck for the German gunners, and he knew it. He had become the only visible target, and the machine gunner did not neglect the opportunity. Bullets churned up the ground at Winters's feet and buzzed around his ears like mosquitoes as he bounced back and forth across the road, frantically grabbing men, yanking them to their feet, and pushing them forward.

"Get going!" Winters yelled. "You're gonna die here. Move!"

The men were stunned, less by the German fire than by the sight of their mild-mannered lieutenant suddenly transformed into a raving madman. At first they gaped at him in awe, then the discipline they'd forged during two years of training returned. Rader moved out, followed by another man, then another until all were charging ahead under the withering fire. Winters ran with them, encouraging them forward, as they poured down the road and into Carentan.

While the Germans were focused on Winters and the men attacking down the road, Welsh closed in on the machine-gun position. He yanked the pin from a grenade and lobbed it through the window of the building. The explosion silenced the gun.

Behind the wheel of my rental car and with Paul beside me and Forrest in the backseat, I followed Easy Company's route down rue d'Auvers, now lined with new homes and businesses, and turned left onto rue Holgate. As we drove, Paul explained that the miniseries depicted the attack as the men charging straight down a single road, when in fact they had to make the turn onto rue Holgate.

At the bottom of the sloping rue Holgate, where it meets the rue de la Guinguette, we parked the car by the small train station that serves the Cherbourg to Paris rail line. Across the tracks is a small plaza formed by rue Holgate and the present-day rue de la 101eme Airborne and rue de Verdun. On one corner sits the café, which the miniseries mislocated by placing it, and its machine-gun nest, at the end of rue d'Auvers and eliminating the turn onto rue Holgate.

"In the series they simplified it into one intersection," Paul said. "But they actually came into the town, turned left, and then came down here. So there were actually two intersections. They encountered some fire at the first intersection, but the main fighting was here in this plaza."

In my mind, I saw the men of Easy charging down the rue Holgate and across the tracks, which were also not shown in the miniseries. Where we were now standing, they fanned out and moved house to house, throwing a grenade through a door or window, then kicking open the door, running inside, and shooting at anyone in sight.

Gazing across the plaza, Forrest pointed to a building on the left. He vividly recalled a woman peeping out of a doorway, watching the Americans crossing the railroad tracks.

"It wasn't a good place for her to be, because when we approached a house, the first thing we did was throw a hand grenade inside," he said. "Things started cracking and she took off."

Most of the buildings Easy's men entered were empty, and Forrest added, "Every now and then we found some wine."

While Easy fought their way across the plaza, Carwood Lipton was struck in the upper thigh and crotch by shrapnel. One of the first to reach him was Forrest Guth.

"He was pretty badly hit, and we got him some aid," Forrest said.

Lipton was scooped up and carried to safety by Floyd Talbert, who first checked the frightened man to make sure "everything was okay."

He didn't have far to take his comrade. While Winters insists that the aid station established by the company physician, Lieutenant Jackson Neavles, is long since gone, Paul is not convinced. On the southwest corner of rue Holgate and rue de la Guinguette, diagonal from where my car was parked, is a house Paul believes was the actual aid station.

"The only reason I think that is I was doing a tour here about four years ago and a guy in his early thirties came down and said to me, 'I just bought this house. Was it involved in the war?'" Paul said.

Paul showed him a wartime photo of the area that included the house.

"He said he was adding some space and a new window to make a new bedroom, and said under the floorboards and inside the walls of the building were hundreds of bandage wrappers with 'Carlisle, Pa.' on them," Paul told us. "If hundreds of bandage wrappers are there, and the house is in close proximity to the fighting, doesn't it make sense that it was an aid station?"

Easy Company charged across the tracks, through the plaza, and along rue Holgate, soon entering a much larger plaza where the street intersects rue Sebline and rue du Dr. Caillard. Once littered with bodies, shattered trees and debris, this open expanse is now a municipal parking lot and the site of the town's popular carousel—a pleasant oddity considering the hell that descended on this place.

Talbert recalled, "I spotted a German who was seated behind a tree. I could see his shoulder protruding. I shot him with my M1 and he came spinning down from behind the tree. I didn't kill him and he rolled over and attempted to elevate his gun. I shot him a second time and finished him. I finally got a look at him. He looked so young."

Here in this battle-torn plaza Father John Maloney moved back and forth, under fire, comforting the wounded and giving the dead and dying last rites.

"It was like having the Lord Himself come down to visit you," Guarnere recalled.

The chaplains and medics, Wild Bill said, "were the real heroes."

Another man wounded during the fighting in Carentan was Clancy Lyall. The Texan and future Easy Company man was attached to 2nd Battalion headquarters at the time, when he had an unfortunate run-in with a German bayonet.

"We had to run around this corner to throw grenades into a house where these German paratroopers were," he said in an interview in 2009. "We ran like hell, zip, zip, zip. All of a sudden I ran around a corner and here's this poor German with a rifle in his hand. He's frozen stiff, and so am I, and it went in maybe about a quarter of an inch. That's all. I shot him, then I started shaking like a leaf."

The stomach wound landed Lyall in an army hospital in England until August, when he returned to active duty and was assigned to Easy Company, then billeted back in Aldbourne.

Easy continued across the plaza and along rue Holgate for another block, entering the Place de la Republique, Carentan's main square, where rue Holgate and rue de la Halle intersect. At the southern end of this square, a winged statue honoring the French town's war dead gazes down rue Holgate.

Fanning out across the square, Winters ordered, "Secure this intersection. Clear those buildings to the right." During the fight, Guarnere recalled that Shifty Powers of 3rd Platoon "picked off a couple of snipers." Powers had a sharp eye and "could pick out movement a mile away."

"He was from the mountains in Virginia, born and raised with a gun in his hand, not like us city slickers," Guarnere later said.

German small-arms fire slackened as the enemy was rooted from their hiding places, but moments later, explosions began rocking the town.

"Mortars," Winters yelled. "Take cover!"

The Germans had the intersection zeroed in and as houses were ripped apart, flying chunks of steel and masonry struck several men. One private was killed outright. Ed Tipper was severely wounded in the head and both his legs were broken when a mortar shell blasted a building he was securing.

The attack was going "by the book," Tipper told me. The paratroopers were assisted by "three machine guns and they had only one."

This house likely served as an aid station during the fight at Carentan, and may have been where Winters, Lipton and Blithe were treated.

The rue Holgate in Carentan. Easy charged down this street during the June 12 attack.

But an uneasy feeling pervaded the men, Tipper said, and some thought, "This is too easy. Maybe it's a trap."

Tipper recalled seeing some houses that might be concealing enemy machine guns, so he and a few others decided to secure them.

"I cleared out one house, and as I was coming out, they began dropping in mortars," Tipper told me in 2009. "It was a trap, because they had the distance measured. They dumped a whole lot of mortar rounds in on us very quickly and wounded eight or ten or twelve guys right at that moment and I was one of them. That was the end of the war for me."

Welsh got to Tipper quickly and yelled for a medic. Talbert arrived next.

"I saw Ed Tipper being hit. It looked like half of his face, including one eye, was gone," Talbert said in a postwar interview. "I thought he was finished and went on because the fighting was really heating up at that point."

Tipper went from the aid station to a field hospital and, eventually, back to England and finally the United States. He would spend the next year in the hospital, but despite the grievous nature of his wounds, he made a remarkable recovery, although he endured a great deal of plastic surgery, including a glass eye.

"When I realized how badly I was wounded I thought my life was over," he told me. "I thought I couldn't live any kind of a normal life; couldn't get a license to drive a car, maybe be in a wheelchair or have a walker. None of that happened. I lived a totally normal life."

Talbert assumed his friend did not survive his wounds. Later, Talbert's mother wrote him a letter saying Tipper had visited her.

"I wrote back and told my mother that it couldn't be Tipper, that Tipper had been killed in front of me at Carentan," he recalled. "I could not believe he had lived through the ordeal."

Tipper confirmed the story with me, saying Talbert told his mother "whoever is claiming to be him is an impostor."

The rain of mortar shells ceased as suddenly as it had begun. Fearing the lull might signal a counterattack, Winters decided to check the company's ammo supply. Walking by the hotel in the intersection where a dead German machine-gun crew lay sprawled, a voice called, "Lieutenant Winters. Is it safe to cross?"

It was Strayer. The battalion commander and his staff, directly across the Place de la Republique from Winters, crouched by a building with a unique, multi-arched portico, if the miniseries is to be believed.

"That's where, in the series, Colonel Strayer asks if it's safe to come out," Paul said, pointing to the building, which still bears its distinctive façade.

Regardless of where this incident took place, the depiction in the film is based on truth.

"Yes, sir," Winters replied to Strayer's inquiry.

Winters told me he was irked by Strayer's question in light of the fact that his men had just bled to secure the area. To emphasize the point, Winters stepped into the middle of the street. Strayer nodded, then hurried across, his staff trailing behind. Winters smiled and shook his head in disgust.

"That was typical of Strayer," Winters told me. "Don't lead the way if someone else can do it instead."

Strayer was no sooner out of sight than something slammed into Winters's left shin with the impact of being hit by a baseball bat. He involuntarily gasped in pain, and hobbled to the side of the road.

"Goddammit," he said, less from pain than out of anger for knowing he had stupidly exposed himself to show up Strayer. Welsh ran to Winters and helped him into a sitting position on the sidewalk.

"Let's get that boot off," Welsh said. Doing so, he examined the wound. "It's not deep. Maybe I can get it."

He drew out his trench knife and began probing.

"Ouch! Dammit, Harry, you're all thumbs," Winters winced. "Just help me to the aid station."

Winters limped his way to the aid station, quite likely the house Paul pointed out to us at rue Holgate and rue de la Guinguette, where Neavles treated his injury. It was here that Winters noticed Private Albert Blithe sitting with his back against a wall, seemingly unhurt. Neavles, noting Winters's questioning gaze, told him Blithe was suffering from hysterical blindness. Winters knelt in front of the young man.

"Blithe," he said. "It's Lieutenant Winters. Can you tell me what's the matter?"

"Everything just went black, sir. I can't see a thing. I'm sorry. I'm truly sorry."

Winters patted the distressed young man's shoulder and told him he'd soon be sent back to England and to just "hang tough." He rose

The square in Carentan. Dick Winters was wounded near this spot.

and limped away. He'd barely taken five steps when Blithe called to him, saying, "I can see. It's okay. I can see. I think I'll be all right."

Winters walked back to him. Blithe looked into Winters's eyes, and the lieutenant said gently, "That's good, Blithe. But why don't we send you back with the rest and get you checked out properly to make sure you're okay."

Blithe asked permission to stay with his platoon. Winters would have preferred to send him back, but relented.

Winters told me how he felt enormous pride in Blithe. The young man was so terrified he literally lost his eyesight. Yet once given a few reassuring words, he had snapped out of it and was ready to return to duty.

"Blithe could've taken the easy way out," Winters said during one of our interviews. "But he chose to stick with his friends."

Blithe would be wounded on June 20. Point man on a three-man patrol led by Guarnere that included Private Joseph A. Lesniewski, Blithe spotted a German sniper, but rather than fire his rifle, he inexplicably reverted to his training days and pointed at the German with his hand.

"Sniper, bang, bang," he yelled.

The German got off a round from his Mauser that struck Blithe in the neck.

Guarnere and Lesniewski dragged the injured man to safety. Blithe's war was over. (Blithe would recover and remain in the army, serving in Korea in the 1950s.)

"He did exactly as he was taught in training," Winters later told me. "Unfortunately, this wasn't training."

Guarnere said Albert Blithe, whose nickname was Alby, was unjustly treated in the miniseries, which depicted him as being frightened. Wild Bill noted that "everybody was scared."

"Blithe was a good soldier," Guarnere later said. "That's why I put him on point."

Instead of bodies and chunks of blasted buildings, today the winged statue in the Place de la Republique overlooks an expanse cluttered with cars. Like the broad plaza a block to the north, it is a municipal parking lot in the midst of a bustling retail district. After parking my Opal near the statue, we got out and walked around and listened as Paul told us of a tragedy that occurred here, in large part because of Maxwell Taylor's oversight.

In mid-June, Taylor held several award ceremonies here in the square to hand out medals to deserving men. During one of these ceremonies—historians argue over which one—children from Carentan were enlisted to hand out flowers to each recipient. Taylor was to receive his flowers from nine-year-old Danielle Laisney, who was standing just a few feet away from him. What Taylor did not take into account, but should have, was that the Germans were just two miles away, and an artillery spotter, or possibly a French traitor, noticed the gathering and reported it. Before long, shells came whistling in.

"One of the first shells just decimates little Danielle, and her blood splatters all over Maxwell Taylor," Paul told us. "A medic ran up and tried to save Danielle's life, but she died here in the square, and some people say that was the day Maxwell Taylor changed as a person. He became much more sensitive to losses."

Danielle's mother still lives near the square and retains the bloody dress her daughter wore that sad day.

A shell also blasted one of the wings off the statue. The wing is still missing.

As we departed from the plaza, an intoxicated French driver—drunk even though it was eleven o'clock in the morning—backed his car into my rental. Instead of realizing he had hit something and pulling forward, he gunned his engine and actually pushed my car backward for several feet. A report with the man's name and address was filed with the gendarmes, and we continued on. The damage to my car was slight, but I smiled at having the dubious distinction of being "hit" in almost precisely the same spot where Dick Winters had been wounded.

The taking of Carentan is the source of another confusing tale. In his book, Compton recalls none of the fighting described in other works, including my own and Ambrose's. Compton wrote that the company "walked through" Carentan, which was "like a ghost town." He recalled the destruction, but assumed it was caused by units moving ahead of them, although in fact, no other units had advanced ahead of them during the attack.

"They show Carentan in the series like it was some big, high-powered battle, but I never saw any of that—not on the way in, anyway," Compton wrote. "When we walked through, we didn't have to fire a shot. It was already slaughter alley."

Forrest Guth said Easy Company took Carentan twice, the first time without firing a shot. Then, he said, "we had to pull out."

"This taking of Carentan twice story has just begun to surface," Paul told us. "I think what happened was that while moving into their attack position, they passed through the outskirts of town and assumed the whole place had been taken."

Time plays tricks on human memory.

After Carentan, the 101st advanced to a position about two miles outside the town, forming a protective cordon in the event of a counterattack, and as a jump-off place for launching an offensive thrust.

Easy Company was on the division's far right, their line ending at the Cherbourg to Paris railroad track with nothing beyond their unguarded flank but swampland. As the company approached a hedgerow situated on high ground, German mortar and small-arms fire poured down on them. Easy returned fire as Winters quickly deployed the men along the tangle of hedgerow just to their front. Keeping his head under the flying lead, Winters crawled along the line, giving encouragement to the men.

Recalling the fight to me years later, Winters said, "The most important thing you can do as a leader is to move around and let the men know you're there, that you're watching out for them, and that they're not alone. You have to keep your own head down, pop up and take a shot or two, and then keep moving."

Dusk brought a lull to the fight, but the night was far from quiet. Just after midnight a German patrol began firing weapons and shouting insults at the Americans. Winters cautioned his men to be alert for a possible attack. None developed. A few hours later the darkness was pierced by a shriek as Sergeant Talbert, wearing a captured German rain poncho, was bayoneted by Private George H. Smith Jr. Talbert had attempted to wake Smith up for guard duty, but emerging from the haze of sleep, Smith mistook Talbert for an enemy soldier.

Gordon later said in a postwar interview, "I was sent out to an outpost with my machine gun together with Guth and Sisk. Since we were too exposed and had no way of withdrawal, our squad leader, Sergeant Talbert, ordered us to move back. Tab picked up a German camouflage poncho. He wore it and still had his pistol, the barrel of which I had looked into earlier on D-day night. It was a big .45-caliber military revolver his mother had gotten from the police chief in Kokomo, Indiana, and sent to him.

"So Talbert had the gun in his hand and was waking [George H. Smith Jr.] up. Smith, in a state of exhaustion and confused, saw this enemy camouflage garment and immediately assumed it was a German. He jumped up and started lunging at Talbert. He got Talbert right in the chest with his bayonet. Later, Tab was in the ambulance at the same time I went to the aid station. Both of us rejoined the outfit for other campaigns."

Talbert, in a postwar interview, recalled Smith looking "wild-eyed."

"I kept yelling at him, shouting who I was, and thought that he would eventually cease attempting to stab me," he noted.

Talbert, gun in hand, could have shot Smith, but thought he would "become rational at any time."

"That didn't happen," he recalled. "Some other guys came to my assistance and they finally calmed him. I was rushed back to the first aid station. When the medics attended me, they discovered that a small black Bible, which I had in my front left pocket, had diverted the bayonet thrust, which caused it to miss my heart and lungs."

Forrest said his friend Talbert "thought he was dying."

"I was outposted with Gordon and Sisk in an exposed position on the far right of the main line," Forrest recalled. "The night was dark and cold. Floyd came to our position and told us to pull back. He was wearing a camouflaged German poncho to keep him warm. Then he headed out to check the rest of the line."

That was when Talbert was stabbed by Smith.

"His mother gave each of her sons a Bible when they entered the service and told them to carry it close to their hearts for protection," Forrest remembered. "It probably saved Tab's life."

While Talbert was being taken to the aid station, Winters spoke with Lewis Nixon, who had come up from Sink's headquarters. Nixon told Winters that "headquarters thinks we've run into a German counterattack heading toward Carentan." Nixon said Easy was going to attack at 0530 provided the Germans didn't strike first. Winters told James "Punchy" Diel, his acting first sergeant since Bill Evans was still missing, to alert the platoon leaders.

Easy endured a fitful night's sleep, interrupted by spurts of harassment fire. Winters had his men up and ready for the dawn attack. He placed his machine guns to provide support and deployed his mortars to the rear, where Guarnere began presetting the ranges.

At that moment German mortar shells began dropping on the Americans. "Take cover," Winters yelled, and men dove for their foxholes as the explosions tore into the hedgerow. The ground vibrated from the blasts. Hot steel and wood splinters filled the air above the cowering men. The barrage was short. When it let up, Winters leaped to his feet and began racing along his line.

"I told the men to get ready, that the Germans were coming, and to mark their targets," he told me.

Silently, solemnly, men removed ammo clips from their bandoliers and grenades from their belts. They placed these on the ground in front of their foxholes where they could be easily and quickly reached.

The German counterassault on the 101st was led by the 6th Parachute Regiment, which the 506th had just pushed out of Carentan. All along the regimental line, toughened German paratroopers began pouring small-arms fire on the GIs' line. The Americans fired back and slugs from both sides bit into the earth, thunked into tree trunks and clipped off branches. Spent brass casings tinkled melodically onto the ground. Men shouted and cursed in English and German, sometimes in anger, other times in pain or shock as a bullet found flesh.

Guarnere wrote that he kept running back and forth between all of the platoons and not just his own, encouraging the men.

"We couldn't let the Germans take Carentan," he said. "Too much was at stake."

Gordon was firing his machine gun when mortar shrapnel splintered a wooden fence near a post that he had been using to prop his weapon. A shard of steel pierced his leg and shoulder. Rod Strohl had been hit at the same time.

Above the roar of the battle Winters and his men heard a frightening new sound: tanks. Poking their prows over the crest of the ridge, the armored behemoths blasted away at the American line, their shells tearing through the trees and bursting with a roar.

The sudden and unexpected arrival of the tanks rattled Fox Company, which fell back in confusion. The retreat would cost Captain Mulvey his job, which Winters told me he felt was unjust.

Our guide, Paul Woodadge, agrees with Winters. Paul, who lives just a few miles from the site, has studied this fight in-depth, just as he has many others, and believes Fox Company "was in the wrong place at the wrong time." Paul thinks the German attack was coming at an angle, crossing Easy's front, to strike directly into Fox, which was also under assault on its other flank and was in imminent threat of being totally enveloped.

"Easy's on the right flank and they're seeing German tanks go across their front," Paul said.

Mulvey's men thus took the brunt of the hit as Germans drove a wedge between them and Easy, which may be why Frederick "Moose" Heyliger, who would later briefly command Easy but who at this time led the 81mm mortar platoon for 506th headquarters, recalled, "There's no line."

"[Fox] was the advance company and suddenly they've got Germans all around them, and they just fell back to try to link up with people on their left and right," Paul believes. "It wasn't that they were retreating."

Again, Paul's assessment reinforces what Winters said when he insisted to me in 2004 that Mulvey did not deserve to be sacked.

But whether the firing was deserved or not, Fox fell back, forcing Dog Company to do likewise, although D Company's Ronald Spiers and his platoon, out in front of Easy Company's line, held their exposed position in an abandoned house for several hours. Hence, Spiers's later writings about the "lost platoon" at Carentan.

With the fallback of D and F companies, Easy's left flank was now exposed. As the Germans pressed their advantage, the Americans gave ground as company after company, battalion after battalion, were pressed back toward Carentan itself. Only Easy Company, on the far right, held fast in the teeth of the German firestorm.

"We were out there on our own," Forrest recalled to me. "Had we known it at the time, it would have been a lot scarier. It was bad enough as it was."

Except for the loss of D and F companies, Winters was oblivious to his precarious situation. All he knew was that he had been ordered to hold. Moving in a crouch along his line, he scurried to the far left. There he found Welsh and 1st Platoon trying to defend the gap vacated by Fox Company.

"Thank God, I'm glad to see you," Welsh sighed with relief. "The Krauts are trying to push through. I didn't know if I should pull back or what the hell to do."

"We're staying and holding, Harry," Winters said. "Keep pouring it on 'em. Don't let them flank us."

Shortly after that encounter, a German tank lumbered toward the gap where Fox Company had been.

"When a tank is coming at you, you can do one of two things," Forrest told me. "First, you try to get out of the way. If you can't, you try to get up close because they can't shoot down on you if you're close."

Welsh chose the latter method. He grabbed Private John McGrath and the two ran into the open. McGrath carried a bazooka while Welsh held a satchel containing several rockets. McGrath knelt as Welsh jammed a rocket into the rear of the bazooka. Once loaded, Welsh tapped McGrath on the head and the private fired. The rocket streaked at the tank, only to carom harmlessly off. Welsh hastily began reloading and Winters could hear McGrath shouting, "You're gonna get me killed, Lieutenant." The tank fired its main gun at the two men, but being on higher ground, the gunner couldn't depress the barrel enough and the shell passed overhead, slicing off some young saplings.

"Hold your fire until I tell you," Welsh said.

He waited as the tank climbed a small rise, then said, "Fire."

The rocket hit the tank's soft underbelly, pierced the thin armor and detonated. The tank exploded, belching smoke and flame. Carrying its dead crew, the tank rolled a few feet forward from its own momentum, then came to a smoldering stop. By that time, Welsh and McGrath were back in the cover of the hedgerow. The destruction of the tank had a sobering effect on the other armored crews, who halted their vehicles in place.

Strayer by now had managed to push Dog and Fox companies back on line, although not quite to their original positions. Still, it was enough to secure Easy's flank and the hard fight continued through the day. Around four thirty that afternoon Winters heard the bellowing roar of engines to his left. Sherman tanks of the U.S. 2nd Armored Division rolled through the fields to Winters's left, machine guns and cannons blazing. One German tank blew up, then another, under the sudden onslaught of American armor. Pressed by the Shermans and taking casualties, the Nazis abandoned their attack. The surviving German tanks shifted into reverse and retreated over the crest. Then the infantry began to fall back, ending what Winters called "a very, very tough day."

"We whooped their goddamn asses," Guarnere recalled.

Up close, the Germans, he said, were "not superhuman."

"They were good, but we were better," he wrote. "We could thank Sobel for that."

This fight would become known as Bloody Gulch, and its precise location, unfortunately, is open to interpretation. The actual ground is about two miles west of Carentan, but of late, Paul said, some guides have moved it farther away. They tend to forget, Paul said, that the town limits have expanded since 1944 and that today, much of the ground has been overrun by houses and roads.

"People on tours tend to go farther out of town to where the hedge-rows are big and scary and it looks more like it does in the TV series," he said.

Paul admits relics, such as mortar shells, have been recovered at the "other" site as "evidence," but said the overall battle was widespread, encompassing both locations, so artifacts are inevitably going to be found. Paul bases his information on much on-site research, and on a thirty-seven-page account written in 1947 by Captain Ronald Spiers, which he found in the archives at Fort Benning. In his report, Spiers plotted the location of Dog Company, and sketched Fox Company's position as well. This allowed Paul and his team to fix the location of Easy Company.

"So we're slowly building up exactly who was where," Paul said. "We're at the point where we just about think we have the positions in line."

Paul explained how Easy's 3rd Platoon, which included Forrest Guth, Earl McLung, Floyd Talbert, C. T. Smith, and Jim Alley, was on the far right and slightly forward in a scouting position. The railway line was "literally six feet away on their right" and they saw German tanks advancing across their front. Paul said the Germans, now reinforced, picked a good time to hit the 101st. The airborne unit was exhausted after more than a week of fighting, ammo and supplies were low, and many noncoms and officers were still missing, and along comes a fresh German division "and the shit hit the fan."

Today, the place Paul is convinced is Bloody Gulch is located west of a nearby cattle market and south of the east-west railway line. The market and some new roads have done what the Germans could not do, overrun Easy Company's line. But the hedgerows to the west through which the enemy attacked remain unchanged.

At least for now.

No visit to Normandy is complete without stopping at the American cemetery overlooking Omaha Beach at Colleville-sur-Mer.

We made this pilgrimage, for that's what a trip to such a place must be, on the second day of our stay in France. Arriving around lunchtime at Les Moulins, where the rue de la Liberation and rue du 6 Juin 1944 merge, we stopped at a little place right on Omaha Beach called the D-Day House. As luck would have it, the only other people dining there that day were an American family from Illinois who knew the saga of the Band of Brothers and felt honored to meet one of the genuine articles and shake his hand.

After lunch I drove my rental car along the elevated D517, the Boulevard de Cauvigny, which parallels the beach, toward Vierville-sur-Mer. I pulled the car to the side of the road. While Paul and Forrest remained inside, I got out, descended the concrete stairs, and stepped onto the beach. I walked toward the surf, aware that I was totally alone on Omaha Beach. There was not a human being to be seen to my left or right anywhere along the expanse of sand. It was just me and history.

I was standing in the Dog White sector. Here, G Company of the 116th Regiment, 29th Division, stormed ashore that morning, into a hail of machine-gun and small-arms fire coming from Germans entrenched in the bluffs behind me. To my left as I faced the English Channel was Dog Green, where the bloodbath depicted in the movie *Saving Private Ryan* occurred. As I immersed myself in my surroundings, I was keenly aware that weather and surf conditions were much as they must have been on that day sixty-four years earlier. The sky was gloomy and overcast, and a brisk, damp wind kicked up white-capped waves, which pounded the beach. Missing, thankfully, was mine-tipped steel or wooden beach obstacles and the unimaginable hell of the battle.

As I had done earlier on this trip, at Brecourt Manor, at Marmion Farm, in the field where Lieutenant Meehan and his men died, and at Utah Beach, and would continue to do throughout the trip, I attempted to place myself beside those brave soldiers storming the beach. I tried to conjure up the sight of hundreds of ships at sea, the Higgins boats swarming ashore through the waves, men loaded down with gear struggling through the roiling surf as bullets kicked up water spouts and clanged off the steel obstacles, the horrible sound of men being hit and crying out for "medic" or "mother," and the tide running red with blood.

But there was no way I could succeed. I had not been there on June 6, 1944. But I was there now. I removed a jar from my pocket, scooped up some sand, and returned to the car.

Standing on Omaha Beach that day was one of the most powerfully emotional experiences of my life.

* * *

Like Omaha Beach, the cemetery overlooking it was a place I had to see. For Forrest, it was yet one more chance to visit with his friend Terrence "Salty" Harris.

The rectangular-shaped cemetery at Colleville-sur-Mer encompasses 172.5 acres, with its main paths laid out in the shape of a Latin cross. The largest memorial is a semicircular colonnade housing battle maps depicting not just the beach landings and airborne operations on D-day, but the American military campaign in western Europe up until May 8, 1945, when Germany surrendered. Within the open arc of the memorial stands a twenty-two-foot bronze statue depicting "The Spirit of American Youth Rising from the Waves."

The grounds are absolutely immaculate, and the grass perfectly manicured with an underground drainage system to run off excessive rainwater. On these hallowed grounds stand 9,387 headstones, both crosses and Stars of David, beneath which rest the remains of 9,383 men and 4 women, including 41 sets of brothers and 307 unknowns. Of these, 1,006 died on D-day, two-thirds of whom are paratroopers. There is also a memorial called the Garden of the Missing, honoring the 1,557 men missing in action, but whose names are forever enshrined within. The 307 unknowns, because their identities have never been established, are in all likelihood included in this number.

Each grave also denotes a death date, but Paul told us this may not be the day the soldier was killed, but rather the date on which the body was discovered. This is especially true for paratroopers who were not recovered until U.S. troops moved inland and the men of Graves Registration could perform their grim jobs.

Among the rows of headstones stands a limestone chapel, containing a black and gold marble altar bearing the inscription "I give unto them eternal life and they shall never perish."

Each year, about a million visitors tread this sacred ground.

When we arrived at the cemetery we were greeted by Geert van den Bogaert. Geert had worked for Paul as a guide, but he is now employed by the American Battle Monuments Commission, which operates and maintains twenty-four American cemeteries and twenty-five memorials in fifteen countries.

In deference to the aging veteran with us, we rode from the visitors' center to the cemetery in a motor cart surrounded by a clear plastic skirting to fend off the harsh, cold wind blowing in from the Channel. As we drove, Geert told us that one of the important aspects of his job is to learn as much as he can of the nearly ten thousand soldiers buried here. On several occasions, he pointed out the grave of a man and told us some remarkable story of heroism. It's a constant learning experience for the cemetery's historians.

"We still have families who come to the cemetery and tell us the most amazing stories of bravery and loyalty," he told us. "It's very inspiring."

As we drove along the path paralleling the English Channel, the cemetery, with its rows of graves laid out with parade-ground precision, stretched away to our left. In one of these plots, not too far from Ed Tipper's buddy Robert M. Bloser, also of Easy Company, lies Salty Harris.

Harris acquired the nickname "Salty" because, before joining the army, he had attended the naval academy at Annapolis, Maryland.

"He didn't like it," Forrest recalled. "Not enough action, I guess. Salty was restless."

Harris then enlisted in the army, volunteered for the paratroops, and trained with his comrades at Toccoa.

Geert knew exactly where we were going. He halted the cart. We crawled out and, with Paul carrying a small pail of sand and a brush, we walked along the silent white row of headstones until we came to one and stopped. Paul took some sand, sprinkled it on the stone and brushed away the excess. The sand that was not brushed away filled in the engraving on the stone, and the words "Terrence C. Harris, PFC 506 PRCHT INF 101 ABN DIV, June 18, 1944" glittered as if etched in gold.

Forrest was silent as he gazed down thoughtfully at the grave.

"He was a real good man," Forrest finally said. "Gung ho. Rough. Tough. He was a lot of fun and a great friend."

Harris, then a sergeant, had been considered the "ringleader" of the noncommissioned officers' mutiny against Herbert Sobel in the weeks prior to the Normandy jump. Because of that, he and the others had been herded into Sink's office at Littlecote House. There he was busted to private and transferred out of Easy Company. Shortly afterward, Harris volunteered as a pathfinder and was among the first men dropped into France on June 6. As Forrest told the story, I detected a lingering hint of bitterness toward Sink.

Paul picked up on it too, and said the animosity toward Sink over transferring Harris is felt by other Easy Company men as well.

"I had Paul Rogers here and he told me that it was not so much the fact that Harris died," my guide said. "It was the fact that he died not with his friends, not with the people he knew, but among strangers."

Forrest heard of Salty's death after the company had returned to England.

"It's funny," he said, standing there, a hand on the pure white cross. "We were young and we expected some people not to make it, so it wasn't as much of a shock as it maybe should have been. But we did miss him. I still miss him."

For me, physically standing in the cemetery was much more impressive than anything I had imagined from the many photographs I have seen. There are no words to accurately describe the experience, other than to say if you ever have an opportunity to visit there, do so.

As we left, Geert offered me the honor of signing the cemetery's VIP guest book. Not sure if I deserved that special treatment or not, I thanked him and signed. Forrest's name, not surprisingly, is already there.

After Bloody Gulch, Easy Company returned to Carentan, where, Guarnere wrote, the men raided houses for food and booze, specifically Calvados.

"That stuff will straighten you out," he wrote. "Heavy duty."

Winters saw that his men were properly billeted in houses, then he and Welsh bedded down. With his injured leg stiffening up, Winters turned command over to Welsh to give the wound a chance to heal.

Not long after that, it was off to Cherbourg, a bivouac behind Utah Beach, then back to England and Aldbourne to rest and refit. Of the 139 men Easy had gone into battle with on June 6, Winters's June 30 roster showed just 5 lieutenants—Welsh, Compton, Warren Roush, Francis L. O'Brien, and himself—and 69 men. He had 3 known dead—Privates Joseph M. Jordan, Everett J. Gray, and William S. Metzler. The rest were wounded or missing.

Guarnere, reflecting on Normandy, thought about men who had died and how he felt partially responsible.

"But you can't second-guess," he wrote. "You don't know if you'd done it some other way, or ten other ways, if it would have been worse. . . . It's sad when one of our guys got hurt or killed, but you didn't have time to cry. Some guys did. You couldn't let yourself get soft."

After three weeks of combat, he said, the men had bonded.

"We saw and experienced the worst things humans can see or experience," Wild Bill recalled. "We saved each other's lives. It was give and take. The bond really came out."

They also learned that their bodies could endure far more than any of them had expected. The body responds automatically, Guarnere said, "and your brain catches up later."

John Martin noted that he was struck by the fact that so many had fallen and he feared that none of them would make it home alive. Maybe that's why Guarnere said how the men returned to England and lived it up, because "tomorrow we might all be dead."

That thought did not diminish their enthusiasm for another crack at the Nazis.

"When they got back to England, we were ready to go again," Forrest told me.

Forrest and I did not return to England as Easy Company had after Normandy, but rather headed back for our B and B at Haute Addeville and prepared to push on to more battlefields. I enjoyed our stay in France. We were made to feel nothing but welcomed, quite unlike Edward "Babe" Heffron, who wrote that the French "wanted no parts of us," and Guarnere's comment that "most of the GIs don't like the French. They weren't friendly during the war."

Forrest and I did not share Wild Bill's experience.

On the night of November 6, Paul and his staff threw us a farewell party with a lavish smorgasbord of food, prepared by Spencer Henry. Sixteen people attended, including Mayor Daniel Hamchin of Angoville-au-Plain. I signed copies of my book *Biggest Brother*, and Forrest signed copies of *Band of Brothers*, and we posed for photos with the guests.

The next morning, we continued our trip into history.

CHAPTER 7

"THE SITUATION IS NORMAL. WE'RE SURROUNDED."

OPERATION MARKET GARDEN

After being pulled off the line in Normandy, Easy Company was sent to Cherbourg, then to a camp behind Utah Beach, before catching transport ships back to England, and, finally, Aldbourne.

"It was wonderful to be back in Aldbourne," Winters later wrote. "Everyone was glad to see us. It was just like home."

Easy Company had left this Wiltshire village in late May with 145 men. They returned to its hearthsides in mid-July with 74, while the 506th overall suffered 983 casualties, including 231 killed. Those troopers who did not die at the front were returned for treatment. Throughout the summer, the airfields at Membury and Ramsbury droned with the incessant sound of C-47s flying the wounded in, then flying out again, empty, to bring back still more.

Villager Tom Barnes recalled, "They would fly over Aldbourne very low, wheels down, on final approach to Membury. About thirty minutes later, the army ambulances would wind their way down Baydon Hill, almost an endless stream, on their way to the military hospitals locally. One of them pulled up at the bottom of the hill, nearby to where the library is today. As a youngster of fourteen and almost still children, we found all of these activities very exciting, and were quite curious. I walked over toward the parked ambulance, eager to know what was happening, when all of a sudden the back doors opened and a medic got out carrying a galvanized bucket full of blood, and poured it down the hillside drain in front of my very eyes. This vivid memory has stayed with me ever since my childhood, and had an immediate and sobering effect—I was never again curious to see the state of the wounded from the battlefront when they passed through Aldbourne, fighting for their lives."

The death of a man who had stayed in the village affected not just his soldier buddies but the townspeople as well.

Again, Tom Barnes told historian Neil Stevens, "My older sister had been dating a wonderful chap by the name of Earnest L. Oats. He was a giant of a man, very strong, with broad shoulders, and one of the 506th medics at the Farm Lane camp. When they all came back after D-day, I kept asking after Ernie. The other men kept telling me he would be back soon, but that day never came. It gradually dawned on us that Ernie was never coming back."

The unfortunate Oats had been with Stick 68. A few minutes before takeoff, for some unknown reason, he switched places with another medic, Edwin E. Pepping, who was assigned to Stick 66, led by Easy's commander, Lieutenant Meehan. As a result, Oats died when the plane carrying him, Meehan, and the rest of the stick was shot down in the early hours of June 6, 1944.

Ironically, even had Oats not switched, the loss of Stick 66 would have had an impact on Aldbourne. Pepping was also dating a village girl.

For the injured men who were flown back ahead of their units, treated, and returned to Aldbourne, life had changed. Don Burgett, who was wounded early in the fighting and thus became the first of the 101st men to return, wrote how the Green and Hightown were utterly deserted.

"I walked through the gateway of the camp and stopped and stood for a long time in the courtyard," he later said. "It was deserted. The stables were just as we had left them when we departed for our marshaling areas for the invasion. There was no noise, no troopers bustling about, no one doing close-order drill, no officers or noncoms chewing someone's butt, no nothing, just silence. For the first time in many months, I felt a deep loneliness. Opening the door of stable thirteen was like opening the door of a tomb. Memories flooded my mind. How many guys were still alive? The only thing to do was to keep busy, so I gathered up all my dirty laundry and walked to the washhouse and scrubbed everything by hand. I ate some fish and chips I had purchased earlier and went to bed."

When the bulk of the regiment finally returned in mid-July, accommodations changed. Instead of the Quonset huts at Farm Lane, Easy Company was billeted in the Hightown stables, just off the village Green, while Winters and Welsh moved back in with the Barnes family.

Forrest Guth took up residence in one of several large glider boxes on the Green. Guth, something of a weapons innovator— he figured out how to make the semiautomatic M1 carbine fully automatic—had become the company weapons specialist.

"I was always making something out of another," he told me. "I guess that's why I was made the company armorer."

Forrest shared the roomy glider box with the 506th's mail orderly, an advantage since it generally meant he was among the first to get his letters from home.

As for his conversion work, after making a carbine fully automatic, the weapon and the idea were kicked up to division, where both promptly vanished. (Forrest only recalled making one, but Buck Compton, in his book, also claimed to have one of these special carbines, which, as mentioned earlier, he lost during the D-day jump.)

Colonel Sink moved back in at Littlecote House and began getting the men ready for their next action, wherever and whenever that might be.

On August 27, with new battles imminent, Colonel Sink held a memorial service for the fallen at his Littlecote headquarters. At 11:00 a.m. some two thousand men in full dress uniform stood at rigid attention on the fields in front of the estate as the roster of the dead and missing was read, a total of 414 names. At the conclusion of the service, a formation of C-47s flew overhead, and Chaplain McGee read the regimental prayer entitled "Our Heroic Dead." General Maxwell Taylor, the Screaming Eagles commander, whose headquarters was at Greenham Lodge in nearby Newbury, gave a stirring speech. Everybody, it seemed, knew someone who had failed to return, and as the men marched off to the strains of "Onward Christian Soldiers," they all realized that those lost 414 men were just the start.

By mid-September 1944 preparations for the next operation were in full swing. The 101st had experienced a number of false alarms in recent weeks, missions that had been planned for then canceled when rapidly moving ground forces overran drop zones. Still, training continued.

In Ramsbury, Raymond Westall, now seventy-five, told us about the hubbub created by the American preparations. He recalled two transport planes on a night mission crashing into a nearby woods after mistaking ground lights for the airfield. A teenager who worked at an ammunition factory in Chilton Foliat, Westall told Forrest and me that he often ran errands for the GIs, who "paid me well," and sometimes shared their abundance of food with the boy.

"We didn't have anything like that," he recalled. "We were on rations."

Today, thanks to hindsight, we know Easy's next stop was Holland, and that was where Forrest and I now found ourselves. We arrived in what would become the 506th's next destination, the medieval city of Eindhoven, on November 10, following the officious voice on my GPS through the city streets to reach our lodgings, the Sandton Hotel. Located along what was known as Hell's Highway but is now Stratumseind, it is just a block and a half south of the heart of the old city. I left Forrest at the hotel to rest while I went exploring.

A narrow, lazy waterway that flows south from the Wilhelmina Canal separated my hotel from the oldest part of Eindhoven. The stream is crossed by a small span known as the First Bridge on Hell's Highway. Once over it, I found myself in the historic part of the city, founded in 1232. It was along this narrow, medieval, cobblestone-lined street that British armored vehicles of XXX Corps had rattled on their way toward Arnhem and the Rhine. Throngs of Dutch citizens, many waving orange flags, greeted them.

This was much the same welcome that Dick Winters and the men of Easy had received when they had entered the city ahead of the tanks, coming from the other direction. I remembered Bill Guarnere writing how the people cheered them, women hugged and kissed them, and offered them beer, milk, and apples.

"They knew they were liberated; it was a celebration in the streets," he recalled.

Gruff Wild Bill thought the Dutch were "the most beautiful people alive" and noted they "couldn't do enough for us." This was a far cry from his impression of the French, whom, he said, he never turned his back on.

"A lot of them liked the Germans a little too much," he wrote.

The men of Easy Company all love the Dutch, and most have returned to Holland over and over. The town fathers of Eindhoven even named Dick Winters an honorary citizen of the city in 2006, an honor Winters, unable to make the trip back, accepted, greeting the people via a telephone hookup that was broadcast publicly. He was also awarded the Medal of the City of Eindhoven.

Bill Guarnere made his first journey back to this city in 1954 on the tenth anniversary of the Market Garden drop.

"For twenty-one days we lived in Dutch homes," he recalled. "They had parades. The children put wreaths on the graves of soldiers."

Babe Heffron recalled staying in the home of "Mom and Pop" Vermuelen, who lived at 402 Hoogstraat. The friendship he forged with them lasted until their deaths in the 1970s.

Since *Band of Brothers*, Babe said, "everyone knows us."

"One morning two guys started hollering out to me, they must've seen the eagle on my jacket, and the next thing I know, they picked me up bodily and took me to a pub," he wrote. "Everyone in the bar started clapping and hitting their glasses on the bar."

Forrest agreed. Even though the number of people of Eindhoven who remember the war is growing smaller and smaller, their children and grandchildren still honor the actions of the veterans.

"When we walk down a street, especially if we have our jackets on, people thank us," he told me. "They know the Screaming Eagle insignia."

On the day I walked along this street, the hubbub that followed liberation was a long time in the past and beyond the memory of most of the people I encountered. The place is much quieter now. For one thing, the entire center of the old city is closed to motorized traffic, other than merchants and delivery vehicles. Only walkers and bicycle riders moved around me. Along both sides of the thoroughfare, small shops and bistros were preparing for the day's business. Some restaurants, like die Altstadt, still provided outdoor seating under wide awnings on this balmy November afternoon.

As I reached a large plaza at the intersection of Stratumseind and Kerkstraat, I stopped and gazed at St. Catherine's Church, its twin, jagged spires seeming to scrape the gray sky. Hundreds of bicycles were parked in bike racks or leaning against walls around the plaza, all, I

British tanks roll along Hell's Highway through Eindhoven, September 18, 1944. *U.S. Army*

The same stretch of road in 2008.

noted with interest, unlocked, something no bike owner in his right mind would attempt in America.

The only disconcerting part of this quaint old-Europe scene was the presence of a large glass-domed galleria shopping mall on the square, opposite the church.

I returned to the hotel.

On September 13, 1944, the 506th's officers sat down for a briefing, where they were informed about Field Marshal Bernard Law Montgomery's energetic plan to seize a bridge over the Rhine. Using the U.S. 101st and 82nd and the British 1st Airborne divisions, he would lay a carpet of paratroopers over a sixty-five-mile stretch of road in Holland from Eindhoven to Arnhem.

The 506th was assigned to Drop Zone C, near the village of St. Oedenrode, just to the northwest of the town of Son. They, with the rest of the 101st, would then drive south and seize six bridges around Eindhoven before taking the city itself. Then they would hold open a fifteen-mile stretch of the brick and cobblestone road that would come to be known as Hell's Highway, for the British XXX Corps.

Operation Market Garden, as the offensive was code-named, took off on Sunday, September 17, a bright, calm, sunny late summer day. C-47s, some towing gliders, lifted off from Membury and Ramsbury, turned south, and winged their way toward Europe.

Back in Ramsbury, young Raymond Westall recalled, "All those planes flying overhead, it was so loud. It was just unbelievable."

On board the planes, the paratroopers wondered what awaited them over the drop zone. The veterans recalled June 6, when the sky was a maelstrom of colored tracers, exploding antiaircraft shells, and twisting, burning airplanes. Thus they anticipated a violent welcome. The new men, knowing it was Sunday and that the drop zones were well behind enemy lines, hoped the Germans might be surprised and slow to respond.

But whether they anticipated a hot reception or a cold one, the last thing they expected, or even dared hope for, was no reception at all. Yet, with a few exceptions, that is what they got.

The first intimation Dick Winters had that this jump might be a breeze was when he looked out of the plane's open doorway at the peaceful Dutch countryside flashing by below him. There seemed to be no alarm, no bustle of German trucks or troops. And when the red "ready" light came on and there was no booming of ack-ack guns, his hopes soared still higher.

Some of the Skytrains bringing men in came under German anti-aircraft fire.

"It was a daylight drop and we were all scared," Clancy Lyall told me. "Well, I don't know about all, but I know I was."

He recalled Allied fighters flying air cover and also providing ground support against enemy flak towers.

"We took some antiaircraft fire, but we also had P-38s and Hurricanes with us," he said.

David Webster wrote that his stomach tightened and he hoped the plane would develop mechanical problems and be forced to turn around and go back, "but the engines' roar was as steady as ever."

Webster served in 3rd Squad under Robert Rader, who was assisted by Donald Hoobler. The platoon leader was Floyd Talbert. Webster remembered a new replacement, James Miller, a quiet, friendly, well-mannered kid whose brush haircut and missing front tooth "gave him an engaging, boyish appearance."

Edward "Babe" Heffron of South Philadelphia joined Easy Company after Normandy. Initially assigned to B Battery, 446th Anti-Aircraft unit, he transferred to the airborne in February 1944 and trained at Fort Benning, Georgia. There he buddied up with John Julian of Syspy, Alabama, a young man with a strong Southern drawl, and an Oklahoma farmer named J. D. Henderson, whom Heffron called a "laid-back kid." The three young men made a pact. After the war, they would visit the families of any of them killed in combat. All three were soon assigned to Easy.

Heffron recalled the mood in the plane on the flight to Holland as being tense, with a lot of men praying or lost in deep contemplation.

"When you stepped out of that door," he wrote, "you knew full well you might not be alive when you hit the ground."

At five feet, six inches tall and tipping the scale at 163 pounds, Forrest Guth was lugging over 150 pounds of equipment into the battle, including something he wasn't supposed to have—his jump boots. Before boarding the planes, the men had been ordered to wear ordinary combat boots instead of their beloved jump boots. The order was roundly hated and generally ignored.

"A lot of us didn't like that and we wore our jump boots into Holland regardless of the orders," he told me.

Forrest disguised his by cutting the leggings off his combat boots and wrapping them around his jump boots until the plane took off. Once in the air, he removed the leggings and left them in the Skytrain.

The flight to the drop zone was relatively smooth with only sporadic opposition. Buck Compton recalled that the aircraft came down to about six hundred feet and soared over the British column. Below were long lines of trucks, tanks, and equipment and a partially completed Bailey bridge being built to span the Albert Canal. During the flight, he relaxed by reading *We Jumped to Fight* by Lieutenant Colonel Edson D. Raff, which related the experiences of the 509th Parachute Infantry Regiment in North Africa. Then it was time to give the orders, "Stand up," "Hook up," "Check your equipment," "Sound off for equipment check," "Close up and stand in the door," and "Go!"

"No one was shooting at us this time, at least that's how I remember it," Compton wrote. "I hit the silver circle clasp on my chest that popped me out of my chute and joined up with my platoon."

The men of Easy had arrived at Drop Zone C.

Drop Zone C was also our destination.

We began our tour on November 11, a day when, all over Europe, people were celebrating the ninetieth anniversary of the end of World War I. Television news shows were full of footage of dignitaries laying wreaths and giving emotion-filled speeches that seemed not to need an interpreter to be understood.

Our guide for the Holland portion of our journey would be Marco Kilian, who, with Frank Slegers, owns and operates Militaria Bastogne, a shop located in Place McAuliffe in the heart of Bastogne. The store specializes in World War II military artifacts and reproduction goods, similar to Dead Man's Corner in Normandy. Marco also gives Battle of the Bulge tours in a period American army truck.

"It was their concept," said veteran Herb Suerth, who joined Easy Company after Holland. "It's a nice store and a roaring success."

Marco's wife, Marion, Suerth said, "runs the Men of Easy Company Web site in Europe for me."

Frank and Marco knew the men of Easy Company long before Ambrose made them famous. Marco recalled meeting the veterans, including Bill Guarnere, Carwood Lipton, and Forrest Guth, when he was just eight years old.

"I didn't just hear the stories, I met the people," he told me.

Today, when Easy Company veterans visit their old battlefields, like Forrest was doing with me, Frank and Marco go to great lengths to make sure their stay is safe and comfortable.

"We made a commitment to E Company veterans," Marco said. "When they are over here, we try to help them as much as possible. I like that. We're doing something for them. They saved my parents and my grandparents from starvation. They liberated us, so if I can give something back, I will."

In America, Marco continued, "people simply read or hear stories of the war, but for people like myself, those stories are real. The war is something we can reach out and physically touch because it happened in our towns and cities, on our farms and in our fields. It happened to members of our families.

"If Forrest needs anything," Marco told me, "let us know."

It was a comforting thought.

Indeed, the two men are among those responsible for the Easy Company monuments Forrest and I saw at Brecourt Manor and near the Bois Jacques in Bastogne, as well as ones we would see here in Holland. They also hope to erect a monument in Haguenau, provided they can pinpoint Easy's position in a city radically changed since 1945.

When Marco arrived at our hotel, we loaded into his car and were soon cruising north, out of Eindhoven on the 18 Septemberplein, then merging onto the four-lane John F. Kennedylaan. As we drove, Marco pointed out all of the houses and commercial buildings we were passing, noting that in 1944, "this was all farms and fields."

To reach Drop Zone C, we left the main highway and got onto the N620, which parallels the Wilhelmina Canal. We turned left onto a country road called Molenheideweg, which soon became Sonniuswijk. Pointing to the expanse of green fields to our left, Marco said, "This was the drop zone for the 101st."

The fields were wide and peaceful and, considering the drop was in September and this was November, probably looked pretty much the same now as they did when American airborne troops floated down onto them.

Forrest recalled the pleasant weather and said it was "a great day for jumping" with "lots of sunshine and not much antiaircraft fire."

"It was a nice, soft drop zone," he said.

Reaching a farm on our left, Marco turned onto a long, tree-lined lane. The farm is owned by Twan van der Weal, who was at work in an outbuilding and waved to Marco as we pulled up and exited the car.

"The fields behind the house here were all 506th drop zone," Marco said, sweeping his hand at the broad open expanse to the rear of the farm. Then pointing toward the fields to his right, he added, "The gliders came down in that area."

To emphasize that this was where Forrest and Dick Winters and the others had come down, Marco pointed to another of the now familiar black, highly polished granite plaques dedicated to E Company, bearing the division emblem and the words "The eagle will always scream for our fallen brothers." Nine gold stars angling to a peak above the emblem symbolize the nine men Easy lost in Holland. The plaque is mounted on the brick wall of the farmhouse.

I walked to the edge of the trimmed lawn behind the house and gazed out across the vacant fields toward a distant road called, appropriately enough, Airborneweg. For me, it was very much like being at the High Water Mark on the Gettysburg battlefield where Pickett's Charge was broken in 1863, and I tried to envision that now peaceful stretch of field as it appeared on September 17, 1944. Unlike the Pickett's Charge site, there had been very little carnage here, just a mass of confusion as gliders skidded across the ground and men drifted down to earth under silken canopies. I remember Winters telling me the biggest threat was not from the Germans but from the very real chance of being landed on by another paratrooper or getting beaned by falling gear, such as helmets and weapons, jarred loose by the jolt of chutes opening.

While Forrest called this a "nice, soft drop zone," it was neither nice nor soft for him. His parachute partially failed and he came down hard.

"My main chute didn't deploy right," Forrest told Marco and me.

"It was twisted up and didn't open properly. I tried to pull the cord on my reserve, but we were jumping between six hundred and eight hundred feet, so it was too late to effectively deploy. I hit the ground hard on my right side. Luckily it was a soft field, but I couldn't move. I wore my canteen on my hip and I landed directly on it, and displaced disks in my spine."

Initially paralyzed and in excruciating pain, he called for a medic. As always, Eugene Roe answered the call with a comforting, "I got ya, Goody." Quickly assessing Forrest's condition, he jabbed Guth with a syrette of morphine and got a stretcher crew to carry the injured man from the field.

"They carried me to a cattle barn, where some Dutch girls took care of me," he said, although the pain and morphine blotted out much of his memory.

That "cattle barn" where Forrest and the other casualties were taken and tended by Roe and medic Ralph Spina still stands, attached to the rear of Twan van der Weal's house.

Forrest Guth was Easy Company's only casualty during the Market Garden airdrop, and one of only twenty-four suffered by the entire 506th. Brought forward when Son was taken, Forrest and the others were housed in a field hospital set up in a monastery, which still stands today and serves as a hospital and care center for the elderly. Eventually Forrest was taken to Eindhoven, then on to an army hospital in France. Amazingly, the doctor who would treat him there was Dr. Andres, Forrest's family doctor from back home.

"He told me he thought he was too old and that the army wouldn't take him, but there he was, working in a field hospital," Forrest recalled. "They made him a major."

Forrest's injury did not require surgery—that would come ten years later—but it did keep him off the line for nine weeks. He would miss the entire Holland operation, and return to Easy Company at Mourmelon, France, just weeks before the division was shipped to Bastogne.

Years later, Carwood Lipton, who was 3rd Platoon sergeant and jumpmaster of plane 75, the "Buzz Buggy," recalled, "The flight was smooth and there was no mistaking our DZ. Within an hour the company was assembled on the ground. Only one man was missing. Forrest Guth. Being from Pennsylvania and of German descent, and since he spoke

German rather well, he had been designated as our interpreter. Goody hurt his back on landing and missed the entire Holland campaign."

Twan van der Weal, who was a small child in September 1944, greeted us and told us, through Marco's translation, what it was like living in the middle of the American drop zone. He said that, during the preinvasion bombardment by American planes, the son of a neighboring farmer was killed by a bomb while trying to herd the family's cattle to safety.

His family, van der Weal said, hid in the cellar during the bombardment, and only emerged when they heard American voices outside rather than German.

"We came out and saw all of the American paratroopers coming out of the fields and walking to the road," he said through Marco. "Many of them stopped at our well and pumped water for themselves. They drained the well."

The pump, green from years of corrosion, is still there, unused.

His father also gave the GIs all of the fresh milk he had on hand.

Twan van der Weal did not recall Forrest specifically, but he did remember a wounded soldier who had been hit in the leg by antiaircraft shrapnel while still in his plane. The man jumped anyway, and was treated in the farmhouse kitchen.

In the decades since the war, reminders of that day still rear up. In the weeks after the fight moved on, holes in the roofs of the house and barn created by bomb shrapnel were repaired with parts taken from ruined gliders. For more than half a century, bits and pieces of the battle have been found.

"He still finds debris, parachutes, equipment, in his fields," Marco said. "For fifty-five years, he drove over a bump in the field. Then one day he decided to see what it was, so he dug down and found an American parachute."

In one of the outbuildings, van der Weal and his late father have created a small makeshift museum of artifacts, including glider pieces, a shovel, German and American artillery casings, an American helmet, belt and parachute harness buckles, a Mae West life jacket, mortar casings, pieces of a C-47 that crashed nearby, a seat from a glider, empty ammo clips, a German ammunition box, a German bayonet and parachute ropes, all found in his family's fields.

Climbing back into the car we drove away, our next stop being the Son Bridge.

The Son Bridge was also the 506th's next stop. Assembling on the fields all around the van der Weal farm, they struck out toward the Wilhelmina Canal, about three and a half miles to the southeast.

For some men, it took a little while to catch up. David Webster recalled that he got separated from his company during the jump and came down in an area that was under fire. He spotted three dead men, two paratroopers and the third, a flight crew chief whom he had met back in England at a pub called the Shepherd's Rest. They'd had a few beers together and Webster remembered him as "a nice guy."

"Now he was dead on the drop zone," Webster wrote.

He and the rest of his 3rd Platoon finally linked up with Easy Company, which was "spread out in brambly ditches beside a sandy road" waiting for stragglers to catch up.

Some men totally missed the mark. Babe Heffron and Earl McLung landed on the wrong side of the Wilhelmina Canal and were cut off from the rest of Easy for a while. During the subsequent assault on Son, Babe recalled guarding the road leading to the bridge when some GIs brought up a wounded German prisoner. An elderly Dutch woman soon appeared. She stopped by the injured German soldier and asked him where he had been hit. He pointed at his shoulder, at which point she began clubbing his injured arm with her purse. Babe laughed and told the others "let her go for a while." When they finally stopped her, Babe took her purse, which, he said, was "pretty heavy." Looking inside, they found it contained a brick.

"Every time when you talk to Babe in Holland, he tells that story because he was really impressed by it," Marco said.

Members of the 506th who landed on the correct side of the canal advanced toward Son unimpeded until just outside the town limits. Meeting German resistance, Winters urged his men forward. They had closed to within about fifty yards of the bridge when an explosion lifted the span, throwing wood and stone high into the air. The GIs sought shelter as the debris rained down on them. Rising slightly and brushing himself off, Winters told me his first thought was, "What a hell of a way to die in combat."

"They blew it up right in our faces," Clancy Lyall told me.

As soon as the hail of falling bridge remnants ceased, Winters was ordered to bring up his machine guns to provide covering fire for 1st Battalion, which was going to cross over the canal. As Winters watched 1st Battalion move, he recalled its commander, Major James LaPrade, out in front tiptoeing from rock to timber to rock, carrying just a .45-caliber pistol.

"For God's sake, man," Winters thought. "Carry an M1 rifle if you're expecting trouble. It'll give you a little firepower and won't advertise that you're an officer."

The fighting continued into Son, with Germans defending a strongpoint in the town's church. The house of worship was destroyed, with only its tower surviving. That battered church tower still stands.

By dark, Easy was over the canal, and Son had fallen into American hands.

The bridge that spans the Wilhelmina Canal at Son today is a broad modern expanse that looks nothing like the one the Germans blew into matchsticks in 1944. However, to give us a feel for what had been there, Marco drove us about two miles to the east. There, along Stakenburg-straat, stands an almost exact duplicate of the Son Bridge. Uniquely Dutch by design, its bright red boom perched atop black steel vertical poles lifts the single-lane road surface that carries traffic across the tranquil canal. This bridge is just south of the town of Breugel.

Yet while the actual Son span is gone, debris can still be found littering the woodland to the west.

After Son, Eindhoven was next, and on September 18, the drive continued. As they approached the city, Winters directed Lieutenant Brewer to take the point with his 1st Platoon. The twenty-year-old Californian expertly deployed his men in perfect formation with a thin skirmish line out in front. Brewer ordered the platoon forward but his combat inexperience now became evident. Instead of remaining with the platoon, the gangly six-foot-four-inch officer advanced with the skirmishers. Worse, he waved his arms in obvious gestures of command, his map case and binoculars in plain sight.

"Everyone knew what was coming," Winters later told me. "I had told him a hundred times in training, don't walk around out in front like that, you'll get it sure as hell."

Winters got on the radio and yelled for Brewer to drop back. But it was too late. A shot rang out and Brewer, struck in the throat, went down, Winters recalled, like "a tree that's been felled by an expert lumberman."

Convinced Brewer was dead, Winters took over the platoon and pushed them across the field and into the town as fast as he could.

Brewer's buddy Buck Compton recalled, "We thought [the sniper] was too far away to be effective. Mostly we were just ignoring it. Sort of random, the bullet that hit Brewer."

Brewer would survive.

Clancy Lyall, of 1st Platoon, 3rd Squad, said he was part of a patrol led by squad leader Bob Rader that was out in front on the approach to Eindhoven.

"We got into a firefight with some Germans and took them prisoner," he said. "Then the company moved up and we pushed down the road until we got into Eindhoven."

Easy fought its way into Eindhoven, where Heffron had a close call. An 88 shell struck a department store he was in, blowing out the windows. The concussion threw Babe into the street, where he landed unconscious. When he awoke, he said a young soldier from D Company was asking if he was okay. Except for a slight arm wound and being dizzy, he was.

The 88mm fire was finally silenced by bazooka teams, and the 506th entered the city, rounding up about fifty prisoners.

The 506th's actual entrance into the heart of Eindhoven was impeded, not so much by the Germans as by jubilant Dutchmen. David Webster wrote how people waved orange flags, handed out refreshments, "and generally acted as if the war were over." The paratroopers did not share that feeling of euphoria, Webster recalled, noting that "our feet hurt, our clothes were wet with sweat," and the weight of their equipment bogged them down.

Babe Heffron found a convenient way to carry his load. A Dutch woman, possibly noting Babe's burden, gave him a baby carriage, into which he dumped his weapon and ammo. As he was pushing it along,

Popeye Wynn off-loaded his gear into the carriage as well, at which point Heffron removed his own belongings and told Popeye to push the carriage himself.

Wild Bill Guarnere recalled the celebration in the streets. A woman rushed up with an autograph book and asked the men, "Sign, sign." Guarnere said the men responded by scribbling names like John Wayne, Cary Grant, Kilroy, and the Andrews Sisters. (Years later, on a return trip to Eindhoven, the veterans located this woman and asked her to produce the book. She did and they signed their real names. Guarnere wrote, "We're friends with her now, and with her son, who was born twenty years after the war.")

Buck Compton wrote of Eindhoven, "They shook our hands and slapped our backs. They offered us food—fresh milk and fruit."

He recalled a little girl motioning him down to her level. He bent down and she pinned a little rag doll to his uniform.

"She didn't say a word, but just offered me this small tribute, then disappeared into the crowd," he said. "I still have that doll, packed carefully in my garage."

"Once we got into town it was damned hard to get through," Lyall recalled with a chuckle.

As they walked into the city, Winters told me the reception was quite different from the one they got in France.

"There we suspected everyone of being a sniper," he remembered.

Winters saw an elderly man drag a pair of chairs out of his house and invite soldiers to take a load off their feet. Two of his men did, stretching out their legs.

"I told them to get going. There wasn't time for goofing off," he said.

Remembering what happened to Brewer, Winters tucked his map case and binoculars inside his field jacket and pulled up his collar to hide his silver bars. Carrying just his M1, Winters figured he now looked like any other GI.

Snipers were a very real threat. Clancy Lyall remembered, "On the outskirts of Eindhoven I met a little boy about ten or twelve years old, he had that darned orange band around his arm. He was spotting houses for us, letting us know where the Germans were. He was carrying this short .22 pistol. I gave him my trench knife. It had my name on it."

As he was working his way through the sea of celebrating citizens, Winters stopped briefly by a crowd chanting something in Dutch while men roughly shaved the heads of several women. The women's offense, Winters learned, was that they had been sexually involved with German soldiers. He understood the people's anger. Still, his own mother had raised her son to have an abiding respect for women and this spectacle offended him.

Guarnere saw that as well, but took a harder view, recalling, "They deserved it."

Clancy Lyall said the Germans inadvertently helped ease his way through Eindhoven.

"The Germans lobbed a mortar or an 88 in, and all those people took off. Whoosh. So now we could get about doing our business," he said.

The Germans also provided Lyall with a much-appreciated treat. He and Mike Massaconi placed their .30-caliber machine gun atop a building "with a beautiful field of fire." An enemy mortar shell exploded nearby, opening up a hole in an adjoining building that turned out to be a Heineken beer brewery. Lyall shinnied down a rope and tossed bottles up to his friend, who would "drop them over the side to the rest of the guys."

The 506th managed to get through Eindhoven in good order and the bridge over the Dommel was secured intact. Heffron set up his machine gun by a footbridge over a canal next to a row of homes, facing a secondary road leading into town. Members of the underground approached and said a horse-drawn wagon and eight Germans were coming. The Americans told the Dutch to take care of the Germans if they wanted to. They did and killed all of the enemy soldiers.

Tanks of the British XXX Corps arrived by midafternoon, rolling down the same narrow streets I had walked upon my arrival in Eindhoven. The armored column halted, the tankers stepped down, and, as Winters told me, hastily built fires and heated water. He was appalled. An entire day behind what was a critical schedule, and they had stopped to brew tea.

That evening Winters took out his ledger (men weren't allowed to keep diaries) and wrote, "This total lack of urgency for the need to push on to the Dommel, the 82nd at Nijmegen and the British at Arnhem leaves us feeling bewildered. I can't understand this lack of concern for their fellow countrymen and the absence of a sense of duty toward the mission."

That evening the 101st bivouacked in the fields north of Eindhoven. Twenty-four hours later, German planes were over Eindhoven, blanketing this beautiful city with bombs while the men of Easy Company watched helplessly from the distance. As he watched the glow of the flames light the horizon, Winters told me, he reflected on the joyous crowds that had greeted them in Eindhoven. The Germans now levied a heavy price on the citizenry, killing 227 and injuring another 800. The next day, there would be no happy Dutch faces or orange flags, just sad expressions of disappointment and betrayal. Of that night, David Webster wrote, "great fires began to burn in Eindhoven."

Easy Company's next objective after Eindhoven was to push farther northeast along Hell's Highway and secure the road as far as Helmond, some eight miles away, so that's what we decided to do as well.

First, however, Marco, who still serves with the Dutch army, took Forrest and myself on a quick tour of the General Major de Ruyter van Steveninckkazerne military base. Built in 1940 by occupying German forces, this sprawling base is now home to a Dutch armored unit whose main weapon is, in a nice touch of irony, the powerful German-built Leopard tank, at least a dozen of which were parked around the grounds.

Then we were off along the modern four-lane Europalaan heading for Nuenen, a historic old town that was home to artist Vincent van Gogh from 1883 until 1885. We finally turned off toward Nuenen, where we looped three-quarters of the way around the traffic circle (Europe and England absolutely *love* traffic circles, or roundabouts) and into Nuenen. Marco drove us along the broad brick and cobblestone Boordseweg through the lovely tree-lined center of town. Driving along, it was hard to imagine war had ever touched this place.

But it had. At one spot, Marco pointed out a former monastery that, in 1944, had been defended by some three hundred Germans. Another landmark, at least for *Band of Brothers* fans, is the Café Schafrath by the town park at the intersection with Pastoor Aldenhuijsenstraat. It was here in real life, and in the film, that the men of Easy—hidden behind a low wall surrounding an outdoor seating area—spotted a hidden German tank and tried to warn the approaching British. The café's appearance remains unchanged.

Cruising slowly around the park, we drove down Parkstraat to visit another Easy Company monument at the corner of Beatrixstraat and an unnamed side street. Not fifty feet away, traffic on the Europalaan whizzed by.

The Easy Company monument here is the typical highly polished black granite slab set into an ivy-covered earthen mound. The plaque bears the usual helmet placed atop a rifle, paratrooper jump wings and Screaming Eagle logo, and a legend, "This monument is dedicated to all who fought and is symbolic for all the sacrifices made for the liberty of Holland." It also bears the inscription "Operation Market Garden" and lists the names of nine men lost by Easy Company during the fighting in Holland in September and October 1944, along with nine gold stars. In truth, of the nine, only seven actually belonged to Easy Company. James "Punchy" Diel had been a member of Easy and had served as acting company first sergeant under Winters in Normandy. After France, Winters recommended Diel for promotion to lieutenant. The promotion came through and Diel was transferred to another company, where he served until he was killed in Holland on September 19.

Another who did not belong to Easy is Rue C. McMahan, who was separated from his unit and fought with Easy until he was killed on October 5.

These men, and others like them who never returned, are what Winters was referring to when he addressed a concern by DeEtta Almon, an Asheville, North Carolina, woman he had met before the war and with whom he kept up a correspondence, over future casualties. "Victory is ours," he wrote, "but the casualties that must be paid is the price that hurts."

This small plaza also contains a memorial to the British forces, placed here by the citizens of Nuenen, as well as two benches dedicated to the British and American soldiers.

It is a small but solemn place.

Easy Company did not arrive in Nuenen by car as we did, but riding the backs of British Cromwell tanks.

Webster wrote that he did not like riding these twenty-seven-ton Cromwells because "tanks drew artillery fire like magnets." He noted that, unlike an American tank column, where the turret of the lead vehicle tracks left and right, ever vigilant against an attack, the Brits were "casual" with all tank guns pointing forward.

As they were approaching Nuenen, a German half-track burst out into the open. The tanks opened fire, hitting it, and as its passengers leaped from the burning vehicle, the GIs cut loose with their weapons.

Winters recalled someone, possibly Private Jack F. Matthews, shouted, "Kraut tanks." Jerking his head up, Winters saw the dark squat hulls of German armor materializing from a distant tree line, moving toward Nuenen. The vehicles belonged to the 107th Panzer Brigade, which was counterattacking from Helmond against the advancing Allied troops. Winters estimated the number of enemy vehicles at about fifty, certainly more than he had ever seen in his life. As they spotted the oncoming American column, the Panzers began fanning out across the field ahead, infantry moving up from behind them.

Winters yelled for everyone to fan out as they entered an adjacent field crisscrossed with irrigation ditches.

Babe Heffron recalled the German tanks came rolling out of woods four hundred yards ahead and cut loose. Working their way through Nuenen, John Martin spotted a German tank hiding in ambush in a hedgerow (from the veranda of the Café Schafrath, as noted above), and, as Babe covered him, ran out to warn the lead British tanker. The Brit could not see the enemy tank and refused to fire in order to avoid unnecessary damage to civilian property. As a result, the German got off the first shot, destroying the British tank.

Easy managed to fight its way through the village, but the enemy fire was too intense, and Winters drew his men back to the relative protection of the town, firing as they withdrew. Private Robert Van Klinken reached for a dropped bazooka when he was hit and thrown to the ground. Winters knelt over the fallen Toccoa man, but Van Klinken was dead. Soon after, Lieutenant Buck Compton fell, hit in the buttocks.

"Suddenly I felt somebody had hit me in the butt with one of those wooden paddles from fraternity hazing days," Compton wrote in his book. "I didn't see it or hear it. It just felt like a swat. The force knocked me off my feet. . . . It didn't really even hurt. The blast banged me and down I went."

Trying to assess his condition, he envisioned part of his spine "blown away." He could still feel his legs, so he knew he wasn't paralyzed. Chuck Grant was the first man to reach him, and he began administering first aid; both men were now exposed to enemy fire. Doc Roe soon arrived.

"Roe was fearless," Compton recalled. "He dumped sulfa powder on my wound to prevent infection. . . . I knew somehow I'd get out. I'm not trying to feign bravado, but I wasn't worried. I didn't think I was going to die."

A single bullet had pierced Compton's buttocks, passing cleanly through, leaving four holes in its wake. Heffron recalled Compton telling him that his girlfriend "always said my big ass would get in the way." Babe said Compton, at six feet two and 240 pounds, feared he was too big for the others to carry out, and told them to leave him and save themselves. Malarkey, Babe, Guarnere, Liebgott, and Toye tried to carry him but it was like "picking up a damn elephant." Winters told me he saw three men, Guarnere, Malarkey, and Toye, rip a door off a nearby barn, load the wounded Compton on it, then drag him rearward.

"He was mad as hell that we were trying to help him," Heffron recalled. "Mad as hell. Cursing us all."

Compton does not remember any of this. In his book, all he recalled was being loaded onto the hood of a vehicle, injured butt exposed, for transport to the rear.

The GIs began taking shelter by the houses of Nuenen, firing at the advancing armored vehicles and accompanying German infantry. A Nazi half-track was hit and its crew shot down as they fled the smoldering wreckage. Incoming machine-gun and rifle slugs pinged off the stone walls of the houses. A tank shell tore through the wall of one house and the building blew apart, the concussion flinging GIs to the ground under a shower of wood and masonry. Men were cut by flying glass.

Babe Heffron recalled tanks burning all around, some of which continued rolling despite being manned by dead crews. He was firing his machine gun from a ditch when a tank rolled toward him. Pinned down by German fire, he was unable to rise and get out of the way as the wrecked tank dropped into the ditch. Heffron still does not know how he escaped unscathed. When he did get out and pull back, he had trouble getting through a hedge until he was yanked to safety by John Sheehy. In being yanked, however, Babe lost his rosary.

"To hell with the rosary beads, let's go," Sheehy told him.

Babe stopped to pick up the helmet that had fallen off his head as he went through the hedge and found his beads in the steel pot. In the book he cowrote with Bill Guarnere after the war, Heffron credited Sheehy with saving his life.

"I never forgot what he did," he wrote.

One who did not make it, and whose name appears on the black stone at Nuenen, was replacement James Miller. Heffron found the young man lying on the ground and tried to hoist him over his shoulder, but Mike Ranney said, "Forget it, he's dead."

Babe recalled that before they went into action, he had tried to calm the young man's fears by telling Miller that he, Heffron, had come through Normandy without a scratch.

"Seeing Miller hit me like a ton of bricks," Babe wrote. "I had to sit there for a minute. I didn't even know his first name. . . . I think about Miller a lot. He was just a kid."

"Punchy" Diel was also among the dead here, and Denver "Bull" Randleman was missing, although he later turned up wounded but alive.

In the end, Easy Company retired toward Eindhoven, leaving a shattered and smoldering town behind.

Nuenen today is a large bustling town, surrounded by lush green fields, with no visible sign of the hell that descended upon it that day, save for the black polished stone that bears the names of James Miller, Robert Van Klinken, and seven other men.

After Nuenen, the 506th moved north, toward Veghel, and so did we, driving along the A50, which has largely replaced the original Hell's Highway. Approaching Veghel and crossing the Zuid-Willemsvaart Canal, I noticed that it was not German armor that threatened these small towns today, but industrial sprawl, as we passed modern building after modern building where fields used to be.

We did not stop at Veghel but continued on to Uden. We swung off the A50 onto the N264, the Lippstadt-Singel, and soon merged onto Veghelsedijk, part of the original Hell's Highway, then drove on into the center of town.

Uden was a prime stop on my tour, for it was here that Easy Company had been split in two when a German counterattack cut the single road that was Hell's Highway. Some of the men were still back at Veghel and the rest, under Winters, here in Uden. Trapped, Winters set up his headquarters in the town, in a private residence owned by the van Oer family. I had a wartime photo of the place and was determined to find it.

On September 22, two days after the fight at Nuenen, Winters and his battle-weary men hauled themselves back onto the trucks, this time headed for Uden. According to the Dutch underground, a large enemy force was moving toward the town and Colonel Strayer dispatched 2nd and 3rd battalions under the command of his executive officer, Lieutenant Colonel Chase, with orders to keep the vital road open at all costs.

Because of a shortage of trucks, the battalion was sent ahead in batches of one platoon per company. Accompanied by a trio of British Shermans, or Fireflys, with a six-pounder replacing the American 76mm, Winters and his men set off.

Clancy Lyall said he did not like riding on British tanks.

"Every day at ten, two, and four they'd stop those sons of bitches, get out of the goddamned tanks and make tea," he told me. "The war's over at those times."

The Germans did not call time-out, so the tanks became stationary targets.

"They'd draw fire," Lyall said. "So I'd get off and walk on their left or right flank. I wasn't going to march behind them or in front of them or on them."

After reaching Uden and driving along Marktstraat, the column halted in the center of town. Winters and Lewis Nixon stepped from their jeep, walked to a nearby church, and climbed into the steeple. The church tower gave them a perfect view of the surrounding terrain and a clear view of German armor as it rolled across the fields to their south, cutting the road and their lifeline to the rest of the army. The thought that ran through Winters's mind, he later told me, was, "The situation is normal. We're surrounded."

Winters then spotted about forty German infantry scurrying over the fields, headed straight for Uden. He ran down the church tower steps and outside, hastily put together a defensive line, and beat back this small assault.

Colonel Chase told Winters to set up a defensive perimeter around Uden, then went back to his command post, "wherever the hell that might be," Winters told me, and it was the last he saw of his superior officer until Hell's Highway was reopened. Winters set up his line, posted the tanks, two at the southern end of town and one to the north, then set up his own CP. For that, he selected a corner house owned by a family named van Oer. They were more than accommodating and moved, without argument, to the cellar. Nor did they complain as Winters's men repositioned rugs and furniture, converting the house into a defensive strongpoint. Winters liked the family and the van Oers were appreciative of Winters's concern for them and their safety. (The van Oers' daughter, Nel, became a longtime pen pal of Winters's sister, Ann.)

The men settled in where they could. Clancy Lyall and his buddies first set up a bivouac in an apple orchard, which, he said, "was the worst thing in the world we could do." The Germans knew they were there and the orchard drew 88 fire with the fuses set to create fearful tree bursts.

The battle rumbled behind them as the attacking Germans ran into the advancing Americans. Winters feared for the fate of the bulk of Easy Company and, unknown to him, they fretted that he and his portion of the company had been annihilated.

Interestingly, amid the fighting all around, Uden remained a pocket of relative tranquility. The only action taken against the men in the town was when Winters and Nixon again ascended into the church tower. Spotted, they were fired on by artillery, forcing them to beat a hasty retreat back down the stairs.

"I don't think our feet touched the steps more than two or three times," he told me, chuckling at the memory.

Winters was constantly on the lookout for a possible attack; the only lapse in discipline during this encirclement occurred when he was checking the outposts and found the one to the north almost unmanned. Investigating, he found the British tank commander in a nearby house having a picnic lunch on the living room floor with a young Dutch girl. When Winters entered the room, the young lieutenant poked his head up and gaily asked, "Are my tanks outside yet, old chap?"

Winters told me he "blew up."

"I set British-American relations back a few years," he said.

Once he got the officer back to his tank, he went in search of his own men, under Harry Welsh. He found them across the street in a tavern, asleep. Welsh was sacked out on the bar, but got up when Winters entered.

"He knew right away that he was wrong," Winters remembered. "I told him, 'Harry, do you think this is a good idea?' And he said, 'No.' And that was it. He knew he had messed up."

Winters chalked the incident up to one of the lapses in judgment Welsh was sometimes subject to.

Luckily, Uden was ignored by the Germans. Winters assumed the Germans knew he and his men were trapped, and figured "they could mop us up later." But later never came. The Germans were eventually thrown back, the road reopened, and the two factions of Easy Company were reunited.

My goal in Uden was to find the van Oer home where Winters had established his HQ. With my wartime photograph in hand, I knew I'd recognize it instantly, thanks to its being on a corner and having a very distinctive triangular brick formation directly over the front door.

Knowing Winters and how he would want his HQ to be centrally located, I asked Marco to cruise through the center of town, figuring it the most likely place. I was right. We drifted slowly along Veghelsedijk, which soon became Marktstraat, when suddenly there it was, directly in front of us.

Except for the fact that the first-floor windows, boarded shut during

Dick Winters's HQ in the van Oer home in Uden, 1944. *U.S. Army*

The van Oer home as it appears today.

the war, are now open, the two-story brick house at the corner of Marktstraat and Kerkstraat looks exactly as it did in 1944. We parked the car on the opposite side of Marktstraat and I got out and crossed the street to stand in front of it. Holding the wartime photo of the house in my hands, I stood there while Marco took a photograph. For me, locating this house was important. My friend Dick Winters had stayed here, and it was every bit as emotional for me as was his early childhood home in Ephrata, Pennsylvania, or his family's home at 418 West End Avenue in Lancaster, or the Barneses' store in Aldbourne.

The van Oer family no longer lives here of course. Instead the building at Kerkstraat 44 is the Uden office of Adecco, a European employment agency.

With a last look at the brick building, we moved on.

Uden is a far cry from the quaint smattering of neat brick homes with fine, orderly gardens depicted in the miniseries. It is a sprawling town that has seen rapid growth, and shows little sign of the war. One reminder, however, is a neatly manicured cemetery located along Burgemeester Burgenstraat by the intersection of Herpenstraat. This is the final resting place of 3,008 British servicemen, killed in the fighting in the days and weeks after they had relieved the 506th.

In the end, Montgomery's Operation Market Garden was a failure. The roadway to the Rhine was never secured, and the British 1st Airborne Division was surrounded and nearly destroyed.

There is blame aplenty for the offensive's miserable showing.

"For Operation Market Garden to work, everything had to be timed to perfection, and everyone needed to move fast," Guarnere later wrote. "There was too much stopping and too much inefficiency, not enough of a push."

Guarnere thinks if the Americans had landed on Arnhem, "we would have gotten the shit beat out of us." But, he added, the GIs "would have fought differently, and we may have succeeded."

He also believes that had General George Patton, and not Bernard Law Montgomery, been in charge of the operation, the outcome might also have changed. Patton, Wild Bill said, would have hit the Germans "like brick."

But that's all speculation. Patton, in fact, would most likely have argued vigorously against such a deep penetration along a single, narrow, and very vulnerable corridor.

Following our stop at Uden, Marco headed his car north toward a little finger of land between the Rhine and Waal rivers known as "the Island."

CHAPTER 8

THE STUFF OF LEGENDS

THE ISLAND

Market Garden was intended to end the war by December 1944 by clearing the way for Allied troops to cross over the Rhine and into the Ruhr Valley, Germany's industrial heartland. But poor planning, difficult terrain, and unexpected heavy opposition caused Montgomery's grandiose, and somewhat ill-conceived, plan to fail in achieving that ultimate objective. As a result, when October arrived, Easy Company was sitting in soggy foxholes on an exposed peninsula five kilometers wide between the Lower Rhine and the Waal rivers known as "the Island."

The ground is mostly flat farmland sprinkled with a few small towns and villages, the two largest being Heteren to the east and Randwijk to the west.

The main road west from Heteren, paralleling the Rhine, is Randwijkse Rijndijk, which runs along the top of a dike twenty feet or more above the surrounding terrain. The slopes of the dike are blanketed with heavy vegetation to avoid erosion, while down below, on flat fields, criss-crossed with irrigation ditches, farmers raise carrots, beets, and cabbages as well as apple and pear trees.

The 506th, temporarily attached to the British XII Corps, had been trucked to the Island on October 2 following British reports that the German 363rd Volksgrenadier Division, which had been badly cut up in Normandy that summer, had been reinforced and was now in the vicinity and awaiting redeployment.

The weather here between the Rhine and the Waal was dreary with a mizzling of rain that coated everything and everybody with a wet sheen, guaranteeing that the ground remained spongy, the air misty, and the men stuck in the foxholes miserable. The GIs made the best of life under these drab conditions. Easy's cook, Joseph P. Dominguez, tried to get hot meals to his fellow troopers before the food got cold, while the men comforted themselves by cursing the war, the Germans, the weather, their draft boards, and anything or anyone else that came to mind. Winters recalled keeping up his spiritual morale by attending church services held in a barn, where, along with the worshippers, cows and horses stood nearby, munching on hay and adding their own special aroma to the worship.

Carwood Lipton recalled the damp misery of this place.

"The weather was terrible there, rainy," he wrote after the war. "We were in foxholes that were pure mud, and we were very uncomfortable. The Germans had observation from across the Rhine because they had the only high ground—what there was of it—and lots of artillery, and whenever we were out during the day, their artillery came in. The worst thing is to be afraid and not be able to do anything about it. The thought of shell fire can get to you. You can't fight back. There's nothing you can do but be there."

Babe Heffron recalled rain and flooding, but he also spoke of rats everywhere and pigs that would gnaw on the dead if they were left unattended.

"You saw them in ditches wherever there were dead bodies," he said.

Second Battalion of the 506th had been ordered to take up position at the village of Zetten, and the next day, October 3, they hiked to the front to relieve the British 43rd Division, which had taken a beating at the hands of the Germans a few days earlier.

Expected to cover a six-mile front with a single regiment, Sink spread the men out with 3rd Battalion anchored on the Waal River, with its line stretching east three miles through Opheusden to Randwijk. There, 2nd Battalion took over, extending its line east two and a half miles, ending near the village of Heteren. First Battalion was held in reserve near Sink's headquarters at Hemmen.

All of the battalions were at half strength or less following the hard fighting along Hell's Highway, so the line was stretched dangerously thin. Strayer deployed 2nd Battalion with Easy on the right, Fox on the left, and Dog in reserve, forcing Winters to cover about a mile and a half of front with 130 men. As mentioned by Lipton, with the Germans holding high ground across the river, movement in the daytime was dangerous, so patrols were dispatched only at night.

So it was that in the predawn darkness of October 5, Sergeant Art Youman led a six-man patrol. The enemy had been spotted near Randwijk and his mission was to see what they were up to and discourage them, if possible, by calling in artillery. The patrol never got to Randwijk, running into an unexpected German unit at an intersection about a mile west of Heteren. In the brief action, four men were hit, the worst being Private James H. Alley Jr., who had been struck by sixteen grenade fragments.

Racing back to company HQ at Zetten, where he found Winters, Private First Class Rod Strohl reported the enemy presence.

"Show me," Winters ordered, indicating his map. Strohl looked at it briefly, then pointed to where Randwijkse Rijndijk, running along the crest of a dike, intersects another road, Renkumse Veerweg, leading from a ferry crossing and factory at the river. That location put the Germans halfway between the company CP and battalion HQ. Winters ordered up his 1st Squad and they hurried into the night. As they drew near to the Crossroad, a machine gun ahead of them suddenly chattered. Instinctively the paratroopers dropped to the ground. The gun continued firing and Winters realized the bullets were not coming at them. He advanced the patrol to within about 250 yards of the sound, then ordered them to hold. Winters scurried to the top of the dike, crossed Randwijkse Rijndijk, and went partway down the reverse slope. Below was a field with a ditch about thirty inches deep running parallel to the road at the base of the dike, and just below him, another, shorter gully, running perpendicular. He returned to the patrol and quickly, silently, brought them across the dike and into the ditch he had spotted. He deployed the men and made a quick one-man reconnaissance, hurrying along the ditch parallel to the dike until he reached the Crossroad, then scaling the dike as far as he dared to see what he was up against.

In the road junction ahead was a cluster of Germans, several in long greatcoats, standing in a knot by the gun, firing into the darkness. Their motives made no sense to Winters. Battalion HQ was in that direction, all right, but was at a farm with a tall arched gateway along the

Schoonderlogt road near Hemmen, almost four miles away. Winters returned to the patrol and filled them in, then led them toward the position he had scouted a few minutes earlier. When they reached the Crossroad, Winters whispered to Sergeant William H. Dukeman Jr. and Corporal Burt Christenson to set up the .30-caliber machine gun and to fire on the MG 42. He then assigned each of his riflemen a particular human target. (Some accounts, including the miniseries, say Winters deployed Skip Muck and Alex Penkala with their 60mm mortar about halfway between the intersection and his fallback position in the short trench, but Winters told me in 2003 that he did not have a mortar with him at this time, nor does he mention a mortar in his memoir. As at Brecourt, I'll let the reader decide.)

Stepping back, he softly told the patrol, "On my command. Ready. Aim. Fire."

The machine gun fired high but the riflemen's aim was true. Seven Germans fell. Three ran. Winters opened up on them, then said, "Fall back!"

The patrol raced back along the trench. Unseen Germans fired at them, their tracer bullets streaking by overhead. Muck and Penkala's precisely dropped mortar rounds, if indeed the mortar was there, helped spoil the Germans' aim as Winters and his men took cover in the small ditch, two hundred yards from the Crossroad. Hunching low in the gully, Winters ordered Boyle to get on the radio and tell Harry Welsh to bring up the rest of 1st Platoon and to grab Lieutenant Frank Reis and have him bring up a section of machine guns from Headquarters Company.

Then they waited.

Following the A50 north, we turned off onto Boterhoeksestraat and entered the village of Heteren. Driving slowly through its quiet streets, Marco turned right onto Steenovenlaan, then left onto Randwijkse Rijndijk. We had only gone about a mile from the town along the Rhine Dike road when we reached the historic Crossroad. In the miniseries, it seems as though this place is in the middle of nowhere, but there are small towns around it, all within easy walking distance, with Heteren being the closest, followed by Randwijk to the west and Zetten about halfway between and a short distance to the south.

Marco turned onto the Renkumse Veerweg road that leads to the river and the town of Renkum just beyond, and parked the car. It was a brisk day, with a stiff, cold wind whipping across the wide-open fields, so Forrest remained in the car. Marco and I got out and walked to the intersection. There stands a large stainless steel star, supported by twin uprights. Attached to the uprights are two copper-colored metal plates describing, in English and in Dutch, the action that unfolded in the field beyond on October 5, 1944.

Seven Germans with a machine gun guarded the intersection directly behind where I stood, firing their weapon at unseen targets. Winters and his men were in a shallow ditch about two hundred yards across the field before me and, unknown to the Americans, a larger German unit, at least company strength, was in the adjacent field behind me and to my right, hidden from fire by the Renkumse Veerweg road.

What came next is the stuff of legends.

Back at company HQ, Winters's call for help set off a flurry of activity. David Webster recalled being rousted by Lieutenant Thomas A. Peacock yelling, "The Krauts have broken through. Everybody get up." At first he thought it one of the excitable Peacock's false alarms, but that illusion was quickly quashed.

Meanwhile, at the Crossroad, as Winters and his men waited for reinforcements, they received some German fire from rifle grenades. One burst nearby and a shard of shrapnel struck Dukeman in the shoulder, knifing through his body and piercing his heart. The Toccoa man fell dead. Paratroopers returned fire and killed the three Germans, who were positioned in a culvert near the intersection.

"Duke was a prince of a man," Winters told me.

"He was a Toccoa man," Guarnere recalled. "No matter what platoon you were in, these men were like family. It affects you, but you can't stop to think about it."

As help arrived, Winters crawled some fifty yards away from the men, needing solitude to ponder his next move. None of his choices were good ones. As he saw the situation, he was in an open field almost devoid of cover with about forty men and an unknown number of the enemy beyond the dike road in front of him. To pull out now meant doing so without the protection of darkness. Worse, once the Germans realized that they had the upper hand, they could easily advance along the top of the dike and put down a killing fire on his vulnerable right flank. On the other hand, even if he could retreat, he wouldn't. If this incursion was the prelude to a German attack, the enemy could roll straight down the road and hit battalion HQ at Hemmen from the rear.

Winters prayed for strength, then rejoined the men where Welsh, Peacock, First Lieutenant Frank Reis, and Sergeant Talbert awaited his instructions. Winters laid out the situation as he saw it, then told them he planned to attack.

Winters decided to send Talbert with 3rd Squad to the right, while Peacock and 1st Squad would attack on the left. Winters would lead 2nd Squad up the middle, while Reis and his machine guns provided suppressing fire. His attack signal would be a smoke grenade.

At this point, Winters told me, he felt as if he was reliving a scene in the movie *All Quiet on the Western Front*, with the men lying in a shallow trench, awaiting the signal to go "over the top."

At the order to fix bayonets, Winters recalled seeing Private First Class Donald B. Hoobler's Adam's apple "making the difficult trip up and down his throat." At Winters's signal, Peacock tossed the smoke grenade. The machine guns blazed.

"Follow me," Winters said.

The men wordlessly rose to their feet and raced forward. Winters later reflected that he had never run so fast in his entire life.

"I was very athletic in school," he later said, "but I ran that two hundred yards faster than I had ever run in my life."

Blood pounding in his ears as he ran, his sole focus was on the dike road ahead, and he unknowingly pulled away from the men behind him. Even the occasional strands of barbed wire, strung at shoe-top height, didn't slow him. Although he tripped a few times, Winters kept his feet and sprinted forward.

Feet pounding, the men followed Winters, each fully expecting a devastating fusillade of German fire at any time. Yet amazingly, the Americans crossed the two hundred yards of open ground unmolested. The Renkumse Veerweg road lost elevation the farther it got from the intersection, so where Winters was about to hit it, the bank was just a few feet high. Reaching the embankment, Winters leaped up on the road and was suddenly confronted with a German sentry directly in front of him. The man was hunched down below the level of the roadway to avoid Reis's machine-gun fire. The two men exchanged surprised looks. In that same fraction of a second, Winters also noticed a mass of Germans to his right, many in greatcoats and wearing backpacks. They, too, had ducked below the embankment for cover.

Jumping back down to his side of the road, Winters slipped a grenade from his belt, yanked out the pin and heaved it at the sentry. The German replied by tossing a potato masher grenade in Winters's direction. As soon as he'd thrown the pineapple, Winters knew he'd goofed. Wary of accidental explosion, he had gotten into the habit of taping down the arming lever, so merely pulling the pin was not going to activate the grenade. Before the German grenade could explode, Winters leaped back up onto the road. The German sentry, awaiting the detonation of the American grenade, which he didn't know would never come, again had his head down. Sensing Winters's presence above him, the man quickly tried to straighten, but Winters, his M1 leveled, fired from the hip. At that distance there was no way he could miss. The German, struck square in the chest, was bowled over backward and fell heavily onto the grassy field.

Even as the man fell, Winters swiveled toward the mass of Germans to his right and, still holding the weapon at his hip, began squeezing the trigger.

As Winters recalled to me years later, everything and everyone except himself seemed to move in slow motion. "I was the only one moving at normal speed," he recalled. "It was so unreal." His men, racing up from the rear, seemed to take forever to arrive. The Germans, being fired on from their unprotected rear and following basic human survival instincts when caught like deer in headlights, began to flee. Winters emptied an entire eight-round clip in their direction, then reloaded, emptied a second clip, and inserted a third.

A few Germans regained their discipline and sent a smattering of fire at the lone American rifleman standing on the roadway, but their aim was spoiled as they were jostled by their panicked comrades hurrying to escape. Then the American was no longer alone. Talbert with his squad suddenly crested the hill smack on the German flank. It was, as

Winters later expressed it, a "duck shoot," as Germans spun and dropped. The GIs could hardly miss.

Confused and being raked by a withering fire, the Germans fled across the open field toward a distant clump of trees near an old wind-mill that stood forlornly on the dike. Clancy Lyall said he and Joe Lieb-gott "went over the dike and into a gulley and captured five prisoners."

As the GIs continued to pour a stream of lead into the backs of the retreating Germans, a shout of warning sounded from one of Winters's men. Another entire company of the enemy, who had evidently been on the other side of the Crossroad, now poured over the dike and straight into the blazing muzzles of the GIs. Without hesitation, the Americans turned their weapons on these new targets. More enemy soldiers fell, while the rest joined their comrades in a confused sprint for the distant woods.

As the enemy pulled back toward another dike road, the Steenord road, about half a mile to the east, Winters hastily consulted his map. Taking the radio from Boyle, he called for artillery fire and requested reinforcements, saying he was up against two German companies with just one platoon. Within minutes the air overhead heralded the arrival of the "incoming mail." As the bursting shells pursued the Germans across the field, Winters lifted his binoculars. The enemy, he noted, seemed to be rallying along the Steenord road, which ran parallel to the one he and his men now firmly held. He glanced again at his map and realized the Germans were trapped between the Rhine and Waal rivers. Their only escape across the Rhine was a ferry crossing, which was at the end of the road Winters now occupied, putting him closer to it than the enemy. He knew he had a great opportunity to cut the Germans off and capture the entire lot.

How much of this area today looks as it did in 1944 is uncertain, but the prime components still exist. The main dike running parallel to the Rhine carrying the road to Randwijk remains, although its steep slopes of 1944 are now gentler, as are the slopes of the Renkumse Veerweg road leading to the river. The town of Renkum lies barely visible beyond the river. A factory still stands at the water's edge near the old ferry cross-ing, just as it did when Easy Company tried to advance on it.

The culvert where Germans fired on Easy Company with rifle grenades, killing Dukeman, remains, as does the drainage ditch at the base of the dike along which Winters and his men approached the Crossroad when they fired on the enemy machine gun.

On the German side of the Crossroad, half a dozen cattle lazily grazed in the pasture where the SS men were hunched down until Winters and his troopers poured lead on them. The peaceful meadow bears no sign of the shell craters from the Allied artillery support Winters called in.

Gone also is the windmill Winters told me about, and which was included in the miniseries version of the fight and the hand-drawn map he made for me. My guess is it stood near a farm about a quarter mile to the east toward Heteren.

Probably the biggest change is the Crossroad itself. The meeting of Randwijkse Rijndijk and Renkumse Veerweg, which in 1944 was a straight T intersection, has been reconfigured over the years and now forms a Y.

Walking through a farm gate and out onto the field across which Easy Company charged that day, I was troubled by the presence of a small dike about four feet in height that cuts across the meadow at a right angle from Renkumse Veerweg to approximately Easy Company's attack position. Marco said it's believed this small dike was present at the time, and that Easy Company originally hid behind it prior to their charge, rather than the small ditch I have described above or as shown in the miniseries. However, when Dick Winters and I discussed this fight in our interviews in 2003, he specifically mentioned being in a ditch, not behind a dike. Nor does he mention a dike in his own memoirs, writing, "We were in a shallow ditch." And last, as noted above, during our extensive discussions, he drew for me a map, albeit a crude one, on which he marked his position, the Germans', the roads and the windmill. No mention was made of the small dike.

And if it had been there, there would have been no need for him to attack across the open field. He and his men could have advanced along the reverse side of the small dike, putting it between them and the Germans.

Like the controversy at Brecourt Manor in Normandy—was the fourth gun turned or pointed straight ahead?—here at the Crossroad I

The marker denoting the Crossroad fight. Winters and his men charged across the field beyond the star, routing two companies of SS troops, October 5, 1944.

was confronted with more inconsistencies, specifically the small dike, and whether Winters had mortars in his initial attack or not. I did not charge across this field with Easy Company on October 5, 1944. But what I have read and heard has come from those who did, and it is on their words that I base my conclusions.

The Crossroad fight is similar to Brecourt in that, at Brecourt, after Winters knocked out the guns, he knew he had accomplished his mission and won a victory, and refused to push his luck even though his men, their bloodlust up, wanted to push on. Here at the Crossroad, Winters had also won a victory, routing two German companies with an inferior number of troops.

"They never should have let me attack," Winters told me, satisfaction still in his voice sixty years later. "All I can think is they had bad leadership."

However, unlike Brecourt, here at the Island Winters departed from his usual caution and uncharacteristically tried to push his advantage further, almost coming to grief.

*   *   *

Shortly after the fight at the Crossroad, Fox Company arrived. Reinforced, resupplied, and rested, Winters began advancing along the Renkumse Veerweg, at the end of which was a factory and the ferry crossing. Webster wrote that Hoobler told him Winters was going to attack the factory because "that's where the Krauts are coming from."

"Captain Winters brought the rest of the men across the road and moved us through the gate and into a ditch that paralleled the dike," he wrote. "We lay down and began to wait."

To cover the move, Winters set up a base of fire with his machine guns then leapfrogged his men, platoon by platoon, toward the river. As he closed the distance on the Rhine, Winters could look across the river and see the rooftops of the village of Renkum. Another two hundred yards and they'd have both the factory and the ferry crossing.

Without warning the air above them whooshed with the sound of incoming shells that burst around the advancing men. Unseen until they had made their deadly presence known, German artillery spotters on the high ground beyond the river, Winters later said, had been "watching this whole cockeyed thing" from the time he'd driven the enemy from the Crossroad until he advanced on the ferry.

To add to his woes, the German infantry Winters had hoped to trap were now advancing on his right flank. In a reversal of fortunes, Winters discovered that he was the one now in danger of being cut off. It was time to get out.

"There was no front and no rear," Webster wrote. "From the windmill and the hills beyond the Rhine, the Germans had the observation on us. They laid down a string of mortar and artillery shells in the fields and ditches around us, coming closer and closer and closer. I wanted to get up and run all the way back to our village."

Reversing his strategy, Winters leapfrogged his men back along the road the way they had come. All went smoothly until the GIs regained the Crossroad, where the German fire suddenly intensified. The Germans, he now discovered, had the T road zeroed in and the only reason they had not fired earlier was out of fear of hitting their own men.

Winters now called in artillery support of his own.

The Germans "bombed the hell out of us," Guarnere recalled. The ground was exploding and men were yelling for medics.

"I got to the dike just as Leo Boyle got hit and fell flat on his face," Wild Bill said.

Shrapnel had struck the back of Boyle's leg, gashing his thigh. Guarnere and Burt Christenson tore open Boyle's pants and sprinkled his wound with sulfa powder until medics took over.

As shells rained down, Webster recalled crawling over the bloodied body of a German in a ditch that ended at a hedge. He said Hoobler scaled a small rise, looked over and yelled, "Krauts! Jesus Christ, Krauts." John Martin, Webster, and another man ran toward the hedge to join the firefight that erupted when an enemy machine gun fired a short burst. Webster was hit in the leg, yelling, "They got me." He later regretted the choice of words, thinking he'd seen too many movies. Doc Roe eventually patched him up and sent him limping off to Randwijk.

Clancy Lyall recalled the attack, saying, "We got about halfway across that field when the Germans opened up and we come running back. When we got back, Winters said, 'Aw, shit.' That's the first time I ever heard the man cuss."

In all, Winters suffered twenty-two wounded in this encounter, including Boyle, who would recover, but whose war was over. Winters said he had lost "a very good and loyal friend."

Clancy Lyall also "got nicked" by shrapnel.

When the shelling finally stopped, Winters asked Lewis Nixon for a drink from his canteen. As he took a swig, he noticed his hand was shaking uncontrollably.

"That had never happened to me before," he told me in 2004.

For the rest of his life, he would consider October 5, 1944, the best single day in Easy Company's history. With just thirty-five men, they had attacked across two hundred yards of open ground and routed two companies of SS infantry, about three hundred men. In the entire fight, they had suffered twenty-two wounded and one killed, in exchange for which the GIs had killed about fifty enemy soldiers, wounded an unknown number of others, and captured eleven.

"This action by E Company is, in my estimation, the highlight of all E Company accounts for the entire war," Winters wrote a few years later.

"This action on 5 October demonstrated E Company's overall superiority of every man, of every phase of infantry tactics: patrol, defense, attack under a base of fire, withdrawal and, above all, superior marksmanship with rifles, machine gun and mortar fire. All this was done against superior forces, who had an advantage of 10–1 in manpower, plus the enemy had excellent observation for artillery and mortar support."

Colonel Sink also noted the accomplishment. Four days later, he promoted Winters to executive officer of 2nd Battalion and put Lieutenant Frederick T. "Moose" Heyliger in command of Easy Company. And on October 27, Sink issued a unit citation to Easy Company commending them "for their daring and aggressive spirit and sound tactical ability."

Winters hated leaving the company, but also relished the opportunity to move up to battalion level.

"Leaving Easy Company was the hardest thing I had done in my life," he wrote. "Life in an infantry company is extremely intimate and the result is that men share their collective experiences each and every day."

He was proud of what Easy Company had become, a tough, experienced outfit able to get done any job assigned to it. But he also recognized that those accomplishments were not his doing alone.

"I was fortunate enough to have been part of it," he recalled. "But the cohesion that existed in the company was hardly the result of my leadership. The company belonged to the men—the officers were merely the caretakers."

The company did not like to see Winters go.

"The men were pretty upset when they found out we were losing Winters," Guarnere wrote. "The CO can make or break a company. He can get men killed or keep them alive."

However, the men cheered up at the news of Heyliger's appointment.

Forrest Guth, who never served under Heyliger because he was still hospitalized with his back injury, knew Moose and called him "a good man, down-to-earth."

"We all liked Moose," Guarnere said. "He was a good man, a good officer, always out there in the field with us, and made good decisions."

* * *

Easy Company only went on one mission under Moose Heyliger, and that was to ferry British paratroopers stranded on the wrong side of the Rhine when Operation Market Garden sputtered out. One assignment, but they made two attempts.

On the night of October 22–23, Heyliger and twenty-three men attempted a crossing just west of Heteren and the modern-day bridge that spans the river, just under a mile east of the Crossroad. The river here is fairly narrow and looks deceptively calm. On the far side, a gently sloping shore leads up to an open plain that stretches about sixty yards before meeting a woods.

"They made their first attempt to cross over here," Marco told us as he stopped his car on the Randwijkse Rijndijk. "But the current was too strong and they were forced to come back."

Their next attempt the following night was farther to the west near Randwijk, where a ferry crossing exists today and the Veerweg road meets the Lower Rhine. This time they made it across and brought back 125 grateful Tommies.

A week later, on October 31, Easy Company lost its commander when Heyliger and Winters, walking along a railroad track while on an inspection tour of the company, ran into a nervous sentry.

The tour was Winters's idea. As battalion executive officer, he told me he had no decision-making responsibility, but could only make recommendations. He found life on the battalion level "extremely boring" and was unable to use the skills and instincts he had honed to a razor sharpness as a combat leader. Restless to do something—anything—other than sit on his behind at battalion headquarters, on the afternoon of October 31 he called Heyliger and suggested an inspection tour of the company's outposts.

They began their tour at 2100 hours, 9:00 p.m., and headed for 1st Platoon and Harry Welsh, whose HQ was in a barn near the railroad track that cut through this sector. There was a great deal of enemy activity in the vicinity, so Winters called ahead to Welsh to let him know they were coming. Welsh neglected to relay the information to his sentries. As Winters and Heyliger drew near, walking along a dirt path, a voice called out "Halt."

"I saw him take a deep breath and I thought, 'My God, he's forgotten the password,'" Winters told me. "Then he started to say his name, 'It's Moo . . .'"

The sentry cut loose with three quick rounds.

"I can still see the muzzle flashes winking not fifteen yards away," Winters recalled. "Out of instinct, I dropped and rolled to my left into a ditch."

Heyliger wasn't as lucky. Hit twice, once in the right shoulder and again in the left calf, he moaned and dropped heavily. Welsh arrived almost immediately and assisted Winters in bandaging Heyliger as best they could, especially his grievous leg wound. They also jabbed him with morphine. Heyliger was transferred to a hospital and would remain hospitalized until 1947, although he would suffer from the wound for the rest of his life.

"To the day he died over half a century later," Winters wrote, "he still could not recall the password."

As for the sentry who shot Heyliger, Winters transferred him from the company.

"He was only doing his job," Winters recalled. "But it was apparent that he was very nervous as we approached the outpost. Normally a sentry on the outpost would duck down and hope to recognize a silhouette before commencing fire. The trooper who shot Heyliger, and whose name I don't care to remember, was obviously scared to death. He failed to take any precautions before he opened fire."

Winters said he didn't "know nor care" where the man ended up after the transfer.

In 2004 I asked Dick who the sentry was. He told me, "I tried to forget it, and I've done so convincingly."

As a replacement for Heyliger, Winters told me he was "blessed" with First Lieutenant Norman S. Dike. Winters called Dike "an inexperienced officer from division staff whom his superiors felt needed frontline duty." As was his custom, Winters interviewed all incoming officers—and enlisted men when time allowed—taking the measure of the man in order to get a feel for his strengths and weaknesses. A Yale graduate, Dike came from the well-to-do family of a New York attorney. He was, Winters recalled, "very well spoken" with a "military bearing that was deceiving." This, Winters felt, gave Dike the air of a man who

Dick Winters by the Schoonderlogt Arch, October 1944. *U.S. Army*

believed he had leadership skills far beyond what he actually possessed. Dike did not impress Winters as a combat commander capable of making quick decisions, but he was stuck with him.

The men came to feel the same way. Wild Bill Guarnere called Dike "a real stiff, military-career type, completely inexperienced in combat."

As he was never around when the action started, they soon dubbed him Foxhole Norman.

"We learned right away Dike wasn't a good soldier, let alone a good leader," Guarnere wrote.

On November 25, the 101st Airborne was finally relieved after seventy-two straight days on the line. Their stay in Holland cost the 506th 804 casualties, including 176 killed, 565 wounded, and 63 missing out of 181 officers and 2,429 enlisted men.

The division was loaded onto trucks headed for a rest area at Mourmelon-le-Grand, France, and men began to compute how much leave time they had accumulated. Winters guessed he had forty-five days coming. He was looking forward to a long, well-earned, period of rest.

In that fashion, they left Holland.

Our last stop in Holland was Colonel Strayer's 2nd Battalion headquarters in a farmhouse with an imposing brick arch at Schoonderlogt, west of the village of Elst, and probably not too far from where Heyliger was shot.

Leaving Heteren, we drove south on the N837 (Archterstraat), then turned right onto Uilenburgsestraat. After about two miles, where the road intersects Weteringsewal, it becomes Logtsestraat. The farmhouse, cream-colored with a red-tiled roof and a small cupola in the center, the whole bisected by the brick arch, is about a mile farther along, on the left.

Anyone who knows anything about Easy Company and the *Band of Brothers* has seen the photo of Dick Winters standing heroically in front of this archway, head bare, his helmet tucked under his left arm, his determined gaze focused straight ahead. Featuring a rising sun above the words "Landgoed Schoonderlogt"—basically meaning property belonging to the Schoonderlogt family—and highlighted in gold paint on a white stone slab, this distinctive arch will forever be linked to Dick Winters.

Marco stopped the car, and he and I got out and walked along the brick lane toward the arch. I have a copy of the 1944 photo of Winters in front of the arch that Dick gave me in 2003, and I recall seeing a

The Schoonderlogt Arch as it appears today.

photo of a much older, but no less heroic-looking, Dick Winters standing in front of this arch around 1988, as he stepped back in time.

Now, on this wind-blown autumn day, with brown leaves lining the lane like snowdrifts against the hedges, which were themselves a blend of greens, browns, and yellows, I needed to commemorate my own visit to this site. Handing my camera to Marco, I placed myself approximately where Dick had stood as my guide snapped off two shots.

My visit to Holland now complete, we departed.

CHAPTER **9**

★

"NUTS"

BASTOGNE

Chronologically, Bastogne was not the next destination for the men of Easy Company after Normandy in 1944, but for the sake of convenience it was the next stop for Forrest Guth and me in 2008, since our departure seven days hence would be from Amsterdam. The drive across northern France and into Belgium on November 7 was the longest we would have on this trip, but I consoled myself with the knowledge that every city and town we passed, from Caen and Antwerp, to the smallest village, had trembled under the caterpillar treads of German and Allied tanks, and felt the tread of boots and quite likely heard the whine of bullets.

We made the four-hundred-plus-mile trip in great time and arrived in the center of Bastogne by early afternoon. This was Place McAuliffe, named for General Anthony C. McAuliffe, the 101st Airborne's artillery commander, placed in temporary charge of the entire division while Maxwell Taylor was on leave in the States. Taylor had been ordered to Washington, D.C., by General George C. Marshall, President Roosevelt's chief of staff, to discuss airborne operations and their effect in battle. Ordinarily, command would have fallen to Brigadier General Gerald J. Higgins, Taylor's executive officer, but he too was away, back in London, lecturing new troops on the lessons learned in combat. In the absence of both, command of the division fell to McAuliffe, who was thus the man on the spot when the Screaming Eagles would face their most perilous trial by fire.

After parking the car in Place McAuliffe's huge plaza, I got out and looked around, awestruck. It was a world apart from the photos I am used to seeing of this place, photos that depict the plaza strewn with chunks of masonry, wrecked and burnt-out vehicles, trucks, jeeps, a tank, and all ringed by ruined buildings hollowed out by bombs and artillery.

Today Bastogne is home to about 14,500 people, a far cry from the just over 4,000 who lived here in 1944. Looking around, there is no indication of that devastation to be seen. The entire square is bounded by stores, gift shops, cafés, restaurants, and hotels, many housed in the original, reconstructed buildings, and all adorned with neon lights and signs advertising everything from food items like pizza, burgers, gourmet sandwiches, and even buffalo steak to clothing, candy, Belgian chocolate, and gifts. From the chic to the tacky, it's all here.

Forrest had the same recollections of this plaza as I, only his memory was not from black-and-white photographs, but firsthand experience.

"I helped bring in the wounded," he told me. "And we came down here in a jeep to pick up some food one time. And every time we came, the town was more beat up."

On the southern side of the square sits the circular glass and wood Bastogne Visitors Center.

"Last time I was here," Forrest said, "they had a large cardboard cutout of me standing in there. I wonder what happened to it."

Adjacent to the visitors center sits an American jeep and a Sherman tank, nicknamed "Barracuda." This thirty-ton armored beast had seen action in 1944, and came away the worse for it. Knocked out in December 1944, its steel skin bears the wounds of two German armor-piercing rounds, one in the skirting above the treads on the left side, which possibly entered the crew cabin, a tanker's worst nightmare, and one in the rear, doubtless striking the powerful Continental R975 engine. A plaque tells anyone interested that the tank is symbolic and "recalls the sacrifice of all the fighters for the liberation of Bastogne and Belgium." Between the jeep and the Barracuda is a bust of McAuliffe perched atop a pedestal emblazoned with the Screaming Eagle emblem, forever watching over the city he so stubbornly defended.

Our accommodations here would be in the Collins Hotel on the northern flank of the square, overlooking the plaza. After checking in, Forrest and I prepared for the third leg of our journey into the past.

Our guide here was Reg Jans, who owns BB Tours and who specializes in the fighting around Bastogne and the northern shoulder of the Bulge. So after Forrest and I were settled, I called Reg. He happened to be in Bastogne and we met at my car in Place McAuliffe. We strolled to the nearby Le Nut's café for coffee and a get-acquainted meeting. (References to General McAuliffe's reply to the Germans for his division's surrender, "Nuts," are easy to find in this town.)

The Belgian-born Jans told us he had always had a keen interest in the Battle of the Bulge and studied it intensely, walking the battlegrounds every chance he could. He became quite literate on the subject and people soon began asking him to lead them on tours.

"For a while I was taking people out almost every weekend," Reg told me. "So I decided to start doing it semiprofessionally and see how it goes."

Thus far, it has kept him busy.

Reg said he welcomes tour inquiries, but only from serious-minded visitors. He'd rather avoid those with little interest other than just looking for ways to kill an afternoon.

Unlike Paul Woodadge, Reg had never met Forrest and the two hit it off well.

Here in Bastogne we soon linked up with Marco Kilian and Frank Slegers, whom I discussed in the Holland chapters, and whose shop, Militaria Bastogne, was in Place McAuliffe, almost diagonal from our hotel. We were also joined by several *Band of Brothers* fans who traveled from neighbouring Holland to accompany us throughout this portion of our journey. Ronald Ooms, Jeroen van Can, Frank Gubbels, and Linda Cautaert and her husband, Johan Van den Eede, are regulars on the Wild Bill Guarnere Web site, which is how word spread that Forrest and I would be visiting the area. The same goes for BK Masterson, a San Francisco woman who was about a week into a solo tour that would cover the entire Battle of the Bulge. BK arranged her Bastogne segment to coincide with our trip, even checking into the same hotel.

That evening we all dined at Leo's on rue du Vivier, followed by a stopover at Le Nut's for a fine local beer and to give Forrest a chance to puff on a cigar. This beer and stogie stop before turning in would become a nightly ritual during our stay in Bastogne.

* * *

After their battles in Normandy and a rest and refit in England, Easy Company and the 101st jumped into Holland on September 17, 1944. In action for seventy-three days, the division was pulled from the line and sent to the rear, taking up residence at a former French army base at Mourmelon-le-Grand. To men who had just spent weeks living in waterlogged foxholes in Holland, Mourmelon was like heaven. The former army post featured low stucco barracks that were warm and dry. Perhaps best of all were the indoor toilet facilities, meaning the men no longer had to shiver in the cold while answering the call of nature.

Weapons and equipment were turned in for repair and maintenance and the weary men rejoiced upon the news that training would be limited to close-order drill and calisthenics. Kitchens served up hot food and plenty of it, and gripe as they may about army chow, it was still better than living out of a can, as the men had done for more than two months.

Yet more than hot food, real beds, USO shows, and indoor crappers, Mourmelon offered the war-weary troopers recreation and a chance to unwind. Red Cross clubs were established and athletic equipment issued. Regiments formed football teams and set up game schedules. The men of the "Five-oh-Sinks" and the paratroopers of the 502nd scheduled a Champagne Bowl to be played in Reims on Christmas Day, and bets were already being laid down.

Buck Compton, wounded in the butt in Holland, rejoined Easy. He was looking forward to the Champagne Bowl.

Forrest Guth also returned to Easy, having recovered from his back injury.

Replacements like Chicago-born Herbert J. Suerth arrived in late November.

"Actually, I was in the 101st before they left for Holland," he said during an interview in 2009. "I volunteered for the airborne and went to jump school at Chilton Foliat around the middle of August. Of course, of all things, Captain Sobel was our jump school commander."

He had no idea who Sobel was and had only seen him once. But his presence was felt and his sternness was handed down through his trainers.

"Jump school is run by sergeants, and they're handpicked to be diabolical," Suerth recalled. "And they were. All of them were combat vets, and they wanted to eliminate anyone who was weak-kneed."

He had made three of his five qualification jumps before Operation Market Garden kicked off. Then the weather turned sour and the final two jumps occurred after September 17.

"So we watched all of the planes go over to Holland on a gorgeous, sunny Sunday morning," he said.

He "sat in England" until around Thanksgiving, before being flown to the Continent. However, bad weather forced the plane to return, but back in England, the weather was no better.

"For a while, we had no place to land, and we were getting low on fuel," he said. "It was sort of hairy. We had no parachutes either since we were just passengers."

Finally joining the division at Mourmelon, he was assigned to Easy Company's 3rd Platoon, with Forrest Guth, Walter Gordon, and Paul Rogers. The platoon was led by Lieutenant Ed Shames.

"My squad was led by Shifty Powers," Herb said.

Suerth said he did not feel the alienation some replacements felt when being thrust in among a company of combat veterans.

"I don't remember any of that," he said. "I was bunked next to Earl McLung, and I didn't experience that at all. Maybe I was just ignorant or thick-skinned or whatever you want to call it."

He recalled wanting to attend a large midnight mass in December, just before shipping out to Bastogne, that was to be held in Reims Cathedral, but he had no money.

"I hadn't been paid in months, moving around as I was, and I said to McLung, 'God, Mac, I don't have a cent,' and he gave me, maybe, two thousand francs, which I still owe him to this day," he told me.

Dick Winters took this time to visit Paris, checking into a Red Cross hotel because it was less expensive.

Curiosity lured Winters into the Paris Follies. The smoke-filled, raucous club was packed, he recalled, and he had difficulty getting a seat, but admittedly enjoyed the show.

On his second day of playing *An American in Paris*, Winters heard a voice call his name. He turned to find Private James Alley, who had been wounded by seventeen pieces of grenade shrapnel at the Island in Holland on October 5. Recovered now and ready to return to duty, Alley had been hoping to find someone who could tell him where Easy was billeted. Winters helped Alley arrange transportation.

Eventually, though, even the City of Lights bored the socially reserved Winters. Deciding to spend his last night of leave alone, he boarded the Paris Metro in the center of the city, intending to ride it to the end of the line and back. Unfortunately, when the train reached the outskirts of Paris and he was asked to step off, Winters realized he'd taken the last train of the night. He would have to walk back to his hotel.

Lost in thought, Winters strolled pensively through the city along the Left Bank, next to the Seine, passing Notre Dame Cathedral. Traffic, much of it military, moved around the Arc de Triomphe and lights winked on the steel framework of the Eiffel Tower. After four years of Nazi occupation, the City of Lights had reawakened.

"I spent the rest of the night walking through Paris," Winters told me sixty years later. "It was the best medicine that I could have had. I could relax and it gave me a chance to reflect and be alone."

Back in camp Winters, who had been elevated by Sink to battalion executive officer in October, was informed by Colonel Strayer that he was temporarily being placed in command of 2nd Battalion. Strayer was off to London to attend the wedding of British Colonel David Doby, whom he had befriended in Holland after Easy Company assisted in the rescue of British paratroopers stranded across the Rhine in the failed Market Garden operation.

Strayer's departure meant Winters and Lewis Nixon were the sole battalion officers remaining in camp. Nixon spent much of this time quenching his thirst for Vat 69, his beverage of preference and of which he had a never-ending supply, while Winters caught up on letter writing. On December 13 he wrote DeEtta Almon that he had a piece of white parachute silk he planned to send her as a Christmas present to be used as a scarf. Apologizing that it would be late, he added, possibly contemplating being shipped to the Pacific after the war in Europe ended, "Next year, it'll be a grass skirt so don't complain."

He concluded by saying he was going to spend some time reading his Bible.

"Nothing like a war to make a believer out of me," he told her.

Four days later, on December 17, a messenger entered 2nd Battalion HQ. He handed Winters a memo, saluted, and left. Winters looked at the paper. It informed him that the Germans had broken through in the Ardennes, and that the division was being put on alert for a move.

This was bad news for the company, not just because of what it portended, but also for the fact that most of the men's equipment, sent for repair, had not yet returned. Worse, the men had no winter clothes, and there was little ammo in camp. But none of that mattered now, and Winters knew it. He ordered the men to get ready.

"Here we go again," Winters said.

The next day, December 18, they were ordered up.

"In Mourmelon, we were to refit, get new clothes, new equipment, hot food," Clancy Lyall said. "We didn't get to do hardly any of that because the fighting in the Bulge broke out on the sixteenth."

"The division gathered every available truck in the area to take us to Bastogne," Forrest told me. "There were hundreds of them."

There were, in fact, 380 "cattle cars," as Lyall called them, hastily assembled from all over. Babe said the trucks belonged to the famed Red Ball Express and that he sat up front with the driver, a black soldier who also hailed from Philadelphia, and they chatted during the trip, while overhead, Joe Toye manned a .30-caliber machine gun mounted on a ring turret.

Lugging their weapons and personal gear, the men were shoehorned into the trucks, consuming every inch of available space. The convoy stretched for ten miles as it relentlessly rolled northeastward all that day. In many of the jam-packed trucks, the air took on the stench of vomit as men in the bouncing, seemingly springless trucks succumbed to motion sickness and puked into their steel helmets. Periodically, the helmets were passed to the rear and the contents dumped out over the tailgate.

Herb Suerth recalled the "miserable ride" to Bastogne, "standing up for maybe twelve or fourteen hours in a truck." It was, he recalled, "cold as hell and wet."

"It was about as bad weather as I've ever been out in for a long period of time," he said.

The closer the convoy moved toward the front, the slower the progress became as the unpaved roads were increasingly clogged with traffic, some heading east, but more—too much more, Winters thought—

heading west. These latter were refugees of the previous three days' fighting, units battered under the unexpected and vicious German onslaught.

As the convoy rolled deeper into Belgium, headlights were doused. Ahead, the distant rumble of artillery and the dazzling wink of cannon muzzle flashes grew louder and brighter. Heffron said his driver became more nervous with every mile.

"He knew what we were heading into and wanted to drop us and get the hell out," Babe recalled.

Then the trucks screeched to a halt along a lonely road in a tiny farm village called Mande-Saint-Etienne, and the trucks, or as Suerth described them, "grain carriers," emptied.

"It was nighttime, and I looked around," Lieutenant Jack Foley, a replacement officer with Easy's 1st Platoon, later recalled. "I'm making my first nighttime jump four feet off the ground off the end of a ten-ton truck."

Buck Compton said he could feel the temperature dropping. Fortunately there was no snow, but the "feel" was in the air. Compton wore a new woolen overcoat, but had no other winter gear. His boots were the regular leather ones in which one's "feet got wet and stayed wet," he said. Like many others, he had no long underwear or wool socks. Luckily, he did have a new lined sleeping bag.

Buck ordered an ammo check among his men. Don Malarkey announced that he had one spare clip and a couple of grenades. Compton recalled it was "a hell of a way to jump into a fight." Lacking an entrenching tool, Malarkey spotted a tank sitting nearby with an engineering shovel attached to it. He quickly helped himself, and thus carried an M1 and a shovel "into combat as my main weapons."

Luckily, the men were able to scrounge extra ammo and grenades from various sources along the way. One such source was Second Lieutenant George C. Rice, supply officer for Combat Command B, 10th Armored Division, who drove up in a jeep loaded down with boxes of ammo. Rice was attached to Team Desobry, named for the group's leader, Major William Desobry. Like the 101st, this contingent of men and tanks had been sent forward to help stem the German tide. Hearing the advancing paratroopers were ill-supplied, Rice and another man raced to an ammo dump in the village of Foy and, piling all the ammo boxes they could carry into a purloined jeep and a deuce-and-a-half truck, drove to meet the incoming Screaming Eagles. Stopping along their line of march, Rice tossed his precious cargo out to the men. Soldiers scrambled, some on hands and knees, to retrieve M1 clips and grenades as if they were golden nuggets.

Then the Screaming Eagles shuffled away in the direction of Bastogne and everlasting glory.

"We were rushed by truck to a town none of us had ever heard of, but it was a place we'd all remember for the rest of our lives," Forrest Guth told me.

As it was for the men of Easy Company, Mande-Saint-Etienne was our first stop. Reg parked his car on the same road where the 506th had jumped down from the truck beds at four a.m. on that dark, frosty December 19 morning.

Some four hundred trucks clogged this road between where we now stood and the nearby village of Champs. Except for the fact that this paved road was a one-lane dirt thoroughfare at the time, little else has changed. Still, it is difficult for men like Forrest to pick out things they remember.

"It's very hard for veterans to recognize this place, because by the time they got out of the trucks, there was no snow yet, but it was very foggy," Reg told us. "They could hardly see the steeple of the church because of the fog."

Tiny Mande-Saint-Etienne had become an assembly area for the 501st, 502nd, 506th, and 327th Glider regiments and divisional headquarters, as the Screaming Eagles prepared to establish a defensive ring around the beleaguered crossroad town of Bastogne. The 326th Medical Battalion began setting up a field hospital a mile away at a crossroad called locally Barriere Hinck, near the little hamlet of Sainte-Ode, which would be overrun later that same day as the German wave washed around the 101st.

"The Germans killed almost everybody," Forrest recalled.

Wounded were shot in their beds and a number of officers were taken prisoner, including Major Desobry, who had been hit at Noville earlier that day.

It was across these fields, partway between Mande-Saint-Etienne and Champs, where, during the siege, eighteen tanks of the German 15th Panzer Division attacked in an attempt to pierce the 101st Airborne's ring around Bastogne. Withering American fire stopped the infantry support, but the tanks continued on until most were left smoldering across the landscape. A few broke through to the road before being destroyed. The last tank was knocked out in the center of Champs.

Now a quiet hamlet with sturdy farmhouses of stone, large stone barns, well-worn wooden sheds with rusted tin roofs, and fat cattle who watched us contentedly from a roadside meadow, it is impossible to comprehend the confusion and concern that was felt here by so many men so long ago.

From this spot, Bastogne is just under five miles to the west, so after stretching their legs following the long ride and relieving themselves, the men of the 506th silently pondered their future as the lightning flashes and dull drum roll of artillery fire rippled across these now serene fields.

Adjusting the packs on their backs, gripping their weapons and wishing they had warmer clothes and more ammo, the long columns of men began heading for Bastogne.

As they tramped through the night, the eastern sky glowed a dull red and the crumping of artillery assaulting their ears grew ever louder. The ground began to vibrate from the concussion. Buck Compton said, "You couldn't make it out in the dark, other than seeing a lot of fire and explosions."

Entering Bastogne in combat intervals—columns of two on either side of the road—the 506th tramped along rue de la Roche, turning left onto the rue Pierre Thomas. The town was dark, silent, brooding. Germans had marched through Bastogne in 1914 and again in 1940. They had retreated through it two months earlier, and now they were coming back again.

Few citizens were visible on the streets as the 101st slogged along, although some of those who were offered the GIs coffee. The strong, hot joe was gratefully accepted as the men, chilled by the night, plodded toward their defensive position to the northeast near the town of Foy some three miles away in the direction of the thundering battle.

As Forrest had related to me when we first reached Bastogne, the town had been hard hit by the battle now raging. Bill Guarnere recalled the "sad sight" of the "beautiful town in shambles."

But as they tramped along rue Pierre Thomas, an even more disconcerting sight reached their eyes: hordes of American troops, many weaponless, all looking dispirited, were flooding toward them and away from the fight.

Guarnere remembered, "As we advanced, infantry troops were running toward us, scared as can be."

Suerth recalled, "That was one of the most realistic scenes in the HBO series. I can still remember that."

The retreating soldiers became another source of ammo for the 101st, as the refugees dropped their bandoliers onto a rapidly growing pile. Wild Bill said, "So as we walked past, we fished through it and grabbed whatever we could carry." Top priority was given to weapons, ammo and grenades, while such items as food and clothing were secondary.

"When your hands were full, you threw what ammo you found in someone else's hands," Guarnere said.

Buck Compton later wrote, "It's strange when you're heading to fight a battle to see other men—men in the same army as you—walking the other way."

He said the advancing paratroopers were told the Germans were merciless, that they came out of nowhere and there was no way the GIs could win.

Babe Heffron said the men were members of the 28th Division, the Keystone Division, or, because of the red Keystone patch on their shoulders, the Bloody Bucket (although they may also have been men of the 10th Armored Division). Tough combat veterans who had suffered through the hell of the Huertgen Forest, they had been sent to this "quiet zone" outside of Bastogne to rest, refit, and receive replacements. Like two other divisions on this Ghost Front, including the 99th and the 106th, both "green" units untested in battle, the 28th was totally unprepared for the power of the German counteroffensive. In fact, two entire infantry regiments of the 106th had been overrun and captured. Now many of these defeated survivors had no weapons and no helmets, Heffron recalled. "They threw everything down."

Not just that, but the more terrified of the men urged the 101st not to go forward, that the Germans would kill them, warning "there's a million of them."

The advancing 506th remained steadfast. All they saw was a herd of Americans fleeing the front in a state of panic. Winters told me he felt ashamed for them as well as himself.

"They told us, 'They'll kill you. They'll murder you. Get out while you can,'" he told me. Yet, the resolve of his men never wavered.

"I was proud of them for that," Winters recalled. "We gave them no recognition. We just went about doing what we'd been sent there to do."

All of this passed in review through my mind as Reg, Forrest, and I stood at the intersection of rue de la Roche and rue Pierre Thomas, where Easy turned that corner and headed for the fight.

Even though they were not yet at the front, getting there was almost as dangerous. Reg told us about a tour he conducted for a veteran who had served with D Company, 501st PIR. While advancing on Bizory from Bastogne, the man said he had been hit three times by shell fragments that had come from such a long distance that, while he had felt their sting, they did not pierce his skin.

I asked Forrest if he recalled that night march. He nodded.

"When we came [into Bastogne] we went right through town here and on into the woods," he said. "We could hear the shelling in front of us. As we walked out of Bastogne toward the fighting we met a bunch of our infantry fellas who had been up on the line. They were in full retreat and completely disorganized, and were shouting at us not to go there, that it was hell."

Hell, in fact, was all around where Forrest, Reg, and I were standing.

Behind us Reg pointed out what is referred to simply as the Seminary, affiliated with the nearby Saint Peter's Church. Prior to the war, this large stone structure had been a boys' school, run by priests. Beyond the Seminary, where Place Saint-Pierre meets rue Pierre Thomas, is the Saint Peter's Church with its unique tower that is so prominent in many wartime photos of Bastogne.

A stone wall encloses a parking lot outside the Seminary, giving ac-

Easy Company advances through Bastogne toward Bois Jacques, December 19, 1944. *U.S. Army*

The same intersection in 2008.

cess to a large indoor courtyard protected by a high ceiling of glass panels, affixed to the stone walls by ornate, green-painted iron brackets and support beams. It was in this courtyard and in the Seminary's chapel where the 506th had established its regimental hospital, where men—many with bloody, gaping wounds—were tended. During a Christmas Eve bombardment, the seminary-turned-hospital was struck by a German shell that penetrated two floors, yet failed to explode. Miraculously, the glass dome over the courtyard was never broken. Along the inside of the stone wall opposite the Seminary is affixed a wooden cross that bears thirteen small, dog-tag-shaped memorials. Reg told us that on January 5, 1945, the thirteen men, all with the 501st PIR demolition platoon, had been loading land mines onto a truck when something, possibly the pressure of the mines being stacked atop one another, triggered one of them, tearing apart the truck and blowing out part of the stone wall. (A stone outbuilding now fills that gap in the wall left by the blast.)

"It was like there was an angel protecting these men during the shelling, but then eleven days later you got the truck explosion," Reg said.

The monument was created by artist Andre Cenne, with funds raised for the memorial dog tags by an unnamed ex–American officer, probably a veteran of the 501st PIR. Completed in 1992, its dedication was put off until two of the last remaining survivors could attend. There were delays due to health problems afflicting the now aged veterans. Finally, the two were brought together and the monument dedicated. And just in time. Both men died soon afterward.

On the other side of the stone wall from the memorial runs a paved walking and biking path leading north, out of Bastogne. In 1944, this was a railroad line—removed in 1995—that ran past tiny Halte station, which would become Easy Company's right flank. During the siege of Bastogne, this was known as the "path of the medics," along which first aid men in jeeps ferried wounded from the 506th's line in the Foy–Bois Jacques area, to the hospital in the Seminary, following a track that paralleled the steel rails.

We climbed back into our car and drove out rue Pierre Thomas, in the direction of Foy and the Bois Jacques, or Jack's Woods, just as Easy Company had done sixty-four years earlier.

*　*　*

The 506th's position straddled the Bastogne-Foy-Noville road, the N30, with 2nd Battalion dug in to the right, along a five-hundred-yard front. This stretched the battalion thinly. Strayer, who had rejoined the battalion after hurrying back from London, left most of the tactical handling to Winters. He placed Easy Company on the left and Fox on the right, with Dog in reserve. Battalion HQ was roughly centered behind the two companies on the line.

As they advanced into position, Clancy Lyall said his squad was out in front of the regiment, approaching Halte, when they drew fire, although he said, "it wasn't much."

The 101st's defense of Bastogne began almost immediately with 1st Battalion of the 506th and Team Desobry advancing through Foy to attack Germans pouring south and east from Noville. Through binoculars Winters could see the battle rage throughout December 19 and 20. Although Winters didn't know it until later, 1st Battalion's commander, Lieutenant Colonel James LaPrade, whom he had criticized for crossing the wrecked Son Bridge in Holland while carrying only a pistol, was killed in this action. LaPrade and Desobry were in a house in Foy that was hit by an artillery round. Desobry was wounded and sent to the hospital near Mande-Saint-Etienne, where, as recounted earlier, he was captured when the medical battalion was swamped by men in field gray.

On December 20 the Germans flanked the American forces, slipping behind them and occupying Foy. Ordered by Sink to pull back, the cutoff Americans had to fight their way through enemy lines. Small arms barked and mortars crumped all that day and plumes of oily black smoke from smashed vehicles smudged the sky. Sink ordered 3rd Battalion forward to ease pressure on 1st Battalion and Team Desobry.

The battalion suffered heavily in the fighting at Noville. Moving about eight hundred yards across an open field to the east of the town, C Company of Sink's 1st Battalion ran headlong into a German force securely dug in amid a grove of trees and were raked by machine-gun fire. Men fell like sheaves of wheat before a thresher, and the survivors fled back to the town.

The fighting was intense all around the crossroad hamlet, but the

Americans managed to return to their lines while halting the 2nd Panzer Division and buying time for McAuliffe to solidify his defensive ring around Bastogne.

Reg guided us to the field east of Noville where the Germans had repelled Charlie Company. After parking his car on a paved road that had once been a dirt farm lane, we entered the woods. Like so many forested areas in this part of Belgium, these trees had been planted with the idea of harvesting their lumber. They stand in neat straight rows like so many wooden soldiers. The ground is unencumbered by brush and thorny entanglements, but rather is coated with a lush green grass that is nearly knee-high.

But most remarkably, the German foxholes—larger and better built than those dug by their American counterparts—remain basically intact. A number of these can be found at the wood's edge, bordering the lane. These had been machine-gun nests, their very existence bearing mute testimony to the deadly fire they must have sprayed across the wide, open field immediately to their front.

Standing in a gun pit and pointing toward Noville in the distance, Reg said, "You can see that C Company crossing that field didn't have a chance. They ran right into this line of machine guns. The Germans were firing at them like shooting at ducks."

During the late stages of the fight here at Noville, Reg said, as many as thirty-two German tanks, trailed by infantry, closed in from three directions.

"They were all around, like a horseshoe," Reg said, describing the action that roared across this ground. "The tanks would cross the field to get as close to Noville as they could. Then it was fire, fire, fire, and they'd pull back over the ridges. The Americans who were dug in here stayed low and let the tanks and infantry pass, it was foggy, then they jumped up and turned around and shot at them from the rear."

While Reg talked, a local man walking his dog stopped to chat. He told us his mother was Belgian, but his father was a British soldier.

"He never told a lot about the war when I was a kid," the man said. "I would ask him, 'Tell me something. Have you killed Germans?' He just said, 'It was the most cruel period of my life.'"

The man explained in his uncertain English that his father served initially with the British Expeditionary Force in 1940, and was evacuated at Dunkirk.

"They were thrown into the water, and he told me about the small boats, fishing boats, sent to help them escape," he said. "The Germans with their Stukas [JU-87 dive-bombers] were bombing. And his best friend, standing next to him—they were just talking—and two seconds later he was killed."

Our visitor told us Noville had been nearly destroyed during the war and that "they took down almost every house." But though the town is rebuilt and new trees have grown and the land is healing, reminders of the war still crop up on a regular basis. Just recently, he said, a farmer plowing a field adjacent to us discovered an unexploded artillery shell. After digging it from the earth, he propped it against a tree "twenty meters in the woods" and left it there.

"That was very dangerous, so I called the police because you never know what's going to happen," the man said.

A bomb disposal unit arrived to take care of the shell. In fact, they are regular visitors to this part of Belgium.

"They told me they come one day every week to the region," he said.

Since the fighting that took place here was just one small piece of a much larger battle, visitors seldom come to this spot. For that reason, Reg told us, artifacts are still frequently found, and in fact one of the persons with us picked up a rusted, round disk from the floor of one foxhole that appeared to have been the bottom part of one of the legs of an MG 42 bipod.

We returned to the car and continued on.

While the attack at Noville was sputtering out, 2nd Battalion was settling into its new home in the heavily wooded Bois Jacques. Looking the ground over, Winters instantly hated the position, which offered lousy fields of fire. Yet he knew falling back to look for a better position was not an option.

The men labored to hack foxholes into the frozen earth with their entrenching tools, small shovels whose blades could be cocked at a forty-five-degree angle to double as a pickaxe. Branches were cut

In the Bois Jacques overlooking Foy, foxholes dug by the men of Easy Company can still be seen today.

from trees to form protective roofs over the holes, although a lack of good cutting tools made this task difficult.

Bill Guarnere remembered the ground being dimpled with shell craters and littered with shell casings, shattered trees, corpses, and body parts. Amid this disconcerting detritus of war, they were told to "dig in and stay alive."

The battalion's right flank ended at a railroad track by a small station that, despite its commanding name of Halte, was just a two-story stone house (an attached stone barn was added postwar), set back some thirty feet from the steel rails. Beyond the tracks, the 501st Regiment was supposed to be in position. To Winters's dismay, contact with them was spotty at best.

"First they were here, then they weren't, then they were again," Winters told me. "My concern was that our right flank might be wide open."

His assessment was correct. A day after the regiment's arrival, two companies of Germans, about 150 men, slipped unnoticed through the gap along the railroad tracks and dug in behind 2nd Battalion. This caused confusion on both sides until the Germans were cleared out. Winters recalled how one misty morning, a young German, evidently lost in the fog, approached the 2nd Battalion slit trenches. He removed his greatcoat, hiked down his trousers and squatted over the trench. Winters politely waited until the man had finished the job he'd come for, then raised his M1.

"Kommen Sie hier," he ordered. Startled, the German looked up like a deer caught in headlights.

"Kommen Sie hier," Winters repeated, trying to sound malevolent.

The German raised his hands and stumbled forward. A search of his prisoner turned up some family photographs, a few trinkets and the heel of a loaf of dense, black bread, but nothing of any value. Winters sent the frightened man to the rear.

As he watched the young German being led away, Winters thought, "I wonder how his first sergeant is going to report his disappearance on his morning report?"

Halte station today looks almost exactly as it did when Easy Company first saw it. In fact, it might even look better. Although empty at the time of our visit, renovation work has taken place. And of course, as discussed earlier, the barn is postwar, the railroad tracks are gone and a paved walking-biking trail now passes by and continues on to the north.

Across the former rail line from the station, where the tracks cross the Foy Road, is another of the Easy Company monuments erected by the veterans and their friends.

The monument, dedicated in 2004, is made of gray stone and concrete and similar in design to the one Forrest and I saw at Brecourt Manor, and bears three highly polished granite plaques. The center plaque, and largest of the three, displays the Screaming Eagle emblem and carries the etched likeness of two soldiers bundled against the cold, standing in the snow. One man is gazing at an M1 Garand rifle, stuck bayonet-first into the earth, topped by a helmet and dangling dog tag, denoting the temporary grave of a comrade. The wording simply says "506th PIR 101st Airborne Division, 'E' Company."

The left-hand plaque lists the names of fourteen men of Easy, including thirteen killed in the fighting here in Belgium, both during the siege and in the counterattack that followed. Carved beneath is the legend "The Eagle will always scream for our fallen brothers." At the bottom of the list is Private Eugene Jackson, who survived here in Bastogne but would die in March 1945 at Haguenau, possibly Easy's final combat-related death. His name appears here by mistake, I was later told by Marco Kilian, but remains because Jackson's name is on no other Easy Company memorial. Engraved across the top of the main granite slab are fourteen gold stars in honor of the dead.

The right-hand plaque tells the viewer of Easy Company's stand in the Bois Jacques. The memorial describes the fighting and suffering, noting that temperatures dropped to a bone-numbing eighteen degrees below zero. It tells of twice being bombed and strafed by American planes, the constant enemy shelling, and the Christmas Eve attack by about forty-five Germans that cost Easy one man wounded, Walter "Smokey" Gordon, while the Germans lost twenty-three soldiers. Acknowledging the contributions of all American fighting men, the engraving concludes, "This monument is dedicated to all who fought and is symbolic of what happened to other units during the Battle of the Bulge."

Although the Bois Jacques, which during the war straddled the railroad tracks, has been cut back some two hundred yards, what remains of it stands silent and brooding across the field beyond the monument. As will be described in the next chapter, it was somewhere out in this now-barren field where John Julian was killed on a New Year's Day patrol, and where early on January 2, Donald Hoobler would accidentally shoot himself with a captured German pistol.

Getting back into the car we drove in its direction.

Entering the woods, we left the Foy Road, turning onto a narrow dirt track that carried us deeper into Easy Company's position.

Heffron and Guarnere have both been back here on numerous occasions. Heffron wrote, "You always get that creepy feeling in Bastogne. There's something about those woods. You always get that feeling a shell's going to come in. You feel very unsettled, very uncomfortable. You don't know how the hell you lived through it."

As for Wild Bill, he noted, "Each soldier has his own personal thoughts about what he experienced there. You think of what happened, who was where, who was hit, who died where. You look for the foxholes. Some of them are graves of our buddies." . . . "No place has the same charge as Bastogne. It looks like it did in 1944. The woods are there. The foxholes are there. The place is eerie."

I soon understood what they meant.

We parked the car and shut off the motor, and the sudden silence enveloped us. Even though six decades separated us from what happened here in those frigid days of late December 1944, the impact of walking amid these trees left me haunted by those visions. It haunts me still.

It haunts Forrest too, although repeated visits to this place has eased the memory.

"I think of the shelling," he told us as we stood in the silent woods. "I think of the guys getting hit and yelling for a medic, and trying to get the wounded out. But I've been back here so many times, it's not as painful as it used to be."

The sun does not shine on this ground, leaving the earth covered by a soft layer of brown pine needles, dead twigs and branches. The only green at ground level is the moss that coats the base of many tree trunks and rotting stumps. The trees one sees today, of course, did not stand here in 1944. Many of those were shattered by the constant German shelling, and the ones that survived that hell have long since been removed, but most likely not sold for their lumber. For although the purpose of these trees is to be harvested and sold, for many years after the war the lumber mills would not accept wood grown and harvested from the vicinity of Bastogne. Bullets and shards of steel from bombs and shells embedded in the trunks rendered the lumber unusable for fear of damaging saws and lathes.

As I walked through the woods toward where the tree line ended and the fields leading to Foy began, I moved almost trancelike. To my right, a solitary tree grew dead center in a shell crater, whose ragged edges had been smoothed by sixty years of wind, snow, and rain.

All around me were the foxholes that had been chipped into the earth by Dick Winters, Forrest Guth, Bill Guarnere, Babe Heffron, Carwood Lipton, Walter Gordon, Clancy Lyall, Herb Suerth, and the others. It was in these very foxholes where they shivered in the icy cold and snow. Here they huddled deep when the hail of deadly shells splintered the trees above their heads.

"Buck Compton told me the shells were probably all 88s because they couldn't hear the incoming," Reg told us. "You could hear mortars coming in."

Not too far from where we walked, Bill Guarnere and Joe Toye each lost a leg and Smokey Gordon was hit and paralyzed.

Being there, it was all so difficult to grasp.

Forrest told me that the men "started digging as soon as we got here," and "after every shelling, we'd dig a little deeper."

"The ground was frozen solid and we broke our shovels while we were digging," Forrest remembered. "We were under almost constant artillery or mortar fire. The Screaming Meemies [six-barreled Nebelwerfers whose shells seemed to scream while cutting through the air] scared me to death."

Although Forrest does not recall exactly where his foxhole had been—Reg said it was probably somewhere to the left of where we now were standing, where 3rd Platoon was dug in—he recalled that they had initially dug one-man holes. But as temperatures dropped and snow began to fall—a foot fell on December 21 alone—the men buddied up. Forrest moved in with Bob Mann and Carwood Lipton.

Suerth, being from Chicago, was one of the men who could handle cold better than some others.

"Back home, when the temperatures were twenty below, we went out and played hockey," he recalled. "But at Bastogne, I grabbed all the socks I could and wrapped some extra blankets around my sleeping bag."

The army-issue bags, he said, were "no damned good" after temperatures dropped below freezing.

"I can remember one night when we moved and we did not get our sleeping bags, they had gotten blown up in a truck, and four of us slept in a foxhole on top of one another, and every two hours we'd sort of rotate," Suerth recalled. "That was one of the coldest nights we ever had."

Herb said residents have told him "it was twenty below that night."

Clancy Lyall recalled, "You couldn't get warm. Just no way."

As they dug in, Compton recalled the clouds growing darker and the "smell of snow and smoke was in the air."

Sadly, Reg told us that these foxholes, though original, had become "victims of Hollywood." Since the miniseries, *Band of Brothers* fans and relic-hunters have marred them, dug in them, enlarged them and even slept in them. I noticed discarded trash lying in a few. Some of these defilers were World War II reenactors, living historians who should know better than to alter the integrity of these bits of history.

Unlike the National Park Service here in America, no government entity protects these battlefields from desecration. The land remains private property and thus, vulnerable.

Walking to the edge of the woods, we gazed out across the thousand-yard expanse of rolling open fields separating us from the cluster of dwellings that comprise Foy. In the town, Guarnere recalled, they could watch German trucks unloading ammo and supplies but "couldn't do a damn thing about it."

This was the view Winters and his men would observe during those long weeks of the siege of Bastogne while the division defended the vital crossroad town, its defensive line stretched to the breaking point.

"The front line was stretched out so wide that one day a German with no rifle walked right through our lines and up to the battalion CP looking for someone to surrender to," Forrest recalled. "He just walked through our lines, passed the company CP and ended up at the battalion HQ."

Here, in this cold, dark woods, the men held that fragile line and tried to endure. Bill Guarnere shared a foxhole with Buck Compton. The foxhole also served as the platoon CP. The two men took turns watching the field phone while the other slept. Guarnere recalled how they tried to keep in touch with Captain Norman Dike, who had taken command of the company in Holland, but he was always missing. Dike, whom Winters complained to me was "a favorite of someone back at division," had been assigned combat duty, the men believed, to pad his résumé for future promotion in the army after the war.

"He wasn't worth the room he took up," Guarnere said of Dike.

Dike wasn't the only officer giving Easy Company trouble. Colonel Strayer, the 2nd Battalion commander, often seemed befuddled as well.

After attending briefings at regimental or division HQ, Strayer would gather his battalion staff around him and fill them in. Unfortunately, Winters often found Strayer's information vague and confusing. He cast questioning glances at Lewis Nixon, who would respond by rolling his eyes. After these briefings, Nixon would walk the two miles to Colonel Sink's headquarters in the tiny hamlet of Luzery, just north of Bastogne, to meet with Major Hester for clarification.

"Strayer had no goddamn idea what he was supposed to do," Winters said to me in 2004, his voice still carrying a hint of frustration. "But there's more than one way of skinning a cat and the system Nixon and I had worked. Nixon did a good job. He kept 2nd Battalion out of a lot of trouble."

The siege and the bitter cold went on relentlessly.

Forrest remembered how things would be quiet, then suddenly, from somewhere, shots would ring out in the woods and men yelled "medic." Guarnere echoed the same thing in his book, saying there was "nothing you could do but sit there and take it." And when things were all quiet, Wild Bill complained, one could not appreciate the lulls because everyone was "freezing our skidonies off." As the snow accumulated and temperatures plummeted, the men sat in icy foxholes with no winter clothes or warm, dry socks. Guarnere said he was "never that goddamn cold in my life."

Babe Heffron, Guarnere's best buddy, wrote that the men were given two burlap bags to wrap around their feet. Unfortunately, their jump boots were waterlogged, making the burlap wet. As a result, it froze, making all movement feel "like walking with cinder blocks on your feet." Feet swelled and boots could not be removed, plus the snow fell, not just from the sky but avalanche-like from the heavily laden tree branches, where it cascaded down on men's heads and inside their shoes and clothes as well.

Compton said his feet "turned blotchy and gray," causing them first to burn, then tingle, then have no sensation at all.

"I knew trench foot was setting in," he said.

The only preventative method the men had was to try to keep their feet dry by changing socks as often as possible, draping the wet ones around their necks to dry.

With little action, the men "existed on tension" and trying to keep warm, Compton wrote. German flares burst overhead for no reason other than to prevent the GIs from getting any sleep. And in their glare, Compton said one could see "the man in the foxhole next to you, his face dirty, the rings under his eyes, the tight grip on his rifle." The Germans shelled the woods at night and men were so tired they fell asleep walking. Joe Toye sang to provide entertainment.

Being under an artillery barrage is an especially frightening and horrific experience, Bill Guarnere wrote, saying it is "worse than anything else you can imagine."

"You're going to see some gruesome things," he wrote in his book. "It's those things only a combat veteran knows, that's what bonds you for life, because no civilian could ever understand. In ordinary life, a man will never see his buddy's limbs blown off into trees, or a person explode into thin air, nothing left of him. This is not something you ever forget or can put into words."

He said it "made you sick so you tried not to think about it, but it made you appreciate every day that you were still alive."

Herb Suerth recalled the constant artillery barrages.

"The shelling was incredible," he said. "You could count on it every night."

Especially brutal were the tree bursts, which he and his foxhole buddy, Frank Sobelski, protected themselves from by covering their foxhole with logs.

"Frank was from International Falls [Minnesota], so he had cut pulp wood since he was fourteen," Suerth remembered. "So he had an axe, and I was digging the hole and he cut wood and we had that hole covered up before it was two feet deep. That made a lot of difference."

Lyall said he and Massaconi "just sat there and prayed in our foxhole."

"It was just coming down," he said. "There was no way to get rid of it."

"Tree bursts were the worst," Winters told me in 2004. "You just tried to keep as low as you could until it ended." The rule in the event of tree bursts was to "hug a tree," he said, getting as close to the trunk as possible.

Forrest said the men were constantly listening for the whine of incoming shells.

"You felt so helpless," he remembered. "You kept low and hoped for the best. That's all you could do."

Ammo was running low and the order was to not fire at anything unless they were absolutely sure of their target, and the men felt a deep sense of being alone.

"We were in day-to-day survival mode," Compton recalled. "Build the occasional fire. Melt some snow. Find something to eat. Cook in your helmet. Stay out of harm's way. . . . Just do what you need to do to get through the day."

Winters knew about sagging morale and was constantly moving from foxhole to foxhole, chatting with the men. After each shelling especially, he'd move back and forth, encouraging them and helping them snap out of any post-bombardment stupor. Whenever possible, he rotated men off the line, sometimes back to Bastogne some three miles down the road, to get a hot meal.

"Even getting fifty yards behind the line could help," he told me.

Father Maloney conducted services and communions, always concluding with "God bless you and good luck." Babe Heffron took communion with Skip Muck, whom he recalled as a "likeable, funny guy."

Here in these woods, the men were mentally spent, dirty and hungry. Many had that blank "thousand yard stare" that indicates the limits of one's endurance. Guarnere wrote, "Fear was something that was with you all the time." Friends were being killed and wounded, he noted, but if one stopped to think about it, "you weren't doing your job and you might be next."

Fresh waster was hard to find, and what was found was frozen. Fires were built during the daytime hours, and coffee brewed on small sterno stoves. On occasion, GIs craving a little alcoholic stimulant took a swig of the sterno.

"I don't know what the hell it was, but we drank it," Wild Bill said.

The men felt helpless, Guarnere wrote, and wondered, "Where the hell is the rest of the army? Where's the ammunition, where's the food, where are the clothes, what the hell is going on?" If the Germans didn't kill you, he recalled, freezing would.

"I did more praying than anything else," Wild Bill wrote.

Meanwhile, patrols, American and German, probed the lines and men stood vigil at lonely outposts. Sergeants were in charge of the outposts, waking men up in order to switch guards every two hours.

"Getting to outpost was a little eerie," Guarnere later wrote. "You're out there all by yourself. You never knew if you'd get there alive, or if the men on outpost were alive."

As an officer, it was Compton who oversaw the outposts. He recalled a line of OPs dug in along the woods on one side of a sunken road, with Germans dug in on the other.

"Several nights I took a few of our guys up close to the road and set up a listening post," he wrote. "We'd send one guy across the road to the German side and two others on the American side, just listening."

Winters told me that it was during this period, late December 1944 to early January 1945, that company morale was at its all-time lowest level. It got to the point, he said, where they envied the dead because their faces bore an expression of peace and "their suffering was over."

Forrest agreed. The war and the misery was seemingly endless, he said, and they were jealous of the men who were hit and sent back.

"We were ready to go home," my friend told me.

To minimize a further drop in morale, replacements (once the siege was over and they began arriving) were referred to as "reinforcements." No one asked the names of new men coming into the company because, inexperienced as they were, as many as 70 percent would become casualties in the first forty-eight hours.

"You didn't want to be friendly with them," Forrest said.

Two days before Christmas, the men of Easy got an answer to their prayers. Some 260 C-47s dropped 334 tons of supplies.

"The weather cleared and the planes started dropping supplies," Forrest remembered. "It was like a real Christmas present. We were low on food, very low on ammo and short on clothing. They started distributing shoepacs and white suits, but there just weren't enough for everyone."

He himself obtained a white British-made snowsuit.

Still, it wasn't enough to fend off the growing feeling of despair among the men of the encircled division, and they quietly celebrated a drab Christmas. Winters recalled attending church services presided over by a regimental chaplain, standing amid a curtain of fog and praying beneath the snowy cathedral of the Bois Jacques. Easy Company's cook, Joseph Dominguez, whipped up a vat of bean soup that would serve as a meager Christmas meal. Winters joined the company, and as was his policy, and one that was popular with the enlisted men, officers ate last. Some took harsh advantage of this and sneaked back into line for refills, so that by the time Winters reached the cook pots, all Dominquez had to ladle out was half a canteen cupful of beans and broth from the bottom. Winters looked down at the food and shook his head dismally, thinking, "Oh my God." He ate his pitiful meal in silence.

Herb Suerth recalled burying a dead German on Christmas Day.

"He was just a young kid," Herb told me. "He was about fifteen or sixteen, a pure Aryan, blue-eyed, blond-haired. He was a victim of one of McLung's quick shots, and Shames sent me out to bury him."

Then he enjoyed the dead German's lunch.

"We didn't have much food, so I ate his," Herb said. "I had pork roast, blackberry jelly, and black bread. And I was grateful for it."

Shifty Powers later recalled that it was "cold, cold, cold."

"It was a miserable time," he said in September 2005, during a "Road to Victory" tour of the battlefield. "I remember on Christmas day, for our Christmas dinner, we had half a cup of beans, and most of it was soup. Of course, it was cold."

Ed Shames recalled coming back off patrol and being told there was hot food ready. Either Powers or McLung had shot a rabbit and cooked it. Shames said it "stunk like hell" but was still hungrily devoured.

It was the incessant, dense fog that got to Clancy Lyall. A replacement who joined Easy after Normandy, Lyall recalled, "It was so foggy and miserable and I was scared to death because I couldn't see what was out there. All you could do was hear."

The men were thoroughly fed up with the cold, the fog and the snow. Babe Heffron recalled a story told him by a friend about a sergeant lying wounded in a field hospital. The hospital's radio was airing Bing Crosby, probably an Armed Forces Radio broadcast of the singer's December 21 holiday show, and Crosby began crooning "White Christmas." The wounded sergeant shouted, "Come over here, you son of a bitch. I'll give you a white Christmas." The remark, Heffron wrote, "made everyone's day."

Animosity also grew in the ranks toward their own commander, Maxwell Taylor, when the story went around that, while they were—to use Guarnere's colorful phrase, "freezing their skidonies off"—in Belgium, Taylor had been enjoying Christmas dinner in Virginia.

"We couldn't believe our general left us in a spot like that, and we didn't want to hear no excuses," Babe wrote. "Nobody liked Taylor after that."

Winters agreed. In August 1990, while being interviewed by Stephen Ambrose about the Battle of the Bulge, the author questioned him about this, reminding Winters that Taylor had been ordered to the States.

"That's not quite fair," Ambrose said, responding to Winters's criticism of Taylor,

"Isn't it?" Winters replied.

"He was called back to testify . . . ," Ambrose said.

"I don't want to be fair," Winters said, ending the discussion.

On Christmas Eve, Winters and his men listened in silence, not to Bing Crosby, but to the rhythm of German bombers as they plastered Bastogne. The rumble of detonations rolled across the land and flames from the ruined town gilded the distant sky.

The next day the Germans launched a major assault on the far left of the 502nd and, depending on wind direction, the sound of this desperate struggle reached the anxious ears of the men here in Jack's Woods. What they did not know until later was that, even as this fracas raged off to the west, on the southern end of the encirclement, leading elements of the 37th Armored Tank Battalion, attached to General George Patton's Third Army, had made contact with Company C, 326th Engineers, opening a tenuous corridor. The siege of Bastogne was broken. An airdrop of supplies from an armada of C-47s also helped relieve, to some extent, the misery of the men who had held the Germans off for eight days.

With the siege now broken, supplies and relief columns of men slowly began making their way into the beleaguered town, and the men of the 101st hoped their ordeal was over.

They would soon be bitterly disillusioned.

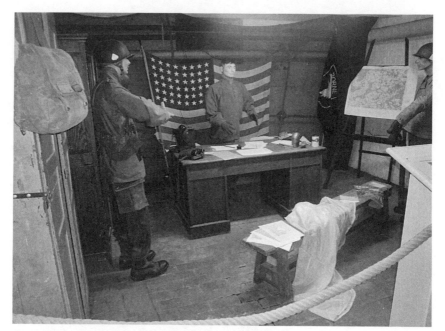

General McAuliffe's basement headquarters in Bastogne, where he replied, "Nuts," to the German surrender demand.

* * *

One boost to morale the men in encircled Bastogne did have was a letter from General McAuliffe responding to a German demand for surrender. His one-word response to the Nazi commander, "Nuts," has become immortal.

That famous reply, and the letter to the troops, had been drafted by McAuliffe in a basement room at a Belgian army base, Heinz Caserne (Heinz Barracks), in Bastogne at 40 rue de La Roche. Now the home of the Belgian 1st Field Artillery Regiment, the base is known as Cave McAuliffe. Overseen by Eric Lemoine, the base adjutant, and Michel Marecaux, first chief corporal, this was one of our stops after leaving the Bois Jacques.

"This was 101st divisional headquarters from December nineteenth until December twenty-seventh," Reg said as we pulled up to the iron gates. "After December twenty-seventh, General Maxwell Taylor returned from the United States and on December twenty-eighth, he moved headquarters to Isle-la-Hesse Castle, a very fancy castle on the outskirts of Bastogne."

The base, used by the Germans from 1940 until 1944, is open only by reservation. We were met at the gate to the installation, admitted, and instructed where to park. McAuliffe's headquarters was in the basement of one of the stoutly built brick barracks buildings, accessible only by a long stairway. It was a slow descent for Forrest, but the aging veteran made it down fine with Reg and me flanking him front and rear, in case he needed assistance. BK was tail-end Charlie in this little procession.

Two of the rooms in this bunkerlike facility depict McAuliffe's headquarters as it appeared in 1944. The first room across from the bottom of the stairway was McAuliffe's communications center. Here mannequins in American army uniforms, overcoats and helmets, work field radios. Communication wires are strung overhead, and boxes of supplies are piled in the center of the room. In one corner, a wounded man lies on a cot.

McAuliffe's office has also been re-created. Three mannequins occupy this room, two representing staff officers, while a third—McAuliffe—stands behind a desk, an American flag behind him, the division flag in the corner to his left and a battle map mounted on an easel.

Lemoine and Marecaux told us that, while none of the furnishings in the room are original to McAuliffe's HQ, they are authentic to the period and the room is a true representation of the general's office. That aside, I was entranced in the knowledge that it was in this drab windowless room with its whitewashed brick walls and heavy water pipes running along the open ceiling that McAuliffe received the German demand.

December 22, 1944

To the U.S.A. commander of the encircled town of Bastogne

The fortune of war is changing. This time the U.S.A. forces in and near Bastogne have been encircled by strong German armored units. More German armored units have crossed the river Ourthe near Ortheuville, have taken Marche and reached St. Hubert by passing through Romores-Sibret-Tillet. Libramont is in German hands.

There is only one possibility to save the encircled U.S.A.

troops from total annihilation: this is the honorable surrender of the encircled town. In order to think it over, a term of two hours will be granted with the presentation of this note.

If this proposal should be rejected, one German artillery Corps and six heavy A.A. battalions are ready to annihilate the U.S.A. troops in and near Bastogne. The order to fire will be given immediately after this two hours' term.

All the serious civilian losses caused by this artillery fire would not correspond with the well-known American humanity.

McAuliffe read the note, and angrily snarled, "Nuts." Then he agonized over an answer until one of his staff officers suggested he simply reply with his first response, "Nuts."

Thus, the German commander received the following reply:

22 December 1944

To the German commander:

NUTS!

THE AMERICAN COMMANDER

He then drafted a letter to the entire division. On Christmas Day, Sink made the rounds of the 506th and read it to his men.

Merry Christmas. What's merry about all of this? We're fighting—it's cold—we aren't home. All true, but what had the proud Eagle Division accomplished with its worthy comrades of the 10th Armored Division, the 705th Tank Destroyer Battalion and all the rest? Just this: We have stopped cold everything that has been thrown at us from the north, east, south and west. We have identification from four German panzer divisions, two German infantry divisions and one German parachute division. These units, spearheading the last desperate German lunge, were headed straight west for key points when the Eagle Division was hurriedly ordered to stem the advance. How effectively this was done will be written in history; not alone in our division's glorious history, but in world history. The Germans actually did surround us, their radios blared our doom. . . .

Allied troops are counterattacking in force. We continue to hold Bastogne. By holding Bastogne, we assure the success of the Allied armies. We know that our division commander, General Taylor, will say: "Well Done!"

We are giving our country and our loved ones at home a worthy Christmas present and being privileged to take part in this gallant feat of arms and are truly making for ourselves a Merry Christmas.

A.C. MCAULIFFE
COMMANDING

His troops loved it.

"We all had a good laugh about that one," Buck Compton remembered.

Heffron believes that if McAuliffe had decided to surrender, the order might not have been obeyed.

"I think they would have gone against orders," he wrote. "As bad off as we were, as cold as we were, as hungry as we were, as sick as we were, I don't think an American Airborne soldier could throw down his gun."

All of that occurred right here in this dreary, unglamorous, dungeon-like room.

Our hosts next took us to a third room, where there was a table set up. Here, Forrest signed copies of the *Band of Brothers* book while I signed copies of my biography of Dick Winters, *Biggest Brother*. Photographs were taken and Forrest, BK, and myself were each given framed, exact reproductions of McAuliffe's immortal letter.

Before leaving Cave McAuliffe, we had one more stop. Directly across the street from the base is Bastogne's old walled cemetery, the burial place of Renee Lemaire, the pretty young nurse depicted in the miniseries, episode five.

According to a commendation letter written by Captain Jack T. Prior, battalion surgeon for the 20th Armored Infantry Battalion, and dated January 1, 1945, thirty-year-old Renee Lemaire volunteered her services at the battalion aid station in what before the war had been a grocery store called Sarma on rue de Neuf Chateau on December 21, 1944. There she helped tend over 150 patients a day, many seriously injured. Prior wrote that the "girl cheerfully accepted the Herculean task and worked without adequate rest or food. . . ."

Lemaire helped change dressings. She "fed patients unable to feed themselves, gave out medications, bathed and made the patients more comfortable, and was of great assistance in the administration of plasma and other professional duties."

During the Christmas Eve bombardment Winters and his men observed from the Bois Jacques three miles away, a German bomb made a direct hit on the hospital. Lemaire, a black nurse from the Congo named Augusta Chiwi, and about thirty wounded patients all were killed instantly. Wrapped in a parachute, Renee Lemaire was reverently buried by the men whose comrades she died helping.

"It is on these grounds," Prior wrote, "that I recommend the highest award possible to one, who though not a member of the armed forces of the United States, was of invaluable assistance to us."

Today, the grave of Renee Bernadette Emilie Lemaire, the young girl who lived at 30 Place du Carre in Bastogne, and who gave her life helping grievously wounded American GIs, is surrounded by a squat iron fence. On her headstone is a picture of a pretty young girl in nurse's garb, a faint smile on her soft, round face, eyes bright with a lifetime seemingly in front of her.

I include her story here because I feel it belongs in this book. In the series, Eugene "Doc" Roe strikes up a friendship with Lemaire. It's a touching episode that shows the human side of war, the warmth of feeling and personal relationships that can be generated even while surrounded by the bloody hell of man's brutality to man.

There is absolutely no evidence that Roe ever met Lemaire, and the episode was purely fiction in that regard. Still, the screenwriter—like me—felt hers was an important story to tell.

To the east of Bastogne stands the huge Battle of the Bulge Memorial. Built in the shape of a star when looked down on from above, this mammoth American monument lists every infantry and airborne unit that took part in this, the largest battle ever fought by the U.S. Army.

It stands on a hill overlooking the town. The ground it occupies is the closest the Germans came to taking Bastogne. The view from the hill is the same one the Nazis had, and they would never get closer.

Along the Colline du Mardasson leading to the monument is the last marker denoting the Route to Liberation, kilometer 1,147, a path that begins with the aforementioned marker 00 at Utah Beach.

Forrest, of course, has been here several times, although this visit included something he had never seen before. Midway between the Battle of the Bulge Memorial and the nearby museum is a new monument presented, its plaque proclaims, by the "City and the Citizens of Bastogne," which reads, "May this eagle always symbolize the sacrifices and heroism of the 101st Airborne Division and all its attached units." Carved in granite, the work depicts an eagle, wings outstretched, its head cocked at a defensive angle, protectively hovering over an upturned American helmet.

Standing by this monument erected to honor the stand he and his comrades made on the bloodstained fields around this crossroad town, Forrest stared at it reflectively.

In contemplation of what the monument means in terms of sacrifice and suffering, Forrest said, "We left a lot of dear friends on that frozen ground, but we tried to put it out of our minds. We still had a war to fight."

"HELL, ALL OF US WANTED TO QUIT"

FOY TO RACHAMPS

On the day after Christmas, when Patton's troops had broken the siege and linked up with the 101st south of Bastogne, the bedraggled men of Easy Company felt certain they'd be pulled off the line to rest and refit. Instead, they soon discovered that they would be part of the American counteroffensive to push the Germans out of the Bulge they had carved with their December offensive.

Still stuck in the blasted, snow-covered Bois Jacques, it was a devastating blow to the paratroopers' morale, already at low ebb from losses and fatigue. Disbelief was everywhere. John Martin spoke for all when he proclaimed, "We're staying here? Are they kidding?"

The truth was, the Americans had no fresh divisions to throw in, and damned few replacements for those units already on the line and depleted by casualties. So with the Germans on the run, Eisenhower and his generals decided to hit the enemy with what they had on hand.

But though the Germans were pulling back, they weren't finished, and as 1944 dissolved into 1945, they sent the Americans defending Bastogne their own special New Year's gift: high-level bombers. On New Year's night lethal flocks of Heinkels and Dorniers droned unseen in the darkness above and dumped their loads on the GIs' heads. Amid this deadly downpour Easy Company burrowed deep into their foxholes as the bombs cut through the perpetual fog, bursting in the woods, shrapnel singing overhead.

The air raid might have been in retaliation for an American barrage the night before. Joe Toye, working the company radio, heard that the

Americans planned to greet the new year by unleashing an artillery bombardment on the German positions. At midnight, guns all along the line erupted. Some fell short, prompting Toye to get on the phone and yell, "Get those shells up. Jesus Christ, they're hitting over here."

The next day, Heffron recalled, the Germans launched an air raid that "beat the hell out of us."

This was the end of a bad day that had gotten 1945 off to an ominous start for the men of Easy. That morning a contact patrol had been dispatched to probe the gloomy forest for the German line. They found it, and Private John T. Julian, at point, was mortally wounded.

Heffron recalled hearing Martin yell that Julian was hit. Babe raced to the scene and found Julian lying in an exposed position, writhing, blood flowing from a throat wound. Babe tried to reach Julian several times, but German fire drove him back. Friends since jump school (unlike in the miniseries, which seemed to depict Julian as a replacement), Babe hoped if he could not drag Julian to safety to at least recover his wallet, or his class ring, or anything, rather than let some German rifle through his friend's possessions after Julian was dead. Try as he might, though, Julian was out of reach, and had to be left behind.

"You never get over something like that," Heffron wrote. "I'm only glad he didn't suffer long. We took care of each other, and I knew what I had to do when I got home."

Julian had been the first man in the company to die in 1945, but between December 19, when they arrived in the Bois Jacques, until the end of 1944, bullets or shrapnel also killed A. P. Herron, Carl C. Sawosko, John E. Shindell, and Harold B. Webb.

Wounds and sickness had plucked even more men from the line, making for grim reading on Winters's morning reports. And now the air raid.

Before the bombs ceased bursting, a cry went out for a medic. It was Joe Toye. He'd been hit in the arm by shrapnel. Luckily, the injury was minor, yet serious enough to send Toye back to Bastogne.

Buck Compton recalled the constant state of anxiety and nervous tension that pervaded every aspect of life on the front line.

"We got to the point where we were always on edge," he wrote. "Not jumpy, just alert—constantly ready to act. Always tense."

The uneasiness, he said, "could make a guy crack before long."

As a commander, Winters tried not to let his personal feelings of loss interfere with his job.

"You look around and you see men hit every day, or getting frostbite or combat fatigue," Winters told me. "Each day the line gets thinner and thinner. Every morning my present for duty roster kept going down. I couldn't focus on each man's loss. I had the rest to worry about."

Two days after Julian was killed, Easy lost Donald Hoobler to a senseless accident.

"Everyone liked Hoobler," Forrest recalled. "He was a character, just like all the rest of them. He was a fun guy. Him and Luz."

Don Hoobler was a Toccoa man, and had spoken often about acquiring a German pistol as a souvenir. He had finally gotten one, after shooting down a German officer on horseback in a brief action along the Foy-Bizory road, when the man tried to flee rather than surrender. The gun, a Belgian-made .32 automatic, did not have a safety.

In the predawn hours of January 3 Hoobler and some other men had been talking, holding canvas shelters over their heads as protection from snow cascading down on them from the thick layer of tree branches above. Hoobler began shaking snow off his canvas sheet when the gun in his pocket discharged.

Forrest Guth was "a couple of foxholes away" when he heard the shot, and was among the first to reach the stricken man, his clothes saturated by a growing stain of dark red blood.

"It looked bad," Forrest said. "It was dark and guys were trying to help him. He was moaning and they were trying to get him out to the hospital. He bled to death before they could get him back. It was so tragic. His loss hit us all."

Babe Heffron was also nearby when the shot cracked through the silent woods. Rushing to the scene, he saw GIs frantically working on Hoobler, ripping away layers of heavy clothes in the dark to try to reach the wound, while Hoobler yelled, "Help me, help me, I'm dying."

The wound was bad. The femoral artery had been severed, and Hoobler died before reaching the hospital.

"A lousy accident and a good soldier gone," Heffron said.

Forrest agreed.

"He was a good guy," he recalled. "It was terrible. We all missed him."

As I stood there in the Bois Jacques I recalled Winters telling me how he had gotten the news at his CP foxhole not from Norman Dike, who should have delivered it, but from Carwood Lipton. When Winters asked Lipton why he and not Dike was telling him, Lipton replied, "I thought I'd tell you since we've known Hoobler since Toccoa."

Winters knew that, "like a good sergeant," Lipton was covering Dike's ass because, as usual, Dike was nowhere to be found.

Winters told me, with a rare depth of feeling he seldom displays, that Hoobler was "a likeable kid" from Manchester, Ohio. His father had died when he was a boy and his mother took on odd jobs to put bread on the table for herself and her son. She became "an enthusiastic fundamentalist," Dick recalled, and began preaching to her friends and neighbors to the point of being overbearing. It quickly made her, and by extension her son, unpopular and misunderstood.

Hoobler "made up for that in the army," Dick told me. He was an "energetic" soldier and outgoing. He liked everyone, and the men exchanged the sentiment. Winters said Hoobler was "always ready to do what was asked of him." He recalled the young man choking down his fear as he fixed his bayonet just prior to the desperate charge at the Crossroad in Holland two months earlier.

But Easy's losses in these bloodstained woods did not stop with Julian and Hoobler.

A day after he was hit in the New Year's Day air raid, the indomitable Toye, his right arm in a sling, rejoined his buddies. Winters saw Toye walking toward the company line and intercepted him, encouraging him to go back and recover more fully and enjoy some hot chow. It had been Toye's fourth wounding, and Winters felt he deserved the rest. But Toye prevailed. His stay would be short. The next day, January 3, a few hours after Hoobler died, German shells fell on Easy Company like a winter snowstorm, shattering trees and spewing hot shrapnel.

"The shelling was unbearable," Guarnere wrote. "I never saw so many shells in my life."

The ground "shook like an earthquake," Wild Bill recalled. And the hard-bitten south Philly boy began to pray.

"When shells are flying over your head and you didn't know where they would land, you started making promises to the man upstairs," he wrote. "I said, 'God, if you get me out of this alive, I'll do anything you want.'"

It was a common reaction, and soldiers in combat made that prayer all the time, although few kept it. However, Guarnere said one trooper later became a priest, so he "made up for all of us scallywags that didn't keep our promises."

During this bombardment, Toye had been caught in the open. He began scampering about, yelling to all to get under cover. Then came a blast and Guarnere heard Toye yell, "I'm hit!"

Wild Bill's friend from Reading, Pennsylvania, lay about eight feet away, one leg blown to bits and hanging off his body, blood crimsoning the snow around him. At first Guarnere thought Toye was dead. Then, realizing otherwise, he jumped up from his foxhole to drag Toye in. As he reached Toye, a German shell shattered the tree next to him, and Guarnere fell beside his friend, his right leg mangled.

"I felt like I was on fire, like someone took a sizzling hot poker and was burning me," Wild Bill recalled. "I thought I was dead."

The two friends lay there side by side, each with his right leg ruined beyond repair.

"Jesus Christ," moaned Toye, suffering his fifth and final combat wound. "What the hell do I have to do to die?"

Lipton, Malarkey, and Heffron ran out to help. Babe recalled both Toye and Bill were "in bad, bad shape," and called the scene indescribable.

"I didn't think they were going to make it," he wrote. "None of us did. If you saw them, you wouldn't have given two cents for them."

Easy's medic, Eugene "Doc" Roe, worked feverishly on both men, patching up Guarnere first. Of Roe, Guarnere said, he was "the best medic we ever had. He was born to be a medic. You could always depend on him." Roe was compassionate and "took care of you mentally, physically, every way."

A jeep carrying a load of 81mm mortar shells happened by, either traveling via the Foy Road or the "path of the medics," and was commandeered to carry the two injured men back to Bastogne. The driver hesitated at being diverted from his mission, until Eugene Jackson yanked out a pistol and threatened the man. Guarnere and Toye were placed on stretchers, loaded onto the jeep, and were soon headed toward Bastogne. As he watched his two friends disappear down the road, now out of the war for good, Heffron would later recall, "they were tough sons of bitches, very courageous men." The loss of one, he wrote, would have been bad enough, but losing both "shook us all up."

"Whenever we lost a Toccoa guy," said Herb Suerth, "it was like, Holy Christ. It affected all of the guys."

But the loss of Easy Company veterans didn't end there. Buck Compton recalled how this quiet forest "was ravaged" by artillery and echoed with screams of "medic."

"It looked like slaughter alley—huge trees blown down, ground ripped up, a whole bunch of guys lying all over the place, some motionless, some gasping, unintelligible words coming out of their mouths," he wrote. "It's a terrible thing to see guys like that. Death was everywhere."

He began to think, "Maybe this time the Germans are really going to get us all. They've been softening us up. Now, this is it. With all these guys wounded, what the hell are we going to do to fight back?"

Compton had seen death before, but this, he wrote, was "unprecedented gore." He called Guarnere and Toye "the two toughest guys in the unit," and to lose them was almost unbearable. What he did next is open to interpretation.

In the miniseries, Compton stares dazedly down at the badly wounded Toye and Guarnere, drops his helmet and sits on a tree trunk, head buried in his hands. He had experienced more pain and death than his mind could handle. His war, too, was over.

Winters believes Compton broke under the intense strain, and that he walked off the line, abandoning his duties as platoon leader. According to what Winters told me, George Luz spotted Compton, weaponless and helmetless, shuffling toward the rear as if mesmerized. He ran to the lieutenant, saying, "You can't leave us, sir." But Compton, Winters said, brushed on by as if Luz was merely a specter in the swirling mist. Luz grabbed Compton and tackled him to the ground, again saying he couldn't leave. But the vacant look in Compton's eyes convinced Luz to let go. Compton rose to his feet and continued walking away, leaving Luz kneeling helplessly in the snow.

Winters saw him next, still trekking rearward through the forest.

"Buck!" he called, jogging toward the dazed man. Winters recognized the symptoms right away. "Buck. Where do you think you're going?"

Compton stopped and looked at him but did not answer. Winters told him to "get back to your platoon."

"Think of your men," Winters told him. "They need you. I need you."

Still no response.

Winters fretted over this breakdown, not just for Compton's sake but also for the impact this could have on the morale of the men.

"Buck, you're an officer, you've got to get ahold of yourself," Winters told me he said. "I can't excuse you for this. If I excuse it for the officers, then what reason do I have to expect the men to put up with the same conditions?"

Compton replied, "I can't take it anymore. I just can't take it anymore. I'm sorry."

In his book, *Call of Duty*, Compton refutes this story, saying he went in search of the ever-absent Dike while also yelling for a medic. Dike, he recalled, had a foxhole "as big as a bedroom," where he would often be found sitting, puffing on a pipe. Coming to Dike, Buck recalled, was like "kneeling before his throne." This time, he could not find his commander, and he "exploded in rage," which others may have interpreted as his cracking up. Compton admitted to sitting down on a tree and crying, but it was out of anger, frustration, and grief, and not combat fatigue—the World War II equivalent of what the First World War doughboys called, with brutal honesty, shell shock.

"I was not shell-shocked or suffering from any mental condition other than what I have described," he wrote in his defense.

Colonel Sink saw Compton limping and took him off the line, saying, "I think you could stand a rest," Buck wrote. Rather than tell Sink he was okay and he would like to stay with the company, Compton complied, which, in hindsight, he believes was the wrong choice.

"If I had it to do all over again, I would have tried to resist his decision," Compton wrote.

He boarded a jeep, but before he left, he said he saw Malarkey and asked him what the other men thought about him leaving. He wrote that Malarkey told him the men considered him "a hell of an officer" and wished him well. In his book, *Easy Company Soldier*, Malarkey also recounts this meeting, confirming the "hell of an officer" quote.

"I couldn't lie to him," Malarkey wrote.

He added, "They wish you the best, Buck."

Then, Malarkey remembered, "we left to go to the different places we each needed to be."

Babe Heffron wrote that he saw Buck roll up his bedroll and press it against his chest. Compton had a blank stare and "a bad look about him," Heffron recalled. He asked, "Buck, where are you going?" to which Compton replied, "I just lost my two best buddies." Then he left. Heffron called Buck "one of Easy Company's best officers," who "was willing to put his life on the line for his men and country without a thought."

"How much personal loss a man can take is a different story," Babe wrote.

He said he doubts any of the men held Buck's leaving against him.

"Seeing your buddies die right before your eyes, day after day, takes its toll, no matter who you are," Heffron wrote. "And when you see two guys like Guarnere and Toye go down it had to affect you mentally."

Malarkey said the men loved Compton, who "would sit down and talk to us, play cards with us."

"He was a soldier's soldier," Malarkey said. "Very compassionate. A good man."

In his interviews with me, Winters was less forgiving, and though the two men remained lifelong friends, Compton's leaving, for whatever reason, remained a sore on Winters's soul that has never healed. As an officer, Winters told me, one had to share the men's hardships. Compton failed that, having lost what Winters called his "mental discipline." Compton was also paying a price for something Winters had always preached against: getting too close to the men. The loss of both Guarnere and Toye pushed Compton over that thin line of stability combat soldiers walk.

Compton never returned to Easy Company after he recovered. Instead, he wrote, as he prepared to head back, he encountered an officer and friend who "knew how to work the system." His friend told him the war was winding down, so why go back and risk dying or being maimed?

The officer helped Compton get stationed in Paris, where he sat out the last months of the war. That, too, Compton believes in retrospect, was a mistake.

"I wish I had just gone back and rode it out with Easy Company," he wrote. "Maybe then there would be no need today to explain all this stuff about my mental health."

Easy Company remained in the Bois Jacques until January 9, when they were moved to a heavily forested "rest area" about three-quarters of a mile to the west in the direction of Recogne. Today, it is a quiet patch of woods about two hundred yards back from the road, but sixty-four years earlier, "restful" was the last word one would use to describe this spot.

"That woods is where Easy spent its two nights of hell," Reg told us as we stopped to gaze at the dark, silent stand of trees. "If you went in there with a metal detector, you could fill a bucket with shrapnel in half an hour. That's where Muck and Penkala got killed."

Reg didn't say it because the miniseries did not depict it, but a third Easy Company man, Richard F. Hughes, also never left that woods alive.

Because this area is seldom visited by the public, throughout the forest one can find foxholes that remain untouched by relic hunters. I walked across ground rippled with "pristine" foxholes, to use Reg's phrase, that have escaped desecration, and whose appearance today compared to 1945 differs only from the normal wear and tear of nature. In these meager earthen shelters, men huddled for warmth and to escape the hot steel of exploding artillery shells.

Any rest Easy might have gotten in these woods lasted just one day. On January 10, the Germans turned the muzzles of their guns on this so-called quiet area.

January 10 would prove to be Herb Suerth's last day in combat. It was around one a.m. when a tank crewman "about fifty yards behind us," he said, foolishly lit a cigarette.

"It was a new tank outfit that had just come in from the States," Herb said. "And they were sitting up on the turrets, and one lit a cigarette, and it was absolutely pitch black. There was no moon. There was nothing. When he did that, about ten guys were ready to kill him."

Within thirty seconds, he recalled, an "88 came right in, they must've zeroed in on that light." The shell dropped a bit short, missing the careless tanker, and exploded less than thirty feet from Suerth.

"It blew me up in the air," he said. "And when I came down and tried to get up, all I could see was the broken ends of both of my legs. I had a compound bilateral fracture of both femurs."

Doc Roe, who had himself been nicked in the heel, jabbed Herb's shoulder with a morphine syrette.

"I was the first one they got to," he recalled. "And I remember laying on the ground and them saying 'this one's dead' and 'this one's dead.' I'm pretty sure I heard it four times."

Of the five men hit by that shell, Herb Suerth was the only one to live. He spent the next eighteen months in army hospitals.

As January 10 dragged on, the loss to Easy continued.

That same afternoon a hail of German artillery shells began screaming in on this "rest area." Everywhere, men hit the ground, trying to pull the earth over their heads, when an 88mm round plunged straight into the foxhole of Skip Muck and Alex Penkala. The two friends died together in a blinding flash.

Babe Heffron's foxhole was about ten feet away from Muck and Penkala and he had been talking to them when the shelling began. George Luz had been out of his foxhole when the first rounds fell and, now exposed, ran for cover. Muck and Penkala yelled for him to hop in with them. Luz dropped to the snow to avoid shrapnel and began crawling in their direction when the shell hit their foxhole. Reaching the smoldering crater, Luz looked in, then moved on and slid in with Babe. He told Heffron, "There was nothing left. They're gone."

When the barrage lifted, Heffron went to the blasted foxhole and later wrote that Muck and Penkala had "vanished into thin air." Knowing that sometimes body parts were thrown up into the trees, he checked. Nothing. Then, like many soldiers do when death strikes so close, he realized in relief fringed with survivor's guilt that had the shell landed a few feet to the left, it would have dropped in his own lap.

Babe later wrote that he thought back a few weeks to when he and Muck had taken communion.

"Muck died in a state of grace," Heffron said. "I still think of Muck every time I take communion."

The loss of Skip Muck was especially devastating to Don Malarkey. When Winters heard the news, he went in search of Malarkey and found him sitting in quiet despair on the edge of his foxhole.

Doc Roe had already visited Malarkey, who had been about a hundred yards away from Muck and Penkala's position during the shelling, and informed him of the death of his friend.

"The shell found them as if it had eyes," Roe told him.

He asked if Malarkey wanted to see Muck and Penkala but Malarkey refused. Years afterward, in his book he wrote, "Later I'd heard that beyond a shredded sleeping bag and a few body parts, there wasn't much to see. That wasn't Skip Muck back there in that foxhole. Skip Muck was sitting on the floor of the PX with me, listening to the Mills Brothers sing 'Paper Doll' on the jukebox. He was getting my food for me when my legs had given out on the march to Atlanta. He was swimming the damned Niagara River at night, a thought that made me want to laugh and cry at the same time, the crazy fool."

Roe gave Malarkey Muck's cross and rosary, which he'd found, saying he knew Muck would want him to have it. He was still clutching it when Winters found him. Knowing how important it was for Malarkey's mental well-being to distance himself from this tragedy, he offered him a few days off the line to serve as his personal runner. Malarkey respectfully declined, opting to remain with the company.

Winters told me he was proud of Malarkey. He knew the man wanted to quit—"hell, all of us wanted to quit"—but his pride would not let him. So he endured like the rest.

"I didn't cry when I learned Skip Muck was dead. That would come later. Much later," Malarkey wrote. "Not that it didn't hurt. Hell, I'd never felt pain so deep. He was like my brother. Hell, he was closer than my brother. But . . . I was too mentally numb to really react. Too tired."

Forrest didn't hear about Muck and Penkala's deaths until some time later.

"I wasn't dug in near them, so I didn't hear about it right away," he said. "But when fellas you know get killed, especially the old-timers, the Toccoa guys, you think 'Oh my God,' but then you just go on. The sadness comes later."

That all happened right here in these woods and among these trees. Since Easy Company arrived here in Belgium, twelve of their comrades had been killed, a number of others were wounded, Buck Compton was lost for whatever reason, and the rest were all suffering from cold and frostbite. And they still had to attack Foy.

We got back into Reg's car and drove on.

The *Band of Brothers* miniseries makes it seem as if Easy Company attacked Foy from their long-held position in the Bois Jacques, which was not the case at all. Having moved three-quarters of a mile west to the "rest area," on January 12 they were shifted half a mile back to the east, the company's right brushing the Houffalize Road (the N30)—the Bois Jacques visible a quarter mile beyond that. A small German bunker, vacant at the time of the attack, still stands its ground nearby.

Reg parked his car along a narrow road that cuts through the woods. Walking cautiously along a muddy trail, and helping Forrest traverse the rutted ground he once crossed so effortlessly six decades earlier, we emerged from the woods onto an open field. The original tree line had been cut back some fifty yards at this point, so we walked out to where the woods had once ended. Across the meadow, the village of Foy stood just as it did then, astride the intersection of the Houffalize Road running north to south out of Bastogne, and the east-west Recogne-Foy road. The town has grown some since January 1945, and the first houses were just a couple of hundred yards away. But when Easy Company stormed across this field, they had 550 yards to cover before reaching the village, a long distance to be sure, but not as long as the thousand yards they'd have had from the Bois Jacques.

It was in these woods to our rear, possibly near where the car was parked, that the company assembled. Winters had been briefed by Colonel Strayer the night before, and spent the rest of the evening in his foxhole, studying attack strategies in a copy of the army manual he carried with him, and "thinking I'd just as soon have a Hershey bar." He told me, "The stuff I was reading in the manual was too elementary for what I needed."

That was also the night Lipton warned Winters that Dike was not up to the job of leading Easy in the attack. Winters knew Lipton was correct, but he also knew he could not relieve Dike prior to the attack merely on suspicion of being incompetent.

Easy Company attacked Foy on January 13, 1945, across this field.

Early on the morning of January 13, the company moved through the trees that once towered over the ground where Forrest, Reg, and I now found ourselves, and gazed, just as we were doing, across the field stretching out before us.

Winters posted two machine guns to give covering fire, and ordered the attack. Across the snow-covered meadow they went, meeting sporadic fire from the town's defenders. Winters watched, holding his breath each time a machine gun stopped firing so the crew could change belts, thinking, "Come on. Come on. Reload."

On the field at Foy again, Forrest recalled the assault down the sloping fields and into the town.

"Coming down over that hill was real tough," he said. "The Germans were hiding their tanks around the buildings and there were guys on the upper floors of the buildings, firing at us."

There were, in fact, only about twenty well-dug-in German infantry in Foy, but there were also a number of armored vehicles, and these were what caused the brunt of the losses. I Company, attacking on Easy's right flank, took almost 65 percent casualties.

"Item Company suffered the most casualties in the attack," Reg said, pointing out the direction of I Company's charge, east of and parallel to the N30.

Then, amid this assault, Lipton's prophecy to Winters came true. About seventy-five yards from the town, the company inexplicably halted, men squatting in the open. Dike had panicked and stopped his company, its troopers now vulnerable and exposed to German fire. Winters couldn't believe his eyes and yelled, "Get moving, get moving." Realizing he couldn't be heard, he snatched up the radio and made contact with George Luz, who was carrying the company's set, and angrily told him to put Dike on the phone.

Dike, seized by indecision, did not take the radio from Luz, and no amount of coaxing or yelling could budge him. Sink, who had come up just as the attack commenced, stood behind Winters, watching the scene unfold. First he asked where Strayer was and why Winters was running the attack. Winters told Sink that Strayer was in the CP. Sink told Winters to "take care of that," meaning the attack, and left.

Angered almost beyond reason, Winters unslung his rifle and took several steps toward the action. Then he stopped himself.

"The movie shows Sink calling me back, but it wasn't that way," Winters told me. "I stopped myself. I told myself I was in command, and I couldn't run out there and take over the attack."

Glancing around quickly, Winters said he looked for an officer, "any officer," he could find to send out to take charge. The nearest was Lieutenant Ronald Spiers, a D Company platoon leader.

"Spiers, get over here!" Winters shouted. Spiers hustled as ordered. "Get out there, relieve Dike, and take that attack in."

Wordlessly Spiers, an almost fearless man, ran forward through enemy fire.

Babe Heffron was manning a machine gun during the assault, running forward next to Dike when his commander froze.

"He couldn't give an order," Heffron wrote. "The Germans were firing at us. Johnny Martin's platoon was up front and they were taking a licking."

"We were sitting ducks out there," Forrest told me. "We had no cover."

Reaching the company, Spiers quickly and efficiently did as Winters had ordered. Dike, meanwhile, trudged rearward in the company of a medic, passing Winters.

"I ignored him," Winters told me.

Interestingly, Clancy Lyall has a different spin on the Norman Dike story. Lyall, who along with Lieutenant Jack Foley was "right next to Dike," said their commander had been shot in the right shoulder. That wounding was what caused Dike to stop, not panic, as depicted in the miniseries.

"People who saw this movie think the man was a coward because he was hollering, but he got shot in the shoulder," Lyall said.

Lyall said he mentioned Dike's wounding to Winters at the film's premiere, saying the filmmakers "shouldn't do that. The man wasn't a coward."

"The man has grandkids, and what are they going to say? 'My grandpa was a coward'? If he was or wasn't, you don't do that shit," Lyall told me.

Lyall said what other veterans say about Dike "is their business," but he feels the movie's treatment of Dike was unfair.

"I don't care if the man was scared or whatever," he said. "You don't go telling everybody. Christ, he was there. That's more than almost everyone else in the world was, right? Every one of us who was there was scared, and if he says he wasn't, he's a damned liar or he wasn't there. That's the truth."

In 1989, Winters stood where we were now standing, on the spot where the attack had begun. He was with Stephen Ambrose and Ambrose's wife, Moira, and was telling the story of the assault on Foy. In what has become one of Winters's favorite stories, he told me how he pointed to two spots on the barren field and said, "I had machine guns set up there and there, where Moira's standing, to provide covering fire." He recalled Ambrose's wife kicking at the dirt by her feet with her shoes, then bending over and picking up objects that turned out to be spent .30-caliber casings from a machine gun. Ambrose, astounded at Winters's sense of recall even though the wood line had been cut back, related the story later to the actor Tom Hanks, who brought it up to Winters in 2002 when they met in person.

In 2008, Forrest did not recall where Winters had set up the machine guns, so I did not have the opportunity to do any shoe-tip "archaeological digs" of my own.

Following Easy's footsteps out into the field, Reg laid out the assault plan.

"Charging from the woods, they attacked this way," he said, pointing toward Foy. "Third Platoon on the right, crossing the road [N30], Second Platoon attacked straight into Foy, and First Platoon swung around and attacked from [the left]."

Reg said attacking Foy from the Bois Jacques where Easy had originally been dug in "was a suicide mission."

"If you read the after-battle report, it states clearly that they attacked from this side," he said.

After a last look at Foy from Easy's jump-off position, we returned to the car. Our next destination was the center of Foy, the same place the company was attacking toward.

Reg parked the car on the Recogne-Foy road, just east of the Houffalize Road intersection, and by a small church that, according to a photo Reg had with him, had its roof ripped open by a shell during the battle.

Another house, directly across the Foy Road on the southeast corner of the intersection, still bears numerous pockmarks on its walls, gouged out by bullets.

"It's amazing after sixty-four years how much damage is still visible," Reg said.

The Houffalize Road running through Foy is wide and modern. A knocked-out German Mark IV tank that had stood just south of the intersection, its silent 75mm gun pointed in the direction of Bastogne, has long since gone to the scrap dealer.

Easy Company's attack carried them across the aforementioned field. During the assault, Third Platoon swung right and crossed the Houffalize Road south of the town, and continued on in conjunction with I Company, which was attacking on Easy's right flank. First and Second platoons continued across the field to the Foy-Recogne road, turned right, and charged toward the main intersection. As they raced past a barn that still stands just west of the intersection's traffic signal, Francis Mellet was struck in the back by a German sniper.

"He shot and killed Frank Mellet right in front of me," Jim Alley said in an interview for *World War II* magazine in 2000. "Shifty Powers got the sniper with a shot right between the eyes."

Forrest also saw Mellet get hit.

"He was a good friend," Forrest told us. "A quiet guy. The sniper got him and he just went down. It was a tragic loss."

Easy Company men Patrick Neill and Kenneth J. Webb were also killed in the attack, and several others were wounded, but had Spiers not gotten them moving after Dike froze, Winters knew the cost would have been much higher.

"Spiers did a wonderful job," Winters told me in 2003.

It was here in Foy that Lieutenant Spiers made his legendary run. Needing to locate I Company, Spiers dashed across the road, straight through the startled Germans, made contact with Item Company, then ran back through the Germans again to rejoin Easy. Amazingly, he made the round trip unscathed.

"I was told when he saw that scene in the movie, Spiers said, 'Did I really do that?'" Reg said.

Reg also told a story concerning the medic Ralph Spina, which, although he has never been able to confirm it, deserves telling. Spina somehow had gotten separated from the company and was being chased along the Foy Road toward the intersection by several German soldiers. Ducking into a small barn behind a house on the southeast corner of the intersection, Spina found it occupied by several wounded enemy infantrymen. Not stopping, Spina ran out the other door. The enemy soldiers pursuing him reached the barn and, thinking Spina still inside, lobbed grenades into the building where, unknown to them, their own injured men lay.

"I've never been able to find out if that actually happened," Reg said, as he showed us the low, squat barn. "But it is an interesting story."

Foy was secured by one p.m., and for Norman Dike, his leadership of Easy Company was at an end. That evening, Sink held a regimental debriefing at his headquarters to go over the day's events. Turning to Winters, Sink said, "Dick, what do you plan to do about Easy Company's situation?"

"I'm relieving Lieutenant Dike from command and replacing him with Lieutenant Spiers," Winters said.

Sink nodded. "Very well."

This appointment sat well with the men. Clancy Lyall called Spiers "one of the greatest."

"He was a good commander," Lyall said. "He put esprit de corps back into the company."

Lyall felt Spiers "wasn't overbearing" and discounted the stories of Spiers shooting POWs or his own men.

"That's bullshit," he told me. "I have nothing bad to say about the guy."

I asked Winters in 2003 where they assigned Dike next. Winters did not know, nor did he care.

"I hope to hell they found something he could do," Winters snapped, still peevish after six decades.

Babe Heffron did not think Dike was a bad officer, just a bad leader of men.

After Foy's capture, the company dug in. Heffron recalled seeing Strayer walking around in fur-lined boots and wondered where he had gotten them, thinking "some officers took care of themselves first."

Somewhere near this crossroad of the N30 and Foy roads, Forrest recalled being ordered to dig in, although he could not recall why, if indeed he ever knew.

"Beats the hell out of me," he chuckled. "They just said I was to dig in here."

Reg said the only way the order would make sense would be if this were a forward observation position, but doubts if that was the case since the Germans had been pushed out of Foy. So the reason for Forrest's mysterious "dig in here" command will probably never be known.

Their respite after Foy would be brief. There would follow a series of quick but tough battles through the villages of Cobru and Noville, ending in Rachamps on January 17, a total distance of less than four miles.

One foggy night during this period, Reg said, the Germans attacked an American roadblock across fields strung with barbed wire. The assault was beaten off, and when daylight came a grizzly sight met the Americans' eyes. Some of the dead Germans still remained standing. Their heavy greatcoats had snagged on the barbed wire, preventing them from falling.

We now followed the route of that running battle, driving northeast along the same road used by the 506th, through the crossroad village of Cobru and ending up on the commanding heights south of Noville.

It was on January 14, after pushing the Germans out of Foy and Cobru, when Easy Company and the rest of the 506th moved against Noville. I recall Winters telling me his plan of attack was to move 2nd Battalion single file across the snow-covered valley separating him from the town, because Noville was on much higher ground, and "I knew the closer we got, the more protection we'd have."

To me, it sounded like a crazy idea. I wondered how on earth moving closer to his objective would make him and his men safer. Standing now on that high ground in person, and seeing it as Dick Winters did, I fully understood.

While the landscape between Noville and Bastogne, about four miles to the south, is mostly rolling woods and meadows, the ground immediately south of Noville rises sharply, as if God, when He created this part of Belgium, dumped millions of tons of extra soil here, possibly for later use elsewhere. Militarily, this would be an incredibly strong point if properly defended, and at some places it was. As 2nd Battalion advanced, Dick told me, he could see 1st Battalion four hundred yards to his left come under intense artillery and small-arms fire, with men being tossed into the air from explosions. But no rounds came down on him.

During discussions with me in 2004, Winters mentioned that when he read the book *Dr. Zhivago*, with its image of troops charging across snow-covered steppes into withering fire, his thoughts returned to the attack on Noville.

This high ground was forested when Winters attacked it, and had been for years afterward. But when we visited the spot, the ground had recently been cleared, allowing us to view the entire American line of approach. The absence of the trees made visible several large craters, reminders of the shell fire on December 19 and 20, 1944, which wreaked hell on this town.

"They used these holes for protection, and covered them with branches," Reg said. "Winters had his CP in one of the holes toward the back. I don't know which one. But for Easy Company, it was very convenient. They just jumped into them, covered them with limbs, and got ready to attack."

Cobru, less than a mile to the southwest, and Recogne, a mile beyond that, were plainly visible, and GIs advancing along that route would come under fire long before they could effectively return it. But, as Winters accurately recalled to me, from the direction he approached, Germans on the hilltop could not depress the muzzles of their big guns enough to impede his advance. I am surprised, however, that he did not at least come under small-arms fire. Evidently, the Germans on this flank were either asleep on the job or too busy angling their fire at the easier targets to Winters's left.

For whatever reason, Winters's gamble worked. By midafternoon the entire 2nd Battalion was safe in the embrace of this quirk of geography. The battalion held its position until dark. Then Winters shifted his men to a draw created by a stream, which still flows across the field below the high ground, at the southern edge of the town. This draw, just to the left of where we now stood, was guarded by a machine-gun emplacement, but the men managed to leapfrog across in small groups. Unlike the rest of the regiment, Winters had gotten the battalion across the open fields and into attack position at the edge of Noville without losing a single man.

"I earned my pay that day," he told me, a smile of satisfaction on his face.

They spent the night on this ground, which Winters remembered as one of the coldest he had experienced so far in the entire Battle of the Bulge. Hoping to catch a few hours' sleep, Winters told me, he curled up on the protective slope of a small knoll, but his violent shivering caused him to keep sliding down, so he gave up on the sleep idea.

The regiment attacked into the town the next day, January 15, meeting sporadic fire. The main bulk of the Germans had pulled out under the cover of night, so the struggle here was over in less than three hours. One German tank remained. Easy's 3rd Platoon commander, Lieutenant Ed Shames, accompanied by Private Jim Alley, initially thought it was American, and Alley shouted, "This way." As the turret swiveled in his direction, they saw the Iron Cross and realized the error. They ducked into a burned-out building as the tank clattered after them. The steel monster sideswiped the building, bringing half of it tumbling down.

The tank kept going as Alley and Shames climbed out of the debris, shaken but unhurt.

Carwood Lipton, now leading 2nd Platoon, had a run-in with the same tank. Ducking for cover, he and several other men slid under a pair of dead Sherman tanks that had been knocked out in the fighting in this town on December 20. The enemy tank stopped. Although the Shermans were useless, the German commander feared their guns may still be operational. Taking no chances on being attacked from the rear as he passed, the German put a round into each Sherman, jarring the teeth and eardrums of the men huddled underneath, but leaving them otherwise unharmed. The tank rolled north, past the hulks, and made its way out of town. If the commander thought finishing off the two Shermans was going to save him, he was mistaken. His presence had been radioed to planes circling overhead, and as GIs watched and cheered, a P-47 Thunderbolt roared in from the sky. With deadly accuracy, the Jug's pilot unleashed a bomb that hit the fleeing tank squarely. The smoldering wreck coasted to a halt.

During the assault, fire from a six-barreled Nebelwerfer, a Screaming Meemie, came howling in. Brad Freeman and Ed Joint were both struck.

"I got hit in the leg and he got hit in the arm," Freeman told me.

He would return to Easy in April.

By now, we had driven from the high ground south of town into the heart of Noville. This crossroad village had been devastated in the fighting, first on December 19–20 as discussed earlier, and then on January 15. War had touched nearly every building. Some had sustained light to moderate damage, with outer walls pockmarked by bullets or shrapnel. Other houses had been reduced to piles of shattered masonry, or stood partially or totally collapsed as roofless shells. Standing across the Houffalize Road from me was the large two-story schoolhouse, which, during the battle, had been partially leveled. A large bomb or shell crater had been gouged out in the street immediately to its front, and a dead German Sturmgeschutz, the turretless tank, lay tilted inside a large crater, its 88mm gun silently aimed at the approaching Americans. Rebuilt after the war, the structure still serves as the town's school.

Just to the south of the school, standing somewhat alone from other buildings, stands a two-story beige-colored house with brown trim, a new row of dormer windows lining its roof. This building was headquarters for Team Desobry and the other GIs fighting here in Noville. Rebuilt after the war, it was in this house that a German shell had burst, wounding Major Desobry and killing Lieutenant Colonel LaPrade back on December 19.

After delivering ammo to the 101st on December 19, Lieutenant Rice returned here to his comrades of Team Desobry, who were also running low on supplies.

"As he drove back from Bastogne, he asked everyone he saw retreating for their ammo and grenades, and he brought it back here," Reg said. "He parked his jeep in front of the CP, and the Germans recognized it as a military vehicle and started to fire at it. One shell missed the jeep and went through the window of this house and exploded, killing LaPrade instantly and severely wounding Desobry."

Directly across the street from this house, where Reg, Forrest, and I stood in a light rain that dimpled the puddles at our feet, is a memorial consisting of a small courtyard surrounded by low stone walls topped by a squat iron fence. Opposite the open gate, and at the end of a short gravel path, is a simple plaque, with the red, white, and black of the Belgian national colors in the upper left and right corners. Flanked by granite flower boxes, the memorial bears the names of eight men from Noville who were among the victims of German retribution.

"When the Americans first arrived in Noville in September, the people celebrated their arrival," Reg said. "When the SS came back on December 21, they found some pictures of the locals celebrating with the Allies. They didn't think it was funny, so they picked out sixty men and lined them up next to the road with their hands on their heads. They told eight of them to clear up the mess and reopen the roads again. When they were done, they rejoined the others who had been standing there for hours and said they were going to take them back home."

Pointing to a building, Reg continued, "They took them back behind there, which was the Café Louis, and when they arrived back there, they saw big holes had been dug. One by one, they were executed, shot in the back of the head. The first one they executed was the priest of Noville, Father Louis Delvaux."

As Forrest and I contemplated this reminder of Nazi brutality, the mizzling rain falling from the steel gray sky seemed an appropriate backdrop.

Easy's final stop in the Battle of the Bulge, and ours as well, was the hamlet of Rachamps, two miles northeast of Noville. (From Foy to Rachamps, Easy Company consistently attacked in a northeast direction.)

Upon arriving in Rachamps, Reg told us about Joe Liebgott and Earl L. Hale, who were holding six German officers as prisoners in a barn in the village.

"The Germans started to shell this town again," Reg said. "Joe and Earl got a little distracted and one of the officers pulled a knife out of his boot and he slit the throat of Hale, but he didn't hit an artery, so Hale lived. Liebgott saw it happen, and he killed all six officers with one spray."

Forrest confirmed the truth of the story.

"Liebgott shot them," he said. "Joe was Jewish and he didn't like the Germans very much."

The story also reaffirmed Winters's statement, when he told me Liebgott "was a killer." (At the Island in Holland when Winters ordered Liebgott to take eleven prisoners to the rear, he had Joe empty his weapon. Then he gave Liebgott just one round for self-defense, and warned him that he expected all eleven men to be delivered alive to headquarters.)

Rachamps is set in a valley between two steeply rounded hills. It was here that the nuns of the village church serenaded the men of Easy, as depicted in episode seven of the miniseries. However, unlike the scene in the film, this physical (and, no doubt, spiritual) respite did not take place in the church, but rather in the nunnery just up the road to the east about seventy-five yards.

"They always misplace the nuns' singing as happening in the church," Reg told us as we stood in front of the building, which is now a school but whose walls still bear scars where bullets struck. "Actually, it happened right here in this convent."

"The nuns were very appreciative," Forrest said as we gathered in the street in front of the former convent. "They brought us food and sang for us. Just bread of some sort, nothing fancy. It was very pleasant after what we had been through."

The convent—now a school—at Rachamps, where the nuns serenaded the men of Easy. January 17, 1945.

The Tree of Liberty, dedicated to Easy Company by the children of Rachamps.

Reg said he brought Babe Heffron here on a tour.

"I asked him if he recognized this building and he said, 'Hell, yeah,'" my guide told me.

Babe said they were here until the morning of January 17, when they were relieved and returned to Bastogne.

At the base of the hill from the convent, near the wall that surrounds the church, the children of Rachamps erected a monument to Easy Company. The square, gold-colored plaque mounted on what appears to be wooden railroad ties shaped like an X, commemorates an "Arbre de la liberté," a tree of liberty, planted September 21, 2002. The young tree grows about ten feet beyond the monument.

"You've seen Easy Company monuments elsewhere," Reg said. "But this was the very first Easy Company memorial."

The 101st Airborne was relieved on January 17 by the 11th Armored Division and sent into corps reserve. It had been exactly one month less a day since they had been herded onto trucks at Mourmelon-le-Grand and ferried to Bastogne. During that time the 506th had suffered 762 casualties, or 37 percent of its strength, including 102 men killed, 601 wounded, and 59 missing.

As for the dead, a temporary cemetery was established at the intersection of the Recogne and Cobru roads. Here, 2,701 U.S. servicemen lay until 1948, when they were disinterred and either sent home at the request of their families or reburied in a more formal U.S. military resting place.

Today, this temporary graveyard is still hallowed ground and is commemorated with a long, low memorial constructed of stainless steel. The memorial, set along the Cobru Road, includes the American and Belgian flags, a black marble plaque depicting a soldier, helmet in hand, gazing out across a cemetery, and two actual grave markers, one cross and one Star of David. The memorial also incorporates a pair of nut trees, to commemorate McAuliffe's reply to the German surrender request. The trees were planted in soil from the two main American cemeteries in Belgium, the fifty-seven-acre Henri-Chapelle American Cemetery and Memorial, where 7,992 American servicemen lie, and Ardennes American Cemetery and Memorial near Liege, with 5,329 graves.

Not by coincidence, if the monument is measured from its lower left corner to the upper right one, it equals 2,701 millimeters—the number of men who once lay under the field it guards.

In the meadow beyond the monument, where brave Americans once lay at rest, a herd of cattle silently grazed. The peacefulness and serenity of this pastoral image seemed fitting.

I asked Reg how many tourists find this cemetery unless they are brought there by guides such as himself.

"Nobody," he replied.

Interestingly, just a short distance south of this former graveyard, along the Recogne Road, is a German cemetery. Here, beneath rows of heavy stone crosses, each marking six graves, lie 6,785 men who never made it back to the Fatherland. Most bear names, such as Captain Fritz Breithaupt, who died Christmas Day 1944. Born August 5, 1892, Breithaupt, at age fifty-two, is the oldest man lying here, while nearby there are soldiers who died at age seventeen. Many grave markers—too many—simply read *"Ein Deutscher Soldat,"* one German soldier, whose identity remains unknown.

"It wasn't that these men were mutilated beyond recognition," Reg said. "But some Americans, looking for souvenirs, took everything, including their wallets and army papers and ID tags, so there was no way to identify them. Looting the enemy was permitted at that time. This happened in both armies."

Unlike 38,563 of their *Deutscher Soldaten Kameraden*, who lie at rest ten miles north of Bastogne in the huge German cemetery at Lommel, these men remain here in Recogne, near where they fell.

There are numerous German cemeteries throughout France, Belgium, and Holland because immediately after the war, the German government did not have the funds to bring them home. Families were told they had to pay for it themselves if they wanted their loved ones returned. Living in a country all but destroyed after having its cities leveled by Allied bombers and its land overrun by armies from the east and west, few Germans could afford such an extravagance, so here these men lie. (Compare this to the U.S. government paying to have 68 percent of American dead returned to their families.)

Saddest of all, this final resting place for what were once brave soldiers fighting for their country, while immaculately maintained, is seldom visited.

* * *

Arriving back in Bastogne, our time here near an end, we all—Forrest, Reg, BK Masterson, myself, and the rest of our *Band of Brothers* friends— gathered for one last time in Le Nut's café. There we talked, took photos, and downed some fine Belgian beer, while Forrest puffed another cigar. Good-byes were said, and Forrest and I retired to the Collins Hotel.

The next morning, under the now-familiar gray and drizzly sky, we headed for Holland, our trip back into history nearing its end.

CHAPTER 11

A PERSONAL PILGRIMAGE

THE STORY OF ANOTHER EASY COMPANY

Around January 20, 1945, as Easy Company of the 101st Airborne was boarding a convoy of trucks that would carry them, eventually, to Haguenau, another Easy Company was advancing eastward across Belgium, helping to push the Germans back to the Fatherland.

This Easy Company was with 2nd Battalion, 334th Infantry Regiment of the 84th Division, Illinois National Guard, the "Railsplitters," whose shoulder patch depicted a white axe splitting a white rail on a bright red circular backing.

Activated on October 14, 1942, at Camp Howze, Texas, the division underwent its training at Camp Claiborne, Louisiana, before being stuffed onto a troop train on September 1, bound for New York and Camp Kilmer. Boarding ships in late September, the division arrived in Southampton, England, in the beginning of October. The Railsplitters, led by Brigadier General Alexander Bolling, waded ashore at Omaha Beach on November 4, where they were met by trucks of the famed Red Ball Express, for a never-to-be forgotten, jouncing trek to the front lines. November 19 found them battling German forces around the city of Gelsenkirchen.

One of the men in the 334th was my future father-in-law, Private Israel S. Gockley, a former member of the 28th Division band who was transferred to the fledgling 84th when the army decided it needed riflemen more than it needed trombone players.

Like Joe Toye of the Band of Brothers, Gockley was born in Reading, Pennsylvania, but soon moved to Ephrata in neighboring Lancaster County. For a point of reference, just one mile away from Gockley's new home lived a young Dick Winters.

Gockley was drafted into the army in 1942. Born in 1915, Issy, at age twenty-nine when his division landed in France, was older than most of the men around him.

When the Germans roared across the so-called Ghost Front on December 16, 1944, Gockley and his comrades were at Gelsenkirchen, near the German city of Aachen.

Dug in on the Siegfried Line, the GIs' name for Adolf Hitler's West Wall defensive system, the Americans got their first look at what separated them from the Fatherland: a network of pillboxes, bunkers, communication trenches, and land mines, with a thousand yards of cleared land for grazing fire.

Here the 84th experienced its baptism of fire, and it came at a cost. Gockley remembered his company sergeant, Vincent Clementi, who had occupied a nearby foxhole.

"A German had fired at us using a captured BAR [Browning Automatic Rifle]," Issy recalled. "Clementi put his head up to see if he could spot the German, and caught a round right between the eyes."

In fact, on its very first day in action, Easy Company lost both its commander, Captain Ledbetter, and his executive officer, Lieutenant Walsh, both wounded and out of the war.

"One of our own tanks ran over Walsh's legs," said Lieutenant James V. Morgia, who would become the company's new XO. "Luckily for him, the ground was very soft, so it just pushed him down, so he didn't lose his legs. He could still walk."

The fight there now over, the men were anticipating a rest.

"When we were pulled off the line we all thought we were going to get R and R in Paris," Issy told me.

That was not to be. On December 21, the 84th dug in along the Marche-Hotton road, on the north shoulder of the Bulge. Within a few days, they had been engaged in numerous firefights as the advancing Germans tried to push toward their goal of Antwerp. These attacks included a Christmas Day visit by German tanks and half-tracks while the 334th was positioned around the town of Menil.

"All hell broke loose," Issy remembered. "They started firing. If the engineers wouldn't have had the road mined like they did, we'd have been goners."

The armored assault was stopped by the minefield, with the exception of one tank.

"It wasn't more than fifty yards from my foxhole and I thought, 'Gee whiz, what do we do now?'" my father-in-law recalled. "Well, there was nothing to do. If we'd run, he'd have gotten us. So we stayed there and the tank got hung up on a fallen tree trunk."

Someone fired a bazooka at the tank, but the rocket bounced harmlessly off its thick armor.

"What we should have done is dropped a hand grenade in the turret," Issy said. "We didn't do that. We took off, and so did the German after he got free. He didn't know how many of us there were. He was in as bad shape as we were."

That was in late December. A month later found the 84th pushing the Germans back toward the West Wall.

By January 13, the 334th was about twenty-five miles north and slightly east of Bastogne, on a line between Halconreux and Bovigny. Their next objectives were Gouvy, about a mile away, Ourthe, a mile or so beyond that, and Beho, this latter about five thousand yards to the east of the American line.

According to the plan, 2nd Battalion was to advance from Halconreux, moving through a heavily wooded area southwest of Beho, while 3rd Battalion, to the left, was to move parallel to the Bovigny-Beho road.

Deep snow and intense cold almost made for unbearable conditions. Men did their best to guard against the elements. Overcoats were discarded and replaced by layers of clothes, often two or three wool undershirts, two shirts, a wool sweater, and two combat jackets, one to wear and another to wrap around one's feet when stationary. Wet socks were replaced by dry ones, with the wet ones placed around the neck to be warmed and dried by body heat. Men let their hair grow and slept with helmets on, to prevent body warmth from escaping through the scalp.

Still, too many layers of clothes made maneuvering difficult, and too few layers made a man too cold to fight. Physical exertion made him sweat, and when he rested, the sweat froze. Thus, men continued to come down with frostbite.

The 334th launched its attack in its sector on January 22. Easy Company was now under the command of First Lieutenant William

"Tommy" Thompson, a Waynesboro, Pennsylvania, man for whom my father-in-law had a great deal of respect.

On February 23, 1945, near Baal, Germany, Issy was ordered by his squad leader and buddy, Sergeant Ivan Beams, to lead a patrol across an open field to scout a patch of woods. Issy considered it suicidal and said he would not do it, nor would he send anyone else. The two friends got into an argument until Thompson hurried over to see what the squabble was about. When Issy told him Beams's plan, Thompson surveyed the terrain and scrubbed the patrol. Later, more than two hundred Germans were flushed from that patch of woods.

"We'd have been dead before we got halfway across," Issy later told me. "Thompson saved our lives."

At Beho, however, the company was being led into action by Thompson's XO, Lieutenant James V. Morgia, of Connecticut. Thompson had earned himself a three-day pass to Paris.

Morgia's orders were to get his company into attack position outside Beho by five p.m. Easy initially was to serve as reserve for Fox Company. Fox, however, became pinned down by German fire from the area of Bovigny. Since Easy was not in a position to help Fox, the 2nd Battalion commander, Lieutenant Colonel Umanoff, and Morgia first returned Easy to Halconreux to evade German detection, then swung toward the large woods south of Beho. Shuffling through the snow, the men crossed a main rail line where two sets of tracks running northwest split, looping around a small woody area before they crisscrossed again, with one continuing northwest toward Bovigny and the other running northeast. The woodland patch between this odd configuration resembles a fish, minus its tail.

Easy Company crossed the first set of tracks, moved through the fish-shaped woods, then reached the second rail line. The company advanced cautiously along the railroad tracks in column, on each side of the rails. The area was laced with antipersonnel mines, Morgia said, but the intense cold—or perhaps the deep snow—rendered them useless. What was not useless, however, was the artillery fire that began falling around them, forcing the company off the tracks and into the large forest that separated them from Beho, and causing a few casualties.

"It was broad daylight, but it was dark in those woods," Morgia told me in an interview in 2009. "We had quite a way to go. We were on the western side of the woods and we had to get to the eastern side to reach the main road to Beho."

Easy's delay meant F Company, which met fewer enemy defenders en route, attacked Beho in conjunction with other elements of both the 334th and 333rd regiments. Ahead, Morgia's men heard the rumble of artillery as Beho was wrested from German control. The town fell around eight p.m.

Easy Company, about 150 men, arrived at the crossroad of the Gouvy and rue d'Ourthe roads, called the Four Corners, just south of Beho at ten p.m., and Morgia was ordered to put his men into a defensive position and sit tight in case the Germans launched a counterattack. The men settled in as best they could.

"I don't know how deep the snow was. I'd say maybe a foot or so. And you couldn't keep warm. It was rough," said my father-in-law, who, due to casualties, was now a sergeant and assistant squad leader.

Beho, in fact, was wall-to-wall Railsplitters. Sleeping space was at a premium and one man slept on a kitchen stove because he could find no level place to lie down.

Around two a.m. a runner found Morgia and ordered him to report to an officers' meeting. There he was told the battalion would move out at first light, heading east toward the town of Audrange (Aldringen on some maps), about two miles away. The battalion's main objective was a cluster of buildings, a farm called the Maison de Neuve, on high ground about a thousand yards from Beho. Easy was to take the lead with George Company on the left. Fox, which did most of the fighting on January 22, would be in reserve.

Easy Company "barely had time to gobble down K rations," Morgia said, when they were on their feet. They crossed the Four Corners and gathered behind a wide loop in the rue d'Ourthe. Jump-off time was 0500.

"We had just the vaguest information about going there," Morgia recalled. "We weren't told about the enemy situation or anything. We were totally in the dark about what to do."

I had wanted to walk the ground of the Maison de Neuve for years, and before embarking on this trip I mentioned the possibility to Reg. My guide, always eager to learn more about the Battle of the Bulge, began researching the fight. Coincidentally, shortly after my inquiries, he was contacted by Morgia for information on the battle around Beho. Reg put me in touch with Morgia.

I had met James Morgia in 1983 at an 84th Division reunion held in Harrisburg, Pennsylvania. I had taken Issy there because it was close to home and I thought he might have a good time and revive some acquaintances, especially with Tommy Thompson, whom he always spoke of so highly.

Issy had never been to a division reunion (and would never attend another), but he had a great time and I will never forget the look of pure delight on his face when he shook hands with Thompson for the first time since 1945.

Twenty-five years later, by pure coincidence, I was back in touch with Morgia, who proceeded to send me written accounts of the fight.

Knowing I would be in Bastogne, just twenty-four miles away, I knew I had to visit Beho, so the day before we departed from Belgium, Forrest and I piled into Reg's car, followed in another by our Dutch friends, Frank Gubbels and Jeroen van Can, and we were off.

It was one of those rare days as we cruised north along the E26 when the sun was out and the sky was a pale blue. Our first stop was Houffalize. Set astride a wide stream in a deep, narrow valley, Houffalize looks like a scene from a postcard. Yet this beautiful town was devastated during the war. We parked by one reminder of those terrible days, a Mark V Panther tank, number 401, of the 116th Panzer Division, permanently on display. From photos on a nearby kiosk, it looks as if this forty-four-ton vehicle, painted in camouflage colors with a large black Iron Cross on its sloping front armored panel, had tried to cross a bridge that could not support its weight, toppled into the stream, and was abandoned.

After posing for pictures by the tank and grabbing a bite of lunch, we went on.

We approached Beho from the same direction as Easy, from the northwest, along the N68. The forest they passed through remains, for the most part, but the rail line is gone, although the grading for its bed can still be seen.

Stopping at the Four Corners, the intersection of the N68 and

N827, we parked. The depression area where Easy bivouacked the night of January 22–23 was right in front of us, and the buildings of Beho lay just beyond. Although I was not there that night, from maps and aerial photos I have of the town, it appears to have hardly grown in size in the sixty-three years since my father-in-law was there.

"According to Jim," Reg said, pointing back the way we had just come, "Easy Company came from the railroad tracks in that direction, and stopped here in this field." Pointing to the Four Corners, he continued. "When they got the orders to move on the monastery, they crossed the road at the intersection and went over that hill."

With a map supplied him by Morgia, we got back in the car and proceeded to follow the footsteps of this other Easy Company.

For some reason, the assault seems to have been delayed, so it was about six thirty a.m. when Morgia led his men forward. A narrow farm lane "with considerable brush and tree growth," Morgia recalled, swung around the meadows and led directly to the Maison de Neuve. During much of the march, Morgia kept this lane about thirty yards to his right.

"It was dark, dark, dark and the snow was deep, deep, deep and it was cold, cold, cold," Morgia recalled. "We weren't sure where the roads were. We didn't know where the crossroads were. It was all snow."

Morgia had no compass; his only guide was the terrain itself. His objective was the high ground, so he knew he was all right so long as he kept walking uphill.

Trudging through what Issy remembered as thigh-deep snow in some places, it took about thirty minutes to make the thousand-yard trek.

Morgia and Easy were now approaching the Maison de Neuve buildings, but because the night was black as India ink they did not know it. Then Morgia sensed rather than saw a shadow to his left. A voice said, "*Halten Sie.*"

"I spoke German, so I knew what that meant," Morgia told me. "Maybe I could have talked to him and bluffed our way by him."

But Morgia wasn't taking any chances. He fired off a shot at the sentry, who sent a round back in exchange. Morgia squeezed his trigger again, but his M1 carbine misfired. "Let's go!" he yelled to his men, and they took off, running on the diagonal away from the sentry. Loping through the deep snow, they soon reached the Beho-Audrange road and some buildings now dimly visible on the company's right.

Easy Company had reached its objective.

After leaving the Four Corners, Reg drove us along the rue d'Ourthe, a narrow paved road that skirts the meadow across which Morgia led my father-in-law and his company that night. All was green now, and cattle munched lazily on grass as they watched our car cruise along. Across the field to the west Beho was visible, and about halfway between us and the town I could catch glimpses of the Maison de Neuve.

As we drove along we spotted a wooded area on our right that at some time during the fighting had been heavily shelled or carpet-bombed from the sky. Reg stopped the car and we exited. The trees, all new growth, conceal and soften this ground, but at one time it had been subjected to intense violence. The passing of years and the natural erosion of rain and snow have smoothed the deep gouges dug into the earth by high explosives, but the craters remain, almost overlapping in some spots.

Moving on, we came to an unnamed road running north to south. We turned left and within moments stopped the car. After years of hearing about this place, I was now here. The Maison de Neuve.

From the air looking straight down, the farm would look like a rectangle of white buildings. A large two-story house, built in 1779, and attached outbuilding form one-half of the rectangle, while a large barn and two attached outbuildings form the other half. The buildings, all of heavy stone walls nearly two feet thick, surround a courtyard that is open on each end, accessing the Beho-Audrange road, which runs east to west beside the farm, and an unnamed road that passes in front of the farm. The two roads, both paved, are former farm lanes, so narrow that two cars traveling different directions would have to pass each other carefully. The roads form a T at the farmhouse.

Since 1945, this farm has been referred to by the veterans as a monastery, and it's easy to see why. Attached to the front of the house is a wooden two-story-high cross that runs from ground level to the roof. In fact, the cross is higher than the roof, and a special peak had been added to accommodate it.

"When soldiers got here and saw this big cross, they figured it was a monastery," Reg said.

The cross is intricately carved to include all of the symbols of Christ's crucifixion. Two hands are nailed to the cross bar, as is a ladder, a hammer used to drive the nails, the spear that pierced Christ's side, and a spear with a sponge atop it, used to ease Jesus's suffering. The carvings include the thorny crown, the sign reading "INRI" placed above Christ's head in mockery, and the Holy Grail, the chalice Jesus drank from during the Last Supper.

A carved wooden plaque on the cross denotes that it was put there in 1904 by Jacob Peiffer and Marian Starcks, although the cross itself was thought to have been placed as early as 1814, and added onto later.

Morgia and his men did not see the tall cross as yet. They were far too busy to play tourist. Arriving on the Beho side of the farm, they quickly pushed forward, passing the farm and crossing the road in front. There they ran into heavy German resistance and shell fire from tanks, and pulled back to the Maison de Neuve, which was still occupied by Germans bypassed in Easy's initial push.

At the farm, Morgia directed his men into position. One platoon he sent into the outbuilding behind the house. My father-in-law's 2nd Platoon under Second Lieutenant Marvin W. Jamison was ordered into the barn, while Morgia took the rest into the farmhouse itself.

"I threw a hand grenade into the house, thinking there might be Germans in there," Morgia told me. "But there were no Germans in the house. They were all in the barn."

He was right. Second Platoon charged into the barn and ran into more than twenty enemy soldiers. In the dark there was yelling, a few shots, and some hand-to-hand grappling as the Americans burst in one door and the Germans tried to flee out the other.

"The Germans were trying to get out. Our men were trying to get in," Morgia recalled.

One American, Staff Sergeant William E. Wright, crawled forward into the barn and lay just thirty feet from a machine-gun position. Armed with a rifle grenade, he fired it so that the missile exploded over the enemy's heads tree-burst fashion, taking out the gun and crew.

When the last of the Germans had gone, Morgia had the mortars set up in the courtyard behind the house and prepared for a counterattack. But Easy's troubles were far from over. Before entering the house, Morgia had spotted three German Mark IV tanks squatted in a straight line just seventy-five yards to the northeast. They now began blasting the buildings. The thick stone walls absorbed some of the shock, but gaping holes soon began appearing. Plus—it was daylight now, about seven thirty a.m.— Morgia saw infantry massing. He knew he needed artillery support.

Earlier that day, at 0600, just as he was readying to depart for the high ground, Morgia had met an officer who told him he was assigned to be the artillery field observer for Fox Company.

"I said, 'How can you do that? F Company is the reserve,'" and added that the man was to accompany Easy.

"The officer insisted, 'No, I'm supposed to go to F Company. Those are my orders.'

"I told him, 'They don't need you today. We may need you on that hill. Just follow us.'" The man finally relented and walked in the rear of the column.

Now, under tank attack at the farm, Morgia ordered the man to call in fire on the armored vehicles a stone's throw away.

"I said, 'Look, there are tanks to the left. Get some artillery just over our heads here and on those tanks,'" Morgia remembered.

The man complied, and within moments shells were screaming in on target. From inside the house, which has no windows on either the northern or southern side, Morgia could not see the effect of the artillery fire. But the shelling by the tanks subsided as the trio of Panzers, dissuaded by the American field guns, evidently pulled back.

German infantry, moving on the farm, was driven back amid a hail of small-arms and BAR fire.

Now—it was around eight a.m.—there seems to have been a lull in the action. But around nine a.m., Morgia spotted trucks in the distance, off to his right. They stopped and men in white snowsuits jumped down from the tailgates. Since his men were also wearing white snowsuits, Morgia at first thought these might be reinforcements. Raising his binoculars, he focused on the first man.

"He was carrying a burp gun," Morgia told me, referring to the Schmeisser machine pistol.

More infantry began appearing—some 250 men of the 20th Panzer Grenadiers—accompanied by the three tanks. Within minutes, the GIs were taking fire from the north, south, and east. Issy Gockley recalled his friend, Sergeant William H. Lumpkin, who was firing his BAR from a second-floor window in the barn, having a shell blast sweep his helmet from his head. Had his chin strap been fastened, Lumpkin would most likely have been decapitated.

The GIs fought a desperate and costly action, slamming fresh ammo clips into the smoking, hungry breeches of their M1 rifles as fast as they could. The barn was riddled by small-arms fire while 20mm shells from the Panzers pulverized the stone walls.

As the Germans pressed closer, the men of Easy faced the very real danger of being swamped by men in coal scuttle helmets.

"We all thought we'd had it," Issy told me. "They seemed to be all around us."

Morgia knew he needed to call artillery down on his own head and turned to the artillery spotter, only to see the man emptying a clip from his carbine into his own radio.

"He said, 'I tell you, this situation looks hopeless. We're in trouble and I can't let the enemy get my radio,'" Morgia told me.

Luckily, Morgia had his own radio operator and he quickly ordered the man to send a message for artillery. He also called up his runner, Private First Class Robert Epley, a Gettysburg, Pennsylvania, boy.

"I said, 'Bob, I don't know if my messages are getting through. You gotta get back to someone in Beho and tell them we may need reinforcements to push these Germans back.' He said, 'I will, sir,'" Morgia remembered. "I knew Epley was a great runner. He was an athlete in high school. He was a good guy. I loved Epley."

Sending the runner in addition to the radio message, Morgia said, was for extra insurance.

"I didn't want to rely on any one thing," he said.

Both the radio message and Epley got through. As Morgia watched the trucks disgorging infantry, he said, the first American shell "hit a truck right on the head." Rounds kept dropping, some no farther than fifty yards from the farm. Luckily for the men of Easy, the Americans' famed knack for accurate artillery fire was dead on target.

Between the shell fire and the stubborn resistance of Easy Company

The eighteenth-century farmhouse at Beho, Belgium. The cross led the men of Easy Company, 334th Regiment, 84th Division, who held this ground to refer to the farm as a monastery.

The men of E-334 fought their way into the barn at the rear of this courtyard in Beho on January 23, 1945.

defending the stone farm buildings, the German attack sputtered out. The battle for the Maison de Neuve was over by ten a.m., but not without losses. Two officers, Lieutenant Jamison of Issy Gockley's 2nd Platoon and 3rd Platoon's Lieutenant Clyde S. Laurent Jr., were dead, and two enlisted men were mortally wounded.

"I helped carry out a man who had a hole through his chest. The medics told me later on that he died. They couldn't save him," my father-in-law recalled.

Fox Company now arrived and Morgia took the time to go into the cellar of the farmhouse. There, huddled for protection, he found the Noll family: Pierre, his wife, Suzanne, and seven children ranging in age from ten years down to sixteen-month-old twins, Georges and Maria Theresa.

After assuring the family all was well, Morgia, who had gone almost without rest for two days, settled down "into a deep sleep."

For his actions at Maison de Neuve, James Morgia was awarded the Silver Star and, later, a pass to Paris. Robert Epley was given a Bronze Star.

Getting out of the car at the farm we approached the house. A small thin man in his mid-sixties, dressed casually in black slacks and an aqua V-necked sweater, approached. This was Georges Noll, the same person who, sixty-three years earlier, as a toddler, hid with his family in the cellar as the battle raged around their home. Noll lives at the farm now, just as his father and his father before him did. In fact, the farm is occupied by the fifth generation of the Noll family.

Noll told us, with Reg translating, that his family moved to the farm around 1880.

"This goes back to his great-grandparents," Reg told us.

Originally, the family did not own the farm, but worked it for a wealthy landowner who lived elsewhere and came to stay in the maison, or mansion, every summer. The workers lived in one of the two outbuildings attached to the barn.

"My family lived here during the war," he said, confirming Morgia's story. "My family was hiding in the cellar."

Having been a toddler at the time, Monsieur Noll was not real helpful about details, although he did say some 84th Division veterans had visited the farm in the past.

Pointing to a barn across the intersection, diagonal from the mansion, Noll said there had been a lot of fighting around what was then a one-story sheep barn, and that it had caught fire and burned down.

"His father told him a lot of Germans got killed in that barn," Reg translated.

Morgia, on the other hand, could not remember any buildings catching fire, and could not confirm the farmer's story.

Standing there by the mansion, Reg pulled out his cell phone and called Jim Morgia in Connecticut. We told him where we were, and he was truly amazed. Morgia has never been back to the farm since that day, although he had always hoped to return. We described what we were seeing and it jibed with his memories.

"That's wonderful," he said. "You're really there."

With Monsieur Noll's blessing, I explored the farm, walking through the courtyard to the big stone barn. Unlike in 1945, when all of this ground was snow-covered dirt, everything is now paved, the roads and the courtyard. But the buildings were almost unchanged. The thick whitewashed stone walls remain, although in some places they have been patched, usually by more stones, and repainted.

The outbuilding opposite the house has one huge spot where a major section of wall was blown out, doubtless by German tank fire. Unlike elsewhere, this place was repaired using brick instead of stone.

The telltale pockmarks of bullets also pepper these walls.

I approached the big barn that I recall Issy talking about so vividly on those rare occasions when he chose to remember the war. Poking my head inside, I became the center of attention for about a dozen cows lying on the straw and eyeing me curiously with their big brown eyes.

It was almost impossible to conjure up an image of the confusion and intense emotion experienced by Issy Gockley, Bill Lumpkin, Bill Wright, and the other men of 2nd Platoon of Easy Company as they stormed through the very doorway I was now standing in and grappled with German soldiers trying to escape through the opposite door.

The yelling, shouts of anger or pain, the gunfire, Wright's bursting rifle grenade taking out a machine-gun crew simply did not jell with this image of lazy cattle, peacefully munching on straw and watching this strange person carrying his digital camera.

Yet it happened right here amid these rows of water troughs and milking stalls.

I snapped a photo and returned to the car.

Like many veterans of World War II, Israel Gockley, who died in 1995, was not quick to share his memories, keeping them buried inside, tucked away in a place where they were seldom allowed to escape. Quite likely the reason was because those memories were so filled with terror and violence, like his images of what happened here at Beho. And, just as likely, it's because so many of those memories are steeped in sadness.

"I remember a young fellow who was sitting on a log and showed me a picture of his young child, which he never saw, and his wife," Issy once told me. "As we moved out he was near the end of the line. The Germans threw an 88 in and he was killed."

Climbing back into Reg's car, my guide twisted the key, started the motor, and we were off. As we drove down the Beho-Audrange road, I glanced back at Maison de Neuve one more time.

"I made it, Issy," I thought with the deep satisfaction of having honored his memory. "I was here."

CHAPTER 12

HAGUENAU

SETTING THE RECORD STRAIGHT

Haguenau is a modern French city sitting astride the Moder River, and it would be Easy Company's next stop after the Bulge. It was intended to be ours, too, but Forrest persuaded me otherwise.

"They changed the place so much," he told me. "They even changed the course of the river. You can't see any of the places we crossed."

The rejuvenation of the city following the devastation of war was remarkable, and of all the places Easy fought in, Haguenau, Forrest told me, is now the "most beautiful." But with rebuilding for the future often comes destruction of the past.

"When we were there on one of our tours, we couldn't find anything," Forrest said. "The whole front is changed. The riverbed has been changed. There are houses all over the place. You can't see any of the old stone houses that were there. We aren't even sure where we crossed. We couldn't even find a person who knew anything about it. I could make some guesses and maybe find some approximate spots, but it's all been redone."

So sacrificing approximates in favor of definites, and with time at a premium, I decided to skip a physical visit to Haguenau and spend more time at other locations. But I include it in this book because Haguenau is still the site of Easy's final combat experience in World War II, and the place where Hollywood screenwriters changed historical fact and slighted my friend Forrest Guth. It's a slight I intend to correct.

As they bounced along dirt roads in jeeps and trucks, the men of Easy Company were thoroughly pissed off. After thirty-six days of almost constant contact with the enemy in the snow-shrouded forests of Belgium, the 101st Airborne Division was told it was going into corps reserve for a break. Instead, the battle-weary men now found themselves jostling their way to Alsace to help defend against what was rumored to be another German attack.

"I thought, 'My God, doesn't the army have any other troops who can plug those gaps?'" Winters told me in 2004.

By the circuitous route they took, it was thirty-six hours and 160 bone-jarring, butt-numbing miles to the town of Drulingen, where they arrived on January 26. Their stay there was brief, and they were soon back on the road along what Sink told Winters was "a little stream called the Moder River."

When they arrived they quickly discovered that the "little stream called the Moder River," normally thirty to forty feet wide, was presently swollen by snowmelt so that in many places it was a football field in width. Swiftly flowing, muddy brown water frothed and swirled, and treacherous currents produced by the flooding would make sending out contact patrols a difficult and dangerous venture. The Five-oh-Sinks were positioned on the division's left along a thirty-five-hundred-yard length of the Moder stretching from Weikersheim to Pfaffenhoffen. To Sink's right was the 501st, the center of Taylor's line, with the 327th Glider on the 501st's right. The 502nd was put in reserve.

The 2nd Battalion was in Haguenau to relieve a regiment of the 79th Division. Opposite them was the German 25th Panzer Grenadier Division, which the 79th had been fighting since January 8.

Life in Haguenau wasn't too bad. For one thing, the men had indoor accommodations, a luxury they had not experienced since leaving Mourmelon for Bastogne on December 19. Every platoon was assigned a house, Babe Heffron recalled.

"We could even do OP duty sometimes from inside a house," he said, as if this was an amazing thing, which, perhaps, it was.

Action at Haguenau was "pretty low-keyed," Forrest told me.

"The war was winding down and both sides knew it," he said. "No one wanted to take any chances."

Clancy Lyall recalled it being "a quiet place," although "every once in a while you got a mortar shell."

There was sporadic firing back and forth, Forrest recalled, as well as artillery shell fire. The Germans, Heffron noted, possessed a huge railroad gun that "had us on edge."

"They'd fire one round from that railroad gun and you could feel the ground shake," he said. "Once or twice a day they fired that damn gun."

The artillery piece was dubbed Alsace Annie, a fifteen-inch railroad gun whose heavy-caliber shells made a *chug, chug* sound like a railroad locomotive as they passed overhead, and just could take out a house.

Still, to the men of Easy, being in Haguenau was better than any foxhole, and the men settled in and made themselves comfortable, both by accommodation and other creature comforts.

"We used to go through the crashed Allied or enemy airplanes when we got time and took everything we could use," Forrest recalled. "They had pistols, machetes, . . . just different kinds of items. I got a shearling jacket [fur-lined leather with a big furry collar] from a crashed aircraft. Since we had no proper winter clothing, I grabbed the coat. I wish I had found it earlier when I was still in Bastogne."

Supplies arrived from the rear as well, including sixty-one hundred pairs of winter shoepacs, arctic socks, felt insoles, and six thousand yards of white cloth, enough to make two thousand snowsuits.

"Oh my, how we could have used them six weeks earlier at Bastogne," Winters told me years later.

David Webster rejoined 2nd Battalion about this time, following his wounding at the Crossroad in Holland. He was riding to the front in a truck with other replacements, he recalled, and glaring at the dismal landscape and bare, "slimy brown" hills, thinking, "God, how I hate Europe." After arriving back with the battalion, he was surprised to find Winters gone and replaced by Spiers. He recalled Spiers's "reputation as a reckless, savage man" and that he "was glad to have him for a company commander."

On the way to Haguenau, Webster was told "half the town is ours, half is Krauts. The rumor is we're going to take the other half." The move forward was done with haste, and Webster recalled sitting down for chow when the call came to "hit it. We're moving out."

"The army never changed," he wrote.

Assigned to 1st Squad, 1st Platoon, he and his comrades "arrived at night, cold rain falling . . . banging of tailgates, men talking excitedly." He wrote that he "gulped down the fear that always came over me when we moved into a new position at night."

The trucks had stopped in the middle of a wide street, where gutted white houses studded with black shell holes lined the sidewalks. Debris in the streets had been bulldozed aside to form mounds five feet high. Webster spent the first night in Haguenau on outpost duty, never a pleasant prospect for him, especially when an occasional shell arced unseen overhead and exploded in the distance.

To get to the outpost, Webster wrote, he had to first cross some two hundred yards of open parade ground, paved in stone and surrounded on three sides by a trio of three-story-high Victorian brick barracks with steep slate roofs. Already heavily shelled, the parade ground was zeroed in on by German artillery spotters and men had to quickly scurry across close to the northernmost building. The platoon CP was in the west barracks, accessible by a steep stone stairway ten feet wide.

Webster was part of a patrol led by John Martin that included Joe Liebgott, Bob Rader, Clancy Lyall, and a new man. Staying close to the CP, they dashed across the parade ground and into a stable. After crawling through a hole in the rear wall, they crossed a cratered field fifty yards wide to what was once a "neat and placid home of a middle-class family" but was now pockmarked by machine-gun bullets that "criss-crossed the ghostly white façade." They scurried across the yard of the house and through an iron gate, then double-timed down the road that led toward the Moder River about a hundred yards away, to another house. There they made their way down an artillery-shattered driveway to the garage, entered and passed through it, then moved on to the next house, which served as the outpost.

When not risking their lives trying to reach their outposts, the men were treated to a few luxuries in Haguenau. The army set up portable showers in which as many as 215 men an hour could rinse away weeks of grime. Entire companies lined up to feel the invigorating sting of hot water on their weary bodies. The men had access to news from the outside as issues of *Yank*, *Stars and Stripes*, and the division's own newspaper, the *Kangaroo Khronicle*—Kangaroo being the division's code name—were widely distributed.

Seven of Hollywood's most recent movies circulated the camps, including *Buffalo Bill*, starring Joel McCrea, Maureen O'Hara, and Linda Darnell, *Mrs. Parkington* with Greer Garson and Walter Pidgeon, and the Alfred Hitchcock suspense film *Saboteur*, with its hair-raising climax atop the Statue of Liberty, although this latter brought about a bit of home-sickness to men who had not seen Lady Liberty in over two years. A Red Cross club arrived, giving the men a chance to mingle, drink coffee, eat doughnuts, or listen to the latest Big Band music and maybe, if they were lucky, dance with a Red Cross girl under a silky canopy of draped parachutes.

But perhaps best of all, the Screaming Eagle shoulder patches they were ordered to remove as they approached Bastogne could now be sewn back on. The division had resumed its identity.

Not surprisingly, cases of frostbite and combat fatigue dropped dra-matically.

Amid all of this, and even with the Germans just across the river and the air overhead rippled with incoming or outgoing artillery shells, there was a realization that the war was winding down.

"There was just a feeling, and you began to tell yourself, 'I might just make it after all,'" Winters told me in 2004. "So you start to walk easy, watch where you step."

In the midst of this feeling of "maybe I'll make it" came word that Colonel Sink wanted Winters to send a patrol across the Moder to snatch German prisoners. Such patrols were conducted on occasion by men of both armies.

"The war was about over," Clancy Lyall told me. "Everybody knew it. Even the Germans. We weren't going to take any chances unless we had to. We'd fire across. They'd fire across. We'd send a patrol out to catch a prisoner, and so did they."

He recalled one German patrol that was spotted halfway across the river and was decimated by American small-arms fire.

Winters was unhappy with the thought of risking men's lives on so difficult and, he believed, foolhardy a mission.

"It's a tough job to approach a man with a rifle or behind a machine gun who is in a defensive position and persuade him to come with you as your prisoner of war," Winters told me. "And what's it going to accom-plish? All we're going to find over there are enlisted men. And what can they tell us? Their guys are probably dumber than ours, and our fellas don't know what the hell's going on. And there's a real good chance of someone getting hurt and us having nothing to show for it. I don't like it."

Earlier in the war, Winters would never have griped about such an order, because raids were a tactically sound decision. One sent out contact patrols as a means of intelligence gathering. But at this stage of the war, men were no longer willing to take needless risks. Nor was he willing to risk men's lives on dangerous and pointless patrols. No one wanted to become what could be the war's last casualty. Winters was also keenly aware that the men were tired and manpower was thin. Instead of having two battalions on line and one in reserve, Sink reversed it, placing one on line and two in reserve. Since 2nd Battalion was now holding the line, this headache patrol fell in Winters's lap.

Winters handed the assignment to Spiers, who selected Sergeant Ken Mercier to lead it. A new young officer, Second Lieutenant Hank Jones, approached Winters and asked permission to go along. Winters denied it, due to the young man's inexperience. Jones persisted and Winters relented. Jones could go, although Mercier remained in command of the patrol.

One more person who was needed for this patrol was a man who could speak and comprehend German, and for that Mercier turned to—not David Webster, as depicted in Hollywood's version of this patrol—but my friend and traveling companion, Forrest Guth.

In his book, *Parachute Infantry*, Webster wrote that he had considered volunteering for the patrol, perhaps to replace Melvin W. Winn, a newer man. However, he must have reconsidered, writing that he was "frankly relieved not to have been chosen, for a patrol in a city as settled and heavily mined as Haguenau was bound to be a rather unquiet venture." Instead, he manned a machine gun with orders to provide covering fire for the patrol's withdrawal.

In fact, David Webster was not the volunteering type, preferring to remain in the background and just do his job. He did this quite successfully. So much so that when his book was first released, Winters had no idea who its author was.

"I called up Carwood Lipton and asked, 'Who is this guy?' and Carwood didn't know," Winters told me. "He made some more phone calls and we finally found out, but I didn't remember him."

Lyall, who would be manning a machine gun to provide suppressing fire for the patrol, and who was in the same squad as Webster, agrees that Webster was not the type to put his neck on the line by going on the mission.

"He didn't volunteer for shit," Lyall recalled. "Whenever they were looking for someone for a patrol, he's not there."

He said Webster kept a diary of his experiences, and "we'd tell him lies like hell, and he'd be writing it down."

Lyall recalled an incident in Holland when he and Massaconi were manning a machine gun atop a dike, "firing like hell because the Germans were trying to infiltrate our line." At the base of the dike were some foxholes with extra ammo boxes for the gun. Webster was the gun's ammo bearer and had "two or three cans in his hole" as well.

"We were running low on ammo, so I hollered three or four times to him and he didn't come," Clancy remembered. "So I took a grenade—I didn't pull the pin—I just tossed it up in the air. He got up there with the damned ammunition before the grenade hit the ground."

Forrest recalled being in his bivouac in a stable by the river when he got word that his interpreting services were needed for the patrol.

"I somewhat volunteered to go on a night mission behind enemy lines in order to capture a prisoner for interrogation," Forrest told me. "They said, 'You, you and you.' I spoke some German, but so did Liebgott."

Since the patrol was made up of Easy Company men, Spiers wanted to tell Mercier how to conduct it, but Winters overrode him. Besides prisoners, his main goal was minimal casualties, and he knew how he wanted the patrol to go about it. He gathered the men together at the riverside and pointed to a large building across the river.

"That's your objective," he told them. "We know the Krauts have an OP in there. Because of the current, the patrol will cross the river upstream on our right flank by D Company's OP and approach the objective. Once you reach the Kraut OP, Mercier, get your flankers out to provide security, then go in. Put a rifle grenade into the building, and close in fast. Get more grenades into the basement windows. That'll stun the Krauts inside. Get in, grab some POWs, and get out. But before you leave, I want a satchel charge on a delayed timer hidden in the building. With any luck, the Germans will reoccupy it before the charge goes off. Get back to the boats as fast as you can. Mercier has a whistle that he will blow when you're pulling back. That's the signal for the covering fire to open up. You'll have blanket support. We have a 57-millimeter anti-tank gun, a .50-caliber and several .30-caliber machine guns, as well as mortars covering your every move. They've zeroed in on every known or suspected enemy position, so woe be to any Kraut fool enough to lift his head."

Winters looked around at the grim-faced men. The plan was as perfect as he could make it.

The patrol moved out on the night of February 18, stopping first at D Company's outpost to gobble down sandwiches and coffee before heading for the boats. The lead dinghy trailed a rope out behind it. Once across, the rope was tied to a pole. The next boatload of men used the rope to pull their way across, but the third dinghy carrying Winn, Roy Cobb, and Thomas A. McCreary capsized, dumping the trio into the icy water. They emerged, drenched, cold, and sputtering, righted the boat and tried again. Again the recalcitrant dinghy dumped them out and they gave up.

Once they were over the river, the action was quick and decisive, as the GIs attacked the house.

"We didn't have much trouble getting the prisoners because they knew the war was nearly over," Forrest recalled. "I yelled 'kum raus, kum raus' and they came out. We captured three Germans, but one was badly wounded."

He did not recall anyone tossing grenades inside the building first as depicted in the film and as laid out in Winters's plan, but figured Mercier must have done so. Nor did Forrest see Eugene Jackson get hit. Jackson had been struck by grenade shrapnel, possibly German, possibly his own. Either way, he would die before he could be evacuated to a field hospital.

"He knew he was dying," Babe Heffron recalled.

With their prisoners and the injured Jackson in tow, the patrol raced for the riverbank and the rubber boats. Mercier blew the whistle and his comrades across the Moder laid down covering fire. The Germans returned fire and orange tracers crisscrossed the sky over the heads of the retreating Americans. Luckily, Forrest recalled, the German fire "wasn't very accurate."

On the bank, the wounded German "began acting up, screaming

and yelling," Forrest told me. His flailing drew enemy fire, and a decision was made to leave him behind as his two comrades were bundled into boats and ferried across the river.

"It was a pretty rough ride back over the river," Forrest said. "Bullets were flying over our heads. You could hear them."

With the patrol safely back across, the firing soon died away, and the quiet of the night resumed. Or almost. The injured man lay there, moaning loudly all night, working on the nerves of the paratroopers.

"Some fellows thought about swimming the river and knifing him, but they finally got him by throwing grenades," Forrest recalled.

The next morning Winters watched with satisfaction as the hidden satchel charge exploded in the building across the river.

"We never knew if any Germans returned to the outpost before the detonation, nor did we care," Winters later wrote. He regretted the loss of Jackson, but the mission had been accomplished successfully.

Forrest Guth was unhappy with the way the screenwriters replaced him with David Webster in the "Last Patrol" episode, and he was not the only one.

"After the 'Last Patrol' episode aired, Winters called me and said, 'What the hell are they doing? That's not the way it went,'" Forrest told me. "He meant that I was on the patrol, and they didn't show me at all. But it doesn't matter too much as long as some people know the truth."

Now everyone who reads this book will know the truth.

Winters's elation at the success of the patrol soon turned bitter, when he received orders from Colonel Sink to repeat the mission and grab more prisoners. Winters couldn't believe his ears. He reddened with anger, but simply uttered a "Yes sir" and saluted. He considered Sink "a magnificent commander," but this time his orders "made no sense."

"He was showing off for his drinking buddy, [Colonel Joseph H.] Harper," Winters told me in 2004. "We were the first regiment to send out a patrol that successfully brought back any prisoners and now he wants to brag and show everyone else how easy it is."

Winters knew that to take any prisoners, the patrol would have to venture even deeper into the German-occupied section of the town, and that this time, the enemy would be on the alert. That presented a very real threat of high casualties among the patrol, for what Winters considered little, if any, tactical gain. The thought of losing men for no good purpose this close to the end of the war revolted him. Earlier in the war, he might have taken the risk, he later told me. But not now. Gathering the patrol around him, he informed them that they were to get a good night's sleep, but that if anyone asked them, they were to say they went across but could not get any prisoners. To make a convincing argument, that night Winters ordered machine-gun and mortar fire on the Germans to imitate covering fire for the nonexistent patrol.

Winters knew he'd just risked his entire military career, and a likely court-martial, by intentionally disobeying an order from his commanding officer. But he was damned if he'd risk any more lives on a foolhardy mission that had little chance of success and a very large chance of turning into a disaster.

"I knew I was getting out as quick as possible after the war was over," Winters told me in 2003. "I had no fantasies of making the army my life. If I had any idea of making the military a career and be a career soldier, would I have disobeyed an order and not sent those men? If someone is going to make it his career, he's not going to have it on his efficiency report 'refused an order.' What kind of officer is that?"

The men who would have made that dangerous foray across the river were forever grateful.

"Winters knew what he was doing," Babe Heffron wrote. "The Krauts would have been ready for us. It would have been a disaster. He led by common sense, not standard operating procedure. He could have gotten himself into big trouble defying orders, but he was willing to take that chance to save a few lives. No one ever said another word about it."

Lieutenant Ralph D. Richey Jr. of F Company, now attached to Winters as an S2 intelligence officer, told him, "That was a classic, sir. You should write that one up for the future."

"No, Lieutenant," Winters said. "That's one report that will never be written."

Fifty-eight years later, Winters told me, "Sink wasn't being mean when he ordered that second patrol. He was proud of what we had done. But it was a dumb, dumb decision."

Winters filed no after-action report on the patrol that never was, nor did Sink ever request one. Did Sink know Winters had orders? Perhaps.

While I was with Paul Woodadge in Normandy, the subject of this patrol-that-never-was came up. Some years earlier, Paul had conducted a tour for Sink's daughter Margaret. At that time he asked her if her father ever knew that Winters had disobeyed his direct order. She said Sink did know, but that he, himself, was just following orders he had received from his superior officer when he assigned the second patrol to Winters. Sink kept the secret from his superiors, just as Winters's men kept it from Sink.

At the end of March, the 101st was pulled off the front and returned to Mourmelon, France. They had been on the line for two and a half months.

Sometime in late March, each regiment in the division held the first of what would eventually become a number of lotteries in which the winner would receive a thirty-day furlough. To be eligible, a man had to have a clean service record and have fought in all of the regiment's campaigns. Thirty-three men qualified. Forrest Guth's name was drawn, and the next day he was packing up to leave. As events developed, he would not be returning.

"Haguenau was the end of my war experience," Forrest said.

It was also Easy Company's last combat experience, and as such, marks the end of this walk back in time.

THEIR ECHO WILL NEVER FADE

Before Forrest Guth departed for home in 1945, he made a stop at the army hospital where Lieutenant "Moose" Heyliger was recuperating from being shot by a nervous sentry in Holland. Heyliger, Forrest recalled, gave him a pistol he wanted Guth to carry back to the States for him. Forrest did.

"The rules said there were some things you couldn't take back, but they didn't care," my friend recalled. "You could take anything you wanted."

Then he sailed westward across the Atlantic aboard a U.S. hospital ship.

Happy to be home, Forrest spent a few weeks with his family and visiting with friends. Yet he still longed to be with his buddies in Easy Company.

"I was glad to be back in the States and all," he told me. "But I missed the fellas. They were family, too."

Then came the time to go back, or so he thought.

"I was getting ready to ship back overseas and rejoin my outfit, but the army wouldn't let me," Forrest said. "The war was nearing its end and by the time I would have been in Germany, the army expected the war in Europe to be over. So I missed all the fun part of it. I didn't take part in the victory celebrations and didn't get my share of the loot from Hitler's Eagle's Nest. It was the biggest hurt when I couldn't get back from the States to join them at Berchtesgaden. I left my barracks bag in Europe, too, with some of my equipment and the souvenirs I'd collected. I thought I was going back and would be able to retrieve it."

Had he known he would not be returning, Forrest said he "would've loaded up." He had picked up a flag, a couple of pistols, and a knife, among other booty, but came away from almost a year in combat with "not much loot at all."

"Well, never mind," he told me. "I was alive and home and had seen enough of war."

Instead of boarding a ship for Europe, Forrest boarded a train for Fort Benning to await the 101st's return from Germany and redeployment to the war in the Pacific.

"We were going to retrain and be reinforced," he told me. "They even gave us Japanese currency."

In June, while awaiting the division's return, Forrest received a four-page letter from Captain Spiers, datelined "Kaprun, 20 miles south of Berchtesgaden." In the letter, Spiers described their trip via "those 10-ton truck trailers" to the "Ruhr Pocket near Dusseldorf" to the Rhine. They conducted a few patrols, he said, then headed for Berchtesgaden in the Bavarian Alps.

"Everyone here has lots of Lugers, P-38s etc.," Spiers wrote. "But I'll be making you jealous. We would have all traded to be in your place."

Updating Forrest on the company, Spiers told him, "Luz fell off a motorcycle and hurt his arm, not seriously. Sgt. Talbert didn't like being 1st Sergeant so I gave him the second platoon." . . . "Lt. Lipton is on furlough in England just now (I mean Scotland) and is very happy, I suppose." As for himself, "I'm waiting out a furlough to England to see my wife and baby." Also "Sgt. Powers was on his way home to the States and the truck overturned and he fractured his skull and he is hospitalized somewhere. Sgt. Strohl is on his way home to the States. Sgt. Chuck Grant got in the way of a bullet from a drunken American and his head is not too good—he is in a German hospital near here and is getting better." Don Malarkey "just got back from a long stretch in the hospital."

Spiers wrote that he was putting a number of men, including Guth, in for the Bronze Star "for meritorious service."

"I am positive they will go this time," he wrote. "So that will mean five more points for you."

The accumulation of points was an important topic to the GIs as the war in Europe ended and the war in the Pacific loomed large in their future. Getting out of the army and making that glorious trip home depended on the number of points one had earned, and the army was stingy with handing them out. Under the Advanced Service Rating

Score established by the army, men received one point for each month of service between September 16, 1940, and May 12, 1945. They also got one point for each month spent overseas during the same time period. Five points were awarded for every decoration, including the Purple Heart, and five points were awarded for each small bronze campaign star a man could pin on his theater ribbon. Lastly, men were given twelve points for each child back home under the age of eighteen, with a limit of up to three children, or thirty-six points. A man needed a total of eighty-five points to qualify for a trip home.

Under those guidelines, however, a GI who had been in the service for three years and had spent two years overseas in combat would have only sixty points. If he had a Purple Heart, Silver Star, or some other decoration and one child back home, his total would be seventy-seven points, eight short of what he needed.

"I think we will also get a battle star for Bastogne and perhaps one for Holland, but all we are entitled to now is two," Spiers wrote. "If we get the other (2), it will be ten more points."

To soothe Forrest's dismay at not being able to return to the company, Spiers told him not to worry, and that the men were just "getting drunk and killing each other," this latter comment referring to the shooting of Sergeant Grant by a drunken replacement, as mentioned above.

Spiers noted that the division was "waiting out coming home and the set up seems to be that we will come home before going to the Pacific. We hope so anyhow. If we do come home, get in touch with us right away and I'll get you right back in the regiment. And if you don't get that promotion when you come back, it won't be because I didn't try. You are a good soldier, Guth, and I hope to see you soon. Don't worry, we'll see you at Benning when we get back."

The letter from Spiers, who was not much on sentiment, surprised not just Forrest Guth, but Dick Winters as well.

"When I showed that letter to Winters after the war, he couldn't believe that Spiers, who was always so tough, would care that much to write back to me," Forrest said.

Forrest liked Spiers as the company's CO, remembering that "he was a good man. He was fearless. He hated the Germans and was rather ruthless. Everyone respected him."

"Of all the officers, I think of him most kindly," Forrest told me. "I think he was the most caring."

Eventually, elements of the 101st began returning to Benning, and whatever came next.

"We thought we were all going to train for Japan," Forrest said.

But the Pacific war soon ended, and Forrest recalled, "We got our boarding passes and went home."

And home is where Forrest and I were now headed.

We had spent thirteen days in Europe, traveling together from Aldbourne, England, across the Channel to Normandy, then into Belgium, and finally Holland. With the exception of Haguenau, we had visited every major field on which the men of Easy Company exchanged fire with the enemy, including Marmion Farm, Brecourt Manor, Carentan, Bastogne, the Bois Jacques, Foy, Noville, Son, Nuenen, Uden, and the Crossroad.

Our last night in Europe was spent at the Ibis Hotel, just a short shuttle bus ride from Schiphol Airport outside Amsterdam. As had happened so often on our journey, a *Band of Brothers* fan, Bart Houx, dropped by to meet Forrest and myself and have us sign copies of my book and Ambrose's. Bart had originally offered to serve as our Holland guide, but our schedules failed to match.

Over dinner that night, I gave Forrest a chance to reflect on the war and his friends.

"It's amazing how much you miss the other guys," he said. "You want to be with them. It was a great group of guys from all over the country, and we had a lot of fun, even though the training was hard work. They're the best friends I ever had."

I asked Forrest about the many replacements who came into the company during the course of the war, and who paid a heavy price for their lack of training before being sent up to the front. Forrest and the other men already on the line didn't know about the assembly-line-style, rudimentary training these new recruits received, which left them ill-prepared for combat, and thought "it was amazing" how quickly many got hit.

"I guess they just didn't know what to look out for," Forrest mused.

Over a cold tankard of Dutch beer, he added, "The war stays with you. It never goes away, although the passing of years softens things. I think about the fellas, especially the ones we lost. A lot of them were good friends. I miss them. When one dies, it's just like losing a family member."

The loss of their comrades and the horrors of war affected these men, both during their time in combat and in the years that have followed. Bill Guarnere wrote how the loss "hits you at night" and said he sometimes got the shakes, but did not cry like some men did while in the solitude of their foxholes.

He said there were days when "you wanted to get hurt and get out," but then one recalled that the war would go on "and you wanted not to let down your buddies." One did not want to be "what they called a goldbricker, trying to get out while you can still fight." Wild Bill recalled thinking, "Lord, get me the hell out of this place," followed, with some feeling of guilt, by "But if I leave, then what's going to happen to my men?"

Carwood Lipton, looking back years later, speculated on how one endures the horrors of war. His answer was simple.

"You're part of a group, an organization," he said. "You develop an intense pride in yourself and in your unit. And you're just sure you're not going to let yourself down or the unit down. You have confidence in the guys around you. You can count on them, and they can count on you."

As for the rigors of incessant combat and the constancy of death, Lipton claimed "it didn't take a lot of adjustment."

"We'd been trained for two years and we'd talked about combat and what it would be like, and we had training exercises where they fired right over us," he said. "As for the dead, the bodies, they don't bother you at all. Enemy bodies make no impression whatsoever. You just don't care. They're the enemy. They're dead and they aren't going to fight you anymore.

"And the bodies of your own men don't affect you for very long. There's a kind of feeling inside of triumph or accomplishment that 'I was lucky enough or smart enough or good enough to keep from getting killed. It's too bad about Joe. He just wasn't able to make it through.'"

I asked Forrest what he thought of the miniseries. Unlike Winters, who told me "they did a pretty good job," Forrest did not like it and blamed "poor casting."

"They don't look like the guys, they don't talk like them and they don't act like the guys," he told me.

Then there was also the fact that he was one of the original Toccoa men the series totally ignored, although a Forrest Guth character was planned and his unique, many-pocketed uniform was re-created from the original. However, the character was never developed and the uniform was given to another actor.

Forrest's sentiments are echoed by others as well, especially by his comrades in 3rd Platoon.

Herb Suerth thought the miniseries "was reasonable as a Hollywood production," despite "some inaccuracies."

"I think there was a lot of politics in the movie within E Company," Suerth said. "Third Platoon was left out completely. Hardly mentioned. Paul Rogers is really upset about that. But those things happen."

He also felt the movie "belittled" Ed Shames.

"Goddammit, Ed was a good platoon leader," Suerth recalled. "He and Paul Rogers knocked out a Kraut tank in Foy with a bazooka, for Christ's sake. Just the two of them. Nobody else around. But there was prejudice against Ed."

Clancy Lyall called the movie "about 90 percent correct." He noted some discrepancies between the film and reality, one of which, he felt, was when Winters led the charge at the Crossroad, running way out in front of the company.

"I don't recall Winters ever being that far ahead of us," Clancy said. "Of course, he could have been."

With the end of the war, the men came home and tried to pick up the pieces of their interrupted lives. Some were able to make the transition from citizen soldier to just plain citizen.

Dick Winters went to work for his friend Lewis Nixon at Nixon Nitration Works, in Nixon, now Edison, New Jersey, before eventually going into business for himself. Others took advantage of the GI Bill and continued their education, while a few were not able to successfully make that leap between war and peace.

Forrest's friend with whom he joined the paratroopers in 1942, Carl Fenstermacher, was deeply affected by the war and bore emotional scars.

"He couldn't hold down a job," Forrest remembered.

Fenstermacher died in 1988.

As for Forrest, he enrolled at Millersville State Teacher's College in Millersville, Pennsylvania, where the former company armorer became an industrial arts teacher. He then went looking for a job.

"I found that in Pennsylvania they paid teachers only nineteen hundred dollars a year," he said. "So I took a job in Norfolk, Virginia, where I could make twenty-nine hundred a year."

He met his wife, Harriet, in Virginia, and they were soon married. In his spare time, Forrest took up woodworking and made furniture, as well as lifelike carved birds. He also began refurbishing classic cars.

Forrest and Harriet later moved to Delaware to work, and they continued to live there after their retirement. They were married nearly sixty years when Harriet died in December 2007. She is buried in Arlington National Cemetery and Forrest misses her greatly; he spoke of her often during our trip, and always with a tear in his eye.

But retirement didn't mean the men of Easy Company got to sit out the rest of their lives in peace and quiet. Stephen Ambrose's book, and especially the HBO miniseries, thrust them onto the worldwide stage, and the spotlight continues to shine on them.

Although Winters, in 2006, stopped all personal appearances and has requested that no more fan mail or books for signing be sent to him, many of the others continue to keep busy schedules. Men of Easy Company are regulars every June at the Mid-Atlantic Air Museum show in Reading, Pennsylvania, one of the largest World War II shows on the East Coast.

In September 2008, Forrest, Guarnere, Heffron, Malarkey, and Lyall were flown by the USO to Iraq to meet with American personnel deployed there. It was a long, grueling trip for men in their mid-eighties, and Forrest, for one, suffered for it upon his return with some health issues. But it was a trip they willingly made.

Yet all the publicity the men of Easy Company have been subjected to, and the celebrity status awarded them in the aftermath of the book and movie, leaves them with a sense of uneasiness.

"I think all of the men in other outfits did a great job," Forrest said pensively. "We were no different than any other company. I don't feel we deserve any more credit than any other outfit. Everyone who served should get as much credit as we're getting."

In an interview in *World War II* magazine's special *Band of Brothers* edition, Jim Alley noted that he appreciates the fanfare but hopes "it is not blown out of proportion."

"I know some of the other companies and regiments in the division will be upset by all this attention," he said. "I know that what we went through was the same as any other company in the division. We are not special."

The plane carrying Forrest Guth and me home from Europe landed at Philadelphia International Airport on the afternoon of November 13, 2008. The sun had shone brightly the entire trip across the Atlantic, allowing me to gaze down at the ocean, a view I did not have on the night flight over.

When we landed at Philly, however, it was dark, cloudy, and rainy. Since that condition accompanied us during most of our time in England and on the Continent, this reception back home seemed somehow fitting.

For me, when the wheels touched down on the tarmac, it was the end of a magnificent adventure, one I had dreamed about for more years than I care to remember. It was an opportunity to visit places I had read about in countless books and seen in documentaries, recorded on thousands of feet of newsreel footage.

But more than that, it was an opportunity for me to visit these places with a man, a friend, who had been there, who had lived the experience and could tell me his thoughts and his memories. This made the entire trip far more personal and meaningful than if I had gone on my own or with a group. It brought everything to life.

For Forrest, the trip was yet one more chance to go back, to remember the most defining event of his life, and to revisit the ground he had walked, the places he had fought, and, in the case of Salty Harris, the friends he had left behind.

Such is the case with all the men who go back to those fields.

Herb Suerth said, "It's sort of like going back to visit your old high school or college. You see a lot of things you recognize, but it was a long time ago."

He admitted that "the first time you go back it's a little hair-raising, I guess." His own first trip back to the Bois Jacques in 1978 left him somewhat unnerved.

At the American Cemetery above Omaha Beach, Forrest Guth pays one last visit to the grave of his friend Terrence "Salty" Harris.

"I was there with some of my family friends, and I got sort of spooked," he told me. "And what was bothering me is that I had seen a bunch of signs up in the woods and they were written in red. I didn't know what they meant, and I'm thinking unexploded ordnance, because, God, it was all over the place. You still can find things. No one paid any attention to it in those days. No one knew E Company and the Band of Brothers had spent almost thirty days in those holes. But now it doesn't bother me to go back there. I don't think it bothers most of the guys."

Suerth said his foxhole buddy, Frank Sobelski, had never been back until December 2007.

"It got to him," Suerth said. "Because he went to the Foy monument and the guys' names were all there who had been killed in the Foy attack that he had been in."

Clancy Lyall understands Suerth's feelings, "considering what happened to him there." Lyall, who reenlisted at the war's end and was assigned to the 508th PIR, remained in Europe. He said he held no animosity against the Germans. Assigned to Germany, he hired an ex–German paratrooper, who was "living in a bombed-out house," as his chauffeur "because I knew they were hurting."

"We have a mutual respect for each other," he said. "There's an honor between paratroopers."

Revisiting the places he had fought in during the war, both during that period and later, he said, gives him no bad memories.

Ed Tipper returned to his old battlefields for both the fiftieth and sixtieth anniversary reunions, accompanied by his wife and daughter.

"We went back to the exact place we fought," he told me in 2009.

Some locations, most noticeably Marmion Farm, remain "totally unchanged fifty-some years after we fought there." To me, he noted that he and Forrest are "the only two E Company men still alive who were in that action."

On his first return to Carentan, he told me, he recognized the house where he had been so grievously wounded. Somewhat surprisingly, it made no deep impression on him, as Tipper chooses to focus on the positive.

"We have made friends with people in Carentan and we're still in contact with them," he said to me. "Any time I go back there, they come out and are anxious to meet us. And the relationship has been very good, even sixty-five years later."

The last time Tipper returned to Carentan, he said, the house where he was hit "no longer existed."

Asked by me about his reflections on going back, Tipper thought for a bit, then said, "It was not something I ever dreamed could happen, that fifty or sixty years after the war, I would be back there."

Babe Heffron noted that, on the many trips he and Bill Guarnere have taken, they often hear the sounds of the young men of Easy Company, echoing across time: of men counting cadence, double-timing, pulling back rifle bolts, shouting to each other and kidding around.

"Bill heard it too," he wrote. "Is it all in the mind?"

Perhaps.

But if you visit the now-silent battlefields—whether it is in Europe, Asia, or the Pacific—and you walk in the footsteps of the veterans, all veterans no matter where they served, and you stop and listen real hard, you will hear it too.

The echo is still there, and it always will be.

FORREST "GOODY" GUTH

1921–2009

On August 9, 2009, as this work was with my editor at New American Library, going through the process of being transformed from raw manuscript to the book you now hold in your hands, my good friend and traveling companion Forrest Guth, in the vernacular of the airborne, took that final jump.

Forrest passed away in a hospital bed at Cokesbury Village in Hockessin, Delaware, just a short walk from the cottage he and his late wife of sixty years, Harriet, had shared since 1977.

I had visited Forrest on several occasions, both before and after our overseas adventure. We'd sit in his living room or, more often, his den, talking and going over the stacks of materials he had relating to Easy Company. Sometimes I'd take him a small gift, usually a bag of Lancaster County hard pretzels, which Forrest loved. He'd pour us sodas, open the bag, and we'd talk and munch on the crunchy treats.

On one visit he took my wife and me into his garage and showed off his classic car collection, especially the 1929 Ford Roadster that he had restored and was in the process of sanding and painting. He was immensely proud of this car and featured it in a Christmas card he had made, with him and Harriet standing beside it. My wife and I were also fascinated by the lifelike birds Forrest had so expertly hand-carved and painted.

Forrest missed his wife deeply, and oftentimes on our journey back over Easy's battlefields, he'd talk about her, recalling when they had visited these same locations together in years gone by. At night, he often grew morose over her loss, and during dinner one evening he told me she was in Arlington National Cemetery, "waiting for me."

I certainly understood his pain, but tried to be uplifting, reminding him that he had friends and family here who loved him, and wanted him to stick around for a while. That thought brought a smile to his lips.

Traveling to England and Europe with Forrest was one of the most interesting and fun experiences of my life. It was not only a once-in-a-lifetime chance to visit these battlefields with a man who was actually there, hearing his remembrances and sharing his emotions; it was also an opportunity to see the effect, or legacy, if you will, of what Forrest and his comrades put their lives on the line for, on the people living in the path of the war. Almost everywhere we went, word traveled ahead of us that one of the Band of Brothers was coming, and, as this book relates, we were greeted by well-wishers and Easy Company fans all along the way.

But for me, some of the best moments were those Forrest and I shared alone, talking as we drove the car across England and Europe, in our stateroom as we crossed the English Channel on the Brittany ferry, enjoying a good meal in a nice restaurant, or sitting in Le Nut's in Bastogne, sipping an excellent Chimay beer while Forrest enjoyed a stogie.

Those memories, ones I will cherish all my life, were in sharp contrast to the Forrest Guth I saw on August 8. I had been forewarned about his condition by his daughter-in-law, Cindy, but even so I was shocked. My friend was awake, but he looked so frail, not at all like the spry fellow with the soft, sometimes sly smile that I was used to seeing.

I visited with him for about ninety minutes, not really knowing what to say to him, I was so shaken. I read get-well wishes sent to him, through me, by fans from America and overseas via various Band of Brothers Web sites. He seemed to enjoy that.

Forrest tried to speak to me several times, but his words were so slurred I was often not able to understand what he was saying, even though I put my ear to his mouth. Finally, it was time for me to leave, but I didn't want to. I patted his shoulder gently and told him to "hang tough." He smiled in response.

I started for the doorway a few times, stopping each time, dreading the thought that he might be gone before I could make the drive back to Hockessin. I was correct, although I never dreamed he would pass the next day.

On October 30, one day short of a year after we flew out of Phila-

★

delphia en route to England, I found myself standing in Arlington National Cemetery as Forrest Guth was laid to rest next to his loving wife. It was a solemn military ceremony that began with a service at the Old Post Chapel at Fort Myer, capped off at graveside with a twenty-one-gun salute by a 3rd Division firing squad. I watched the color guard crisply fold the flag into a neat triangle. At the conclusion, I stood for a moment by the grave and said a silent good-bye to my friend and traveling companion.

Forrest's not being here to see the release of this book is the bitterest of disappointments for me. Yet despite that sadness, I am hugely proud to have been the one to take him back to the days of his youth one last time.

I'm happy, not just because Forrest has now been reunited with his beloved Harriet and his friends Walter "Smokey" Gordon, Terrence "Salty" Harris, Carwood Lipton, and the rest. I am also happy for myself, because just before I left that final day, the last thing Forrest said to me, in a soft but clear voice, was, "It's good to see you."

And it was good to see him, too.

Soft landing, Trooper.

ACKNOWLEDGMENTS

When I first undertook this project, I had no idea how it would come together or even how much information I could gather to make it readable, entertaining, informative, and, perhaps most of all, emotional. Thanks in large part to a number of people, the pieces managed to fall into place, and I would like to take this opportunity to thank them all, for their help, their expertise, and their hospitality.

First and foremost is my friend Forrest Guth, who, even though he was not feeling totally fit, endured like the trooper he was, and allowed me to drag him across England and Europe, while tapping his mind for his memories and his emotions. Hand in hand with this is Forrest's family, who entrusted me with his care.

I also thank my agent, Dave Robie, for his support and encouragement, and my editor at New American Library, Brent Howard, who had perhaps more confidence in my writing skills than I did, by believing I could somehow create this unique literary blend of history, memoir, and travelogue.

Thanks also to the men of Easy, especially Herb Suerth, Ed Tipper, Brad Freeman, and Clancy Lyall, for sharing with me their firsthand experiences, and Dick Winters, who, although he was not interviewed for this book, shared many hours of his memories with me between 2001 and 2004. And, naturally, the writings of Bill Guarnere, Babe Heffron, Don Malarkey, Buck Compton, the late David Webster, and others helped complete the picture of what these men endured.

The vivid memoirs of the late Carwood Lipton were used courtesy of Dan Atchison and Jim Rudolph, who manage the Carwood Lipton Web site.

Since this book starts in Toccoa, my thanks goes to Bucky Simmons. I met Bucky in 2006 and again in 2007 during the Toccoa Reunion. He was nice enough to ferry me around the town, telling me the local history, not to mention trips to Camp Toccoa and to the top of Currahee.

Of course, none of this would have worked without the wonderful folks who helped Forrest and me once we were overseas.

For his services in England, I must thank Keith Sowerby, who, despite my misspelling of his name in the early editions of *Biggest Brother*, is a good friend who was most valuable in helping me obtain accommodations in Aldbourne, as well as showing me around the village and surrounding Wiltshire County, and sharing the area's history with me.

Thanks also to Neil and Clive Stevens for allowing me access to the many invaluable interviews they conducted with Aldbourne residents who lived through the "friendly invasion" by the 506th PIR and other GI units. My gratitude also to Neil for his guide services during the last day of our stay in England, and sharing his knowledge with me.

Bruce Steggles was most helpful and informative during his tour of Littlecote House, Colonel Sink's headquarters. Walking those corridors and experiencing that history was awesome.

Once on the Continent, I was again blessed with wonderful guides.

Paul Woodadge's expertise was of the utmost value. Paul has thoroughly examined all of Easy Company's battlefields, as well as the fields of valor of other units, and his knowledge is first-rate. I was especially grateful for his ability to get me onto the field at Brecourt Manor, which is private property. Walking that field where Easy took out the four-gun battery was one of the high points of my visit.

I also appreciated Paul's being able to allow me the chance to sit in the kitchen with Charles de Vallavieille, just as Dick Winters and Smokey Gordon had done with his father, Michel, as shown in a 1988 photo Dick provided me with back in 2003.

Along with Paul, I must thank his lovely wife, Myriam, who dealt with the gendarmes on my behalf after my car was struck by a crazy, drunken Frenchman in Carentan.

Forrest and I appreciated the hospitality of Dick Cooper, owner of the Blazing Sky bed-and-breakfast at Haute Addeville, who let us sample his fine (but strong enough to clear out nasal passages) local Calvados, and who ran into the village every morning to be sure we had fresh-baked bread for breakfast. Thanks also to Spencer Henry, the inn's manager, for his help and concern for Forrest's well-being, and his historical expertise. Spencer, by the way, is also a helluva cook.

Daniel Hamchin, the mayor of Angoville-au-Plain, greeted us warmly. The information he provided me about the heroic medics who set up an aid station inside the village church, while fighting raged outside, ranks as one of the best stories I heard during my trip.

I am also grateful for the wonderful guide services provided to me in Belgium by Reg Jans, who has a thorough knowledge of the Battle of the Bulge. He lives near those fields and walks them almost every day, and that experience shows.

Paul and Reg in Europe (as well as Bucky in Toccoa) also supplied me with some excellent "then" photos that I was able to match up with current shots, and following the trip, they responded faithfully to my many, many e-mail questions for clarification.

My linking up with these two wonderful overseas guides was possible through my friends Linda Cautaert and BK Masterson, who recommended Reg (bbtours@telenct.be) and Paul (www.battlebus.fr) to me.

I am also thankful to Frank Slegers and Marco Kilian (www .menofeasycompany.com), for their hospitality in Bastogne and their help in making Forrest's visit comfortable. Marco's assistance was also most valuable in guiding me to important Easy Company sites in Holland, especially the Crossroad at Heteren.

Eric Lemoine and Michel Marecaux of Cave McAuliffe enriched my visit by allowing me to tour the commanding general's headquarters, and I am grateful for their hospitality and generosity.

Last, my eternal gratitude to my wife, Barbara, for putting up with my running around Europe for two weeks with Forrest and for putting our lives on hold upon my return, so I could write this wonderful book.

BIBLIOGRAPHY

BOOKS

Burgett, Donald R. *Currahee! A Screaming Eagle at Normandy*. New York: Dell Reprint Editions, 2000.

Burgett, Donald R. *The Road to Arnhem: A Screaming Eagle in Holland*. New York: Dell Reprint Editions, 2001.

Compton, Lt. Lynn "Buck." *Call of Duty: My Life Before, During and After the Band of Brothers*. New York: Berkley Caliber, 2008.

De Trez, Michel. *They Way We Were: Cpl. Forrest L. Guth*. Wezembeek-Oppem, Belgium: D-Day Publishing, 2002.

Draper, Theodore. *The 84th Infantry Division in the Battle of the Ardennes*. 84th Infantry Division Historical Section, 1945.

Guarnere, William "Wild Bill," and Edward "Babe" Heffron, with Robyn Post. *Brothers in Battle, Best of Friends*. New York: Berkley Caliber, 2007.

Koskimaki, George. *The Battered Bastards of Bastogne*. Havertown, Penn.: Casemate, 1994.

Koskimaki, George. *D Day with the Screaming Eagles*. Havertown, Penn.: Casemate, 1970.

Koskimaki, George. *Hell's Highway*. Havertown, Penn.: Casemate, 1989.

Malarkey, Sgt. Don, with Bob Welch. *Easy Company Soldier: The Legendary Battles of a Sergeant from World War II's "Band of Brothers."* New York: St. Martin's Press, 2008.

Webster, David Kenyon. *Parachute Infantry: An American Paratrooper's Memoir of D-Day and the Fall of the Third Reich*. New York: Delta, 2002.

Winters, Major Dick, with Colonel Cole C. Kingseed. *Beyond Band of Brothers: The War Memoirs of Major Dick Winters.* New York: Berkley Caliber, 2006.

Wolff, Cpl. Perry S. *Fortune Favored the Brave.* Mannheimer Grossdruckerei, Germany: August 1945.

Currahee Scrapbook, 50Sink / 506th PIR Association, 101st Airborne Division (Reprint), 2002.

MAGAZINES

World War II: Band of Brothers Collections Issue, special edition, 2000, Primedia Enthusiast Publications, Leesburg, Va.

The Gathering of Eagles, Clive Stevens and Neil Stevens, Military Vehicle Trust, self-published booklet, 2004.

WEB SITES

www.carwoodlipton.com: Dedicated to C. Carwood Lipton; site maintained by Dan Atchison and Jim Rudolph.

INDEX